THE SIGN OF
THE FISH

THE SIGN OF
THE FISH

Peter Quennell

THE VIKING PRESS

New York

TO MY FRIENDS AT
GOLDENEYE

CONTENTS

ILLUSTRATIONS

ACKNOWLEDGMENTS

This book contains a number of passages that have already appeared in a somewhat different shape. For permission to reprint them, I am indebted to the Editors of *Country Life*, *Diversion*, *Harper's Bazaar*, *Horizon*, *The London Magazine*, *The Spectator*, *The Times Literary Supplement*, and to the Directors of the *Queen Anne Press*.

I must also express my gratitude to my friends Miss Nancy Cunard, Mr. Augustus John and Sir Harold Nicolson—to Miss Cunard for consenting to read and discuss my references to her late mother: to Mr. John for allowing me to reproduce an unfinished, and hitherto unphotographed, portrait of Lady Ottoline Morrell: to Sir Harold, for giving me the quotation from Omar Khayyám that appears upon the last page.

P. Q.

Prologue

A QUARTER of a century ago I was living in Japan, and occupied a small house behind the grey board fences of a mournful Tokyo back-street. The sense of solitude was often hard to bear, whether a winter snow-storm had buried the diminutive garden, wreathing drifts around the single dead tree and the collection of curiously shaped boulders that were its only ornament, or summer rain fell in dusky vertical lines, and large sombre butterflies, which disregarded the downpour, flapped heavily to and fro above the pitted, steaming earth. Yet life at Eighty-Six Street of the Chrysanthemum Slope had certain minor consolations. One could descend, for example, from our remote suburban neighbourhood, with its network of muddy paths and vast acreage of untidy wooden buildings, to the Ginza, the city's principal thoroughfare, near the railway station and the Imperial Palace. The Japanese, being, as they admit themselves, under the surface of their national self-esteem a somewhat gloomy and inhibited people, welcome the stimulus that is provided by the ugliest forms of modernism, by blazing electric lights and flaring shop-windows, competitive loud-speakers and big advertisements. Many of the shops in the Ginza displayed cheap and gaudy Western goods ; but native merchandise and traditional pastimes had not been completely banished. Pedlars exhibited singing frogs, or offered little cages for the accommodation of tame crickets. *Go*, or draughts, was played on the edge of the pavements, and groups of solemn enthusiasts would gather about the players' stools. The crowd was various and entertaining. Sometimes a massive top-knotted wrestler would drift through in his loosely girded robe ; sometimes a pair of apprentice geisha, their whitened faces round and expressionless beneath huge helmets of shining lacquered hair, would shuffle delicately, hesitantly past. They might be succeeded by a mob of wild-eyed students, shockheaded, with unshaven chins, whose appearance proclaimed their political beliefs, and who at the time were known as " Marxboys ".

After the oppressive isolation of suburban Hongo, a walk along the Ginza always re-aroused the appetite for life. But best of the diversions the street afforded was a visit to an old-fashioned shop that dealt in the apparatus of a writer's study. Here no concessions were made to twentieth-century commercial taste, but every object recalled the famous *literati* of the feudal period when calligraphy was an art that still exercised the highest talents. Here were the miniature slabs of Chinese ink, embossed with ideograms or traditional designs, to which the calligrapher applied his brush, a selection of the brushes he might decide to use, and notebooks bound in coloured paper, frequently splashed or speckled with tiny scraps of gold leaf, in which to jot down a poem or annotate an ancient text. The elegance of this scholarly equipment gave it an irresistibly inviting air : merely to examine it stirred the creative spirit, even in a Western writer, who asked himself why the business of writing was usually so dull and irksome. With such material at his command, need he hesitate to begin a book ? Once or twice I invested in a notebook that was to lend authorship a fresh attraction ; but the result of my investment was always the same—I never failed to spoil my purchase. The soft feathery texture of its pages was far too fragile for a metal-nibbed pen, which dug deep into the yielding rice-paper and left behind a hideous blot. Nor could a Japanese brush be readily held in English fingers. I would moisten an ink-slab, charge the brush's point, then lower it towards the page, holding it carefully upright as my Japanese friends had bidden me ; at which its fine elastic tip would immediately thicken into a clumsy knob, and letters I was attempting to trace be lost in an unsightly smear. That smear seemed yet more disgraceful compared with the beauty and purity of the pages that were still untouched. The virgin paper preserved its air of promise : the blots and scratches I had inflicted clearly told their own tale.

Twenty-five years have elapsed since I left Japan, with few regrets on either side ; but the recollection of a beautiful notebook which, despite the exquisite promise of its unwritten pages, I somehow never learned to employ, remains a convenient and expressive symbol of the difficulties of the writer's task. Meanwhile the problem of authorship generally has become more and more interesting ; and a number of separate questions have continued to require an answer. Is the professional writer, for instance, a distinct sub-species of the human race ; and, if that be true, in which respects does he differ from the majority of thinking and reading men ? What are the origins of the creative impulse ; and why should the promise held out by a sheet of smooth unwritten paper work so strongly and so disturbingly upon a certain type of imagination ? Many answers promptly suggest themselves ; and one at least has the virtue of extreme simplicity. An author writes because he *enjoys* writing. Pleasure, after all, is the basis of every form of art. We recognise art thanks to the pleasure it gives, the sudden involuntary sensation of delight ; and a critic's chief function is to analyse that pleasure and to help us prolong it by following it back to its hidden source. Pleasure and pain, no doubt, are very often closely linked ; but, notwithstanding the protests of writers who assure us that every line they print has been produced at the cost of an intolerable effort, no work of art can ever have reached maturity in which the pleasure-principle did not take a hand, presiding over the work's conception, even though it may have been unaccountably absent from the laborious business of bringing forth. The writer, then, enjoys arranging words and assembling the images they evoke in significant and lively patterns, just as the primitive craftsman and the child enjoy the symmetrical arrangement of shells or straws : there is some instinct in the human mind that responds to the idea of symmetry, and argues us to substitute an æsthetic order for the fruitful confusion of the inhuman universe. But this simplified view of the problem has several obvious limitations. The creative impulse may well be derived from a deep-rooted human instinct, which, like other instincts, is productive of pleasure once we allow it the release it demands ; but the process of gratification, in an organized society, where the individual artist is beginning to appear, is soon complicated by the influence of a very different set of feelings. They blend with the original instinct to give it a redoubled vigour.

This fusion seems to have taken place far back in the prehistoric ages. The earliest artists to produce recognisable masterpieces were the Aurignacian cave-dwellers who, with ruddy metallic pigments and the soot they derived from charred bones, decorated their underground temples over two hundred centuries before the birth of Christ. Many of the sites they chose were almost inaccessible, deep in tortuous limestone caverns, down terrifying passages still scarred by the mark of the cave-bear's claws, behind echoing halls hung with the teeth of stalactites or across the beds of subterranean rivers. Alarming today, how inexpressibly formidable to the Palæolithic huntsman-artist ! To surmount such a barrier of fear, one needs the incentive of a yet more powerful dread. The pictures created seem to reflect a mood of pure enjoyment. Can the painter have failed to delight in the strength and the splendour of the animals he drew, those plunging bison and rampant boars, the tall stags brought down by a flint-tipped shaft, legs quivering and collapsing as they sink beneath their broad antlers, or the droves of shaggy wild horses perpetually galloping toward the cliff's edge ? The huntsman loved the animals he killed, and recollected in the grim tranquillity of a cave the noise and exhilaration of a memorable chase. Nevertheless he must have explored the cavern, and dared to confront

16

its supernatural terrors, impelled by some fear or anxiety much greater than the fears he braved. His painting, beside the pleasure that it inspired, was primarily, archæologists tell us, an act of magical propitiation. Already the complexity of his motives was adding to the richness of an artist's style.

It is odd to consider a Palæolithic huntsman side by side with one of the most sophisticated European poets of the nineteenth century ; but the forms adopted by the creative impulse, and the spiritual conditions in which the creator works, have changed astonishingly little since the huntsman-magician first became an artist. Charles Baudelaire was a visionary poet whose researches into the problems of his own art led him far into the field of criticism, and who believed, indeed, that the true poet must inevitably take up a critic's functions.* The essay in which this statement occurs, an article on Richard Wagner and Tannhäuser, was published during the spring of 1861 ; and it was followed two years later, towards the close of 1863, by *Le Peintre de la Vie Moderne*, a tribute to the genius of Constantin Guys, in which he describes the relationship between an artist and the fascinating spectacle of contemporary life. Meanwhile he was planning a full-length prose-work—the " terrible book " that, were it ever published, would raise against him, he told his mother, the whole of modern middle-class society. But *Mon Cœur Mis à Nu* was never to emerge from a series of fragmentary jottings—notes on his religious ideas and political prejudices, on love and the character of woman, coloured by the strain of romantic misogyny that he owed to his unhappy childhood, together with resolutions for the future and observations on the tragedies of the past. Among these we discover a single sentence, which he no doubt

---

* ". . . Tous les grands poètes deviennent naturellement, fatalement, critiques. Je plains les poètes que guide le seul instinct ; je les crois incomplets. Dans la vie spirituelle des premiers, une crise se fait infailliblement, où ils veulent raisonner leur art, découvrir les lois obscures en vertu desquelles ils ont produit, et tirer de cette étude une série de préceptes dont le but divin est l'infaillibilité dans la production poétique. Il serait prodigieux qu'un critique devint poète, et il est impossible qu'un poète ne contienne pas un critique."

Richard Wagner et Tannhäuser à Paris.

intended to develop into a discursion covering several pages. Baudelaire's sense of frustration and failure—as a human being if not as a poet; for he still kept something of a creator's legitimate pride—had reached during his middle years a point of almost intolerable anguish. " I am at the end of my nervous resources ", he declared in a letter of May 6th 1861, " at the end of my courage, at the end of hope." Yet his critical perceptions remained as fine and penetrating as ever; and the terrible book he now planned was to have been completed by a self-portrait in which the origins of his adult sufferings were traced back to the circumstances of his early youth—not only to the misadventures he had undergone but to the intractable and explosive temperament he had inherited from his unknown ancestors, " *mes ancêtres, idiots ou maniaques, dans des appartements solennels*", victims like himself of a spiritual restlessness they could not appease.

Even as a child, his nature was cruelly divided. " *Tout enfant,*" he recorded in his jottings, "*j'ai senti dans mon cœur deux sentiments contradictoires: l'horreur de la vie et l'extase de la vie*". Here the poet is concerned primarily with the analysis of his own temperament; " *c'est bien le fait*(he adds)*d'un paresseux nerveux*"—such an idle neurotic as he remembered that he had been in youth; but his remark has also a more general bearing on the problem of a writer's character. What Baudelaire believed to have been true of himself, divided between the horror of life and an ecstatic awareness of the joys of living, may perhaps be true of every creative intelligence, and from the resultant conflict may arise the state of mind that impels an artist towards æsthetic activity, that lends an unwritten page the same mysterious attraction as the painter finds in an unblemished canvas or the sculptor in an unhewn block. The feelings that provoke the conflict are not, of course, peculiar to an artist. Most human beings have experienced them in a greater or a lesser degree, an unhappy minority succumbing to the " horror of life ", from which they may presently take refuge amid the shadows of a mental breakdown, the vast majority learning to accept life and gradually smothering their subconscious fears. The writer's condition is exceptional because he can neither accept nor reject; for the contradictory emotions that possess him are not only unusually violent but extraordinarily well-matched. Thus the conflict is never resolved, and the tension it produces never slackens. The creative writer remains in a state of suspense; like Catullus, he both hates and loves; and from the friction and tension of this ambivalent mood he seeks relief in the magical art of writing, which creates at least an illusion of harmony and gratifies his inborn sense of order. Simultaneously, as the caveman-artist did, he renders an ecstatic, disinterested tribute to the bewildering beauty and diversity of the natural world beneath his eyes.

The hint supplied by Baudelaire's journal becomes still more suggestive if we examine his poetic achievement. There the " horror " and the " ecstasy " of which he wrote are reflected in almost equal strength, horror and disgust often predominating and threatening to overcloud his whole vision, but the " spirit of delight " always re-emerging, often in a passage where we expect it least. No poet has been more obsessed by the squalor of contemporary existence; yet when he set out, in *Le Peintre de la Vie Moderne*, to provide his definition of the idea of Beauty, he declared that Beauty was composed of two separate elements —one " eternal, invariable and exceedingly difficult to assess "; the other " relative and a product of circumstances ", discoverable in the changing background of the everyday world and the " fashions, morals, appetites " of the artist's social period. An impassioned student of the age he condemned, he was deeply sensitive to its fascination—to what he called the " *beauté de circonstance*" and, elsewhere, " *le beau multiforme et versicolore qui se meut dans les spirales infinies de la vie.*" Although *Les Fleurs du Mal* was not a title that he had chosen himself, it suggests how closely his love of life was connected with his sense of evil, and how rapidly his spirit oscillated between attraction and repulsion. In the country of Baudelaire's genius, wrote Marcel Proust, " each separate poem is but a fragment . . . which, as soon as one reads it, joins up with the fragments we already know ", until an entire landscape has been created that gradually fills the reader's mind, opening out into immense aerial perspectives, through endless gradations of light and shade. This landscape owes its dramatic quality to the conflict of feelings I have already mentioned. Seldom have the pains of life been described in more expressive imagery, whether the poet evokes the mood of suffocating tedium that swoops down from a dark sky upon the lonely city-dweller—

> *Rien n'égale en longueur les boiteuses journées,*
> *Quand, sous les lourds flocons des neigeuses années,*
> *L'ennui, fruit de la morne incuriosité*
> *Prend les proportions de l'immortalité*

—or recalls those " vague terrors " which sometimes make hideous the hours of the night—

> *Ange plein de gaieté, connaissez-vous l'angoisse,*
> *La honte, les remords, les sanglots, les ennuis,*
> *Et les vagues terreurs de ces affreuses nuits*
> *Qui compriment le cœur comme un papier qu'on froisse ?*

Meanwhile the poetic intelligence still pursues its indomitable course, full of pride in its own powers and the consciousness of its own integrity :

> *Au-dessus des étangs, au-dessus des vallées,*
> *Des montagnes, des bois, des nuages, des mers*
> *Par delà le soleil, par delà les éthers,*
> *Par delà les confins des sphères étoilées,*
>
> *Mon esprit, tu te meus avec agilité,*
> *Et, comme un bon nageur qui se pâme dans l'onde,*
> *Tu sillones gaiement l'immensité profonde*
> *Avec un indicible et mâle volupté.*

The clue that Baudelaire provides, to a conflict at the heart

of every form of literary creation, might be followed through the
work of many European writers. Both Tolstoy and Shakespeare,
for example, seem to illustrate its effects with unusual force and
clarity. Tolstoy it obsessed so long as he lived; his sensuous
appreciation of the world of the flesh—voiced by the novelist
in a dozen brilliant episodes—was perpetually at war with his
sense of sin, derived from nameless emotions of fear and anxiety.
We are told how, on meeting in the street a pair of stalwart
Russian guardsmen, he paused to admire the spectacle of so
much stupid animal well-being, which epitomised the vigour
and beauty of the human race, untroubled by a conviction of sin
and uncorrupted by the poison of thought.* But, if he loved
and admired humanity, he also feared and hated it; and, whereas
in such books as *War and Peace* and *Anna Karenina* the two
emotions are almost equally balanced, in some of his lesser
works, notably *The Kreutzer Sonata*, the balance is entirely lost,
and a rabid loathing and dread of the flesh appear completely to
have obliterated his gentler and more generous feelings. In his
greatest novels they are always evident; and he finds it impossible to withhold his affection from some of the characters he
least esteems. In *Anna Karenina*, for example, there is that
touching, though slightly absurd personage Stepan Arkadyevitch
Oblonsky, whose good health and good nature and unselfconscious devotion to the *douceur de vivre* spread around him a
kind of " restrained radiance " which affects even the neurotic
Levin. True, he has seduced the governess and made his ailing
wife unhappy; but Tolstoy cannot wholly condemn him, because,
despite moral principles, he finds Stepan Arkadyevitch irresistibly appealing and attractive. The good-natured voluptuary's

---

* " Suler tells us how he was walking with Leo Nicolayevitch . . . when Tolstoi
noticed in the distance two soldiers of the guards . . . Tolstoi began to grumble at
them: 'What pompous stupidity! Like animals trained by the whip . . .' But when the
guardsmen came abreast with him, he stopped, followed them caressingly with his
eyes, and said enthusiastically : ' How handsome ! . . . Their strength and beauty,
O Lord ! How charming it is when man is handsome, how very charming ! ' "
Reminiscences of L. N. Tolstoi by Maxim Gorky, translated by S. S. Koteliansky and
Leonard Woolf.

unconquerable love of life corresponds to one aspect of the writer's own temperament.

Shakespeare, too, had his bursts of affection and compassion, counterbalanced by spells of furious misanthropy, when he rounded upon the human race like Prospero reviling Caliban. It is strange that the English, with their innate distrust of psychological complications, should have recognised as their national poet a dramatist so acutely sensitive to the sufferings of a divided nature. Not only in the tragedies of the " dark period ", but in the labyrinthine and elusive *Sonnets*, he portrays a human being who can neither accept the world as he finds it, nor resolve on a whole-hearted rejection of all the pleasure and the pride of life. Hamlet himself speaks with wondering regard of the infinite capacities of his own species—" What a piece of work is a man ! how noble in reason ! how infinite in faculty ! in form and moving how express and admirable ! "—but subjoins the melancholy admission that they have ceased to bring him any comfort. " Man delights not me "—there are times, indeed, when the " condition of humanity " (which his contemporary and Warwickshire neighbour Fulke Greville described with such majestic eloquence) * is represented by the dramatist as not altogether unendurable merely because to abandon life may be to enter a yet more terrifying state. Thus Claudio, in *Measure for Measure*, offered death as a clean alternative to a precarious and ignominious life, echoes Hamlet's most often quoted speech where he weighs our present sufferings against the horrid uncertainty of a future existence :

Claudio: Death is a fearful thing.
Isabella: And shamed life a hateful.
Claudio: Ay, but to die, and go we know not where ;

* " Oh wearisome condition of Humanity ,
Born under one law, to another, bound :
Vainly begot, and yet forbidden vanity,
Created sick, commanded to be sound . . ."
The Tragedy of Mustapha, 1609.

22

Prologue

To lie in cold obstruction, and to rot ;
This sensible warm motion to become
A kneaded clod ; and the delighted spirit
To bathe in fiery floods, or to reside
In thrilling region of thick-ribbed ice . . .

Claudio trembles at the prospect of death with its apparatus of mediæval torments ; but another consideration also deters him from accepting the sacrifice for which his sister pleads. He, too, has known the " ecstasy of living ", and his " delighted spirit " is doubly reluctant to confront the dangers of that unknown realm. Unlike the creations of earlier and later dramatists, whose monomaniac intensity of feeling confines them to a single level, and who appear to have been engendered merely to suffer and inflict pain, Shakespeare's long array of tragic personages, scholars, soldiers, lovers, sovereigns, are characters who have played many parts before they reached their fatal climax, and have already established a firm footing in the world that they must now prepare to leave. Their creator himself, essentially a man of the world and a successful product of his own period, seems never to have lost his grasp on life and, so far as we can judge from the luminous imagery of his verse, never to have outgrown his taste for experience or his keen enjoyment of wordly pleasures. All his contemporaries agree in describing him as peculiarly equable and sweet-tempered ; and to this buoyancy and natural resilience of mind may be attributed no doubt some of the splendid qualities of his poetic style—his gift, for example, of suddenly inserting an image that transfigures and transcends its context. " His delights were dolphin-like ", * says his mistress

---

* " His delights were dolphin-like ; they
                          showed his back above
    The element they liv'd in . . ."
                Antony & Cleopatra. Act V, Scene II.
    These lines (which, although the sense is magnificently clear, should possibly be emended to read : " They showed *their backs* above ") are a characteristic Shakespearian amplification of a comparatively prosaic passage in North's Plutarch : " As the dolphin shows his back above the water, so Antony always rose superior to the

23

of Antony ; and the poet who could scarcely have created Hamlet, Othello, Macbeth if he had not felt he had some share in them, may perhaps have recognised a similar resemblance in the love-intoxicated Roman conqueror, whom he revives as a type of the Renaissance Man, enjoying enormously and despairing passionately.

Yet Shakespeare's own farewell was not to be tragic ; and, when at length he renounced the stage and decided to retire to Stratford, we do not imagine the creative genius deserting him, as " the God Hercules " deserted Antony, passing away across the night to the sound of solemn aerial music. Rather, we assume that there was a gradual slackening of tension, a lessening of the inward strain, and that, once the conflict had ceased to demand expression, he summarily abandoned his talents because they had outlived their use. True, he had no longer a financial incentive : he had crowned his literary career by accumulating a modest fortune. But another commercial dramatist, the ambitious and emulous Ben Jonson, carefully compiled and revised a majestic folio edition of his collected plays ; while John Lyly complained to his readers of the miserable condition in which his comedies appeared, mangled by the same piratical printers who played havoc with Shakespearian texts. Shakespeare, on the other hand, seems to have been singularly insensitive to the good opinion of posterity. Half his dramas remained unpublished in dishevelled prompt-copies ; the " bad quartos " were disfigured by numerous omissions and grotesquely garbled passages. He did not drown his book like Prospero, even in the shallow waters of the Avon, so much as cast it aside with a gesture of supreme indifference.

If at Stratford he began to re-assemble the leaves, he must

---

pleasures in which he lived ". Malone points out that Shakespeare may also have been indebted to Thomas Lodge's *Life & Death of William Longbeard*, 1593 :
" Oh fair of fairest, dolphin-like,
Within the rivers of my plaint . . ."

have prosecuted the task he had undertaken slowly and half-heartedly ; and not until 1623, when he had been dead for seven years, could his one-time associates, Heminge and Condell, at length produce the First Folio. "*Je ne m'occupe plus de ça*", wrote Arthur Rimbaud in 1879 to his admirer Delahaye, dismissing both the poems of his youth and the astonishing prose-poem in which he had said goodbye to literature ; and Shakespeare's attitude towards his poetic works may well have been as frigid and careless. Yet Shakespeare had completed more than half the normal life-span—by Elizabethan standards he was already growing old ; whereas Rimbaud was not yet twenty-one when the imaginative ferment of his adolescence flickered down and abruptly expired. The demonic rebel who had loved and hated life, who had loathed the world and proclaimed his loathing in imagery as repulsive as it is expressive, yet whose earliest recorded poem is a lyrical tribute to the beauty and tranquillity of the only landscape that he knew and the only form of personal happiness he had yet experienced—

> *Par les soirs bleus d'été j'irai dans les sentiers,*
> *Picoté par les blés, fouler l'herbe menue:*
> *Rêveur, j'en sentirai la fraîcheur à mes pieds,*
> *Je laisserai le vent baigner ma tête nue!*

—concluded his literary career by accepting life on the harsh terms that modern society offered. He would become rich and powerful, an unscrupulous merchant-prince, trading in coffee and ivory, negro slaves and smuggled guns.

Few writers have renounced their art as dramatically as Rimbaud or as lightly and casually as Shakespeare. More often the literary mechanism outlasts the writer's creative impulse ; and we have the sad spectacle of a Tennyson or a Wordsworth, both men of exquisite natural gifts, continuing to exercise their talents after the disappearance of any real need. Yet there are artists who never renounce their genius, or whom their demon never renounces. And one thinks, for example—to turn from poetry to painting—of the distracted, wild-eyed old man, in bourgeois frock-coat and high-crowned bowler hat, who had himself driven out every day along the white Provençal roads towards the lion-shaped ridge of grey-and-tawny Mont St. Victoire. Life was terrifying, Cézanne would cry—terrifying, inexplicable, almost insupportable, what with a philistine family, unsympathetic friends and an idiotic town-council that refused to hang his masterpieces. Yet the situation changed as soon as he had set up his easel : " *C'est à la fois si bon et si terrible de s'installer devant une toile blanche!* " Time was pressing : " *Je n'aurais pas le temps de tout dire.*" Yet how urgently what had to be said pleaded for æsthetic utterance ! " *C'est effrayant la vie!* "—terrifying alike because it frustrated the artist and because the promises that it held out were incessantly re-invigorating him and luring him on. Cézanne's unsullied canvas may be compared to the writer's unwritten page, and the ambivalent emotions that the painter described to the poet's sense of ecstasy coupled with a sense of horror. Such divided feelings must necessarily produce confusion ; but from the turmoil that they engender sometimes arises an harmonious work of art ; for the artist reaches harmony and unity by way of strife and inward discord. It was Yeats who, speaking of a young contemporary, regretted that, to go with taste, exuberance and skill, he had not " more chaos in his composition ".

I

Retreat from Parnassus

BENEATH THE precipices of a mountain once sacred to the God of Poetry, but during the winter-months, when he visited the Hypoboreans, haunted by Dionysus and the troop of savage mænads—half-naked barefoot revellers whose wandering torch-flames could be seen from Apollo's threshold as they danced among the crags above—Delphi on its narrow rocky ledge is still the most numinous of ancient sites. The air itself has a peculiar sharpness and freshness, the deep sky an especial radiance ; and across that sky, noiselessly circling and watching, drift the wide-winged mountain-eagles. Both Apollo and Dionysus are types of poetic inspiration ; and both have contributed to the pervading spirit of the place—so wild and remote and solitary, yet beside the ruins of Apollo's shrine, which had incorporated in its portal the admonitory legend *Nothing Too Much*, so subtly and persistently suggestive of the classical virtues of restraint and order. The traveller who reaches Delphi from Athens feels that he is rediscovering a Golden Age—the cliffs are golden overhead : the wings of the circling eagles turn in an unclouded golden light ; while a literary pilgrim may temporarily regain some of the exhilaration of his lost youth, before the effort to manipulate words became a settled daily business. It is in just such a mood that the professional writer of prose returns, now and then, to the idea of poetry, the older and nobler form of writing from which all other literary modes ultimately derive their strength,

The Sign of the Fish

Poetry is the heart of literature, as Delphi was the reputed centre of the earth; and one cannot admit to having failed in poetry without an occasional prick of shame. Yet the aspirant whom Apollo refuses admittance, and who declines to make a second trial, is possibly less misguided than the rejected devotee who continues to hang around the temple precincts.

The pages that follow describe a retreat from Poetry as conducted by the narrator in person; and, although the upshot of the story is negative, it may perhaps have some incidental bearing on the problem of poetic experience. About this problem even the spoiled poet considers he has a right to speak. For is there really so great a gulf between the poet who fails and the poet who succeeds? May there not, at least, be a revealing similarity in the methods that they adopt and the impulses that they obey? But, before attacking the critical side of the question, I must try to sketch in a contemporary background and depict the state of literature at the opening of the nineteen-twenties. I grew up in a literary period when Verse commanded a degree of respect that it lost soon afterwards. The final volume of *Georgian Poetry* appeared in 1922; and its contributors included Edmund Blunden, William H. Davies, Walter de la Mare, Robert Graves, D. H. Lawrence and Harold Monro. Each of them had achieved a measure of renown, and, except for D. H. Lawrence, each was primarily a writer of verse, pursuing his art with a wholehearted passion which the political passions of the 'thirties had not yet begun to dilute and cloud. They were accompanied by fifteen other poets; and, towards the end of the alphabetical list, I had the immense satisfaction of being able to read my own name. I was still a prisoner, at the time, of the English educational system, in a rather characterless and colourless school, presided over by the father of a well-known modern novelist; and the friendly recognition I received from Edward Marsh, that benevolent and gifted personage, who had launched *Georgian Poetry* and continued to carry it on until the end, made class-rooms and red-brick quadrangle seem doubly depressing and claustrophobic.

28

Retreat from Parnassus

I had arrived at *Georgian Poetry* by a roundabout road. Thanks
to the current state of poetic enthusiasm, new anthologies were
constantly appearing ; Richard Hughes, while he was at Oxford,
had announced an anthology of *Public School Verse;* and I had
sent him an odd little production which came out in the original
issue. He and his fellow editor praised it generously—much
more generously than, I think, it deserved ; for it was a piece of
decorative schoolboy whimsicality, calculated nowadays to set
the reader's teeth on edge. But Hughes believed that it showed
promise ; and a number of popular journals who, although my
original aim had been entirely serious and my only reason for
adopting " free verse " was that I had never learned to scan,
imagined that it was a brilliant parody aimed at the extravagances
of modern literature, reviewed it under large headlines in the
columns of the daily press. About this time I met Richard
Hughes ; and Richard Hughes, I suppose, must have presented
me to Edward Marsh. He also, late on a summer afternoon, took
me to visit Edith Sitwell, leading me along a Bayswater street
and up several flights of dusky stairs, to the topmost level of a
block of " mansion-flats ", where we halted slightly bemused
and breathless. Behind that dark uncommunicative door lay
the enchanted realm I longed to enter.

Nor was my first glimpse in any way disappointing. The bell
was rung ; we heard an answering movement ; and there upon
the threshold stood the famous poetess, tall, attenuated and
elegant as one of those sculptured saints and martyrs who keep
guard around the portals of Chartres. Sheathed in a garment of
gold brocade, wearing a toque of gilded feathers and a large
jewelled cross which, I afterwards learned, had originally belonged
to Cagliostro, Miss Sitwell raised a finger to her lips—on her long
pale distinguished hand were several impressive rings set with
big fragments of semi-precious stone—and murmured warningly,
before we advanced, that there was a madman in the room beyond.
Again, I was not to be disappointed. On the end of a small sofa
crouched a haggard foreign poet—the demented Northern bard,

nicknamed " The Icelander ", already portrayed by Osbert
Sitwell in a volume of his five-fold autobiography—describing
the horrible and fantastic visions that pursued him when he
walked abroad, notably a band of little dark men, carrying large
unrolled umbrellas, who perpetually dogged his footsteps, and
harried and threatened him wherever he fled. On the opposite
end of the sofa perched an elderly lady, entirely clothed in black
velvet, and visibly quivering with alarm beneath a wide black
picture-hat. Her profile was aquiline and boldly whitened ; her
lips were summarily painted a brilliant red ; and from under the
brim of her hat appeared an array of yellow Gorgonian curls.
This, I subsequently discovered, was that good and charming
woman, the once fashionable novelist Ada Leverson, whom her
friend Oscar Wilde had christened " The Sphinx ", and who had
sheltered him with heroic devotion while he awaited his second
trial at the Old Bailey. Like many deaf people, the Sphinx
enjoyed talking ; but for the moment she had been reduced to
silence, as the madman, with his glittering eyes, edged close to
her across the sofa, and she shrank away from him against its
arm, doing her best to seem attentive and making tremulous
propitiatory gestures. After the humdrum quietude of my
parents' house, the drama that I was witnessing appeared particularly strange and desperate. At last I had entered the literary
world, in which beauty, lunacy and genius were woven together
into the pattern of everday life.

Later, I often visited Miss Sitwell's receptions, and usually
found the Sphinx attending, always dressed in the same style—
rich black velvet was her only wear—and, although considerably
less perturbed, seated on the same sofa. Many other visitors had
climbed the stairs, including some celebrated and gifted persons—
Wyndham Lewis, for example, stationed moody and pallid beside
the window—as well as a numerous assemblage of country
cousins and favourite lame dogs. The poetess would revive them
with cupfuls of strong Indian tea and feed them upon " penny
buns ", to which a heavy coating of white-of-egg had given the

lustre of antique glazed pottery. Now and then, she would read aloud—not, however, from her own verses, but from a correspondence she was carrying on with an irritable retired soldier who lived nearby, and who kept some noisy domestic animals which frequently disturbed her hours of work. Both neighbours were of an extremely pugnacious turn ; but everyone agreed that the poetess's latest retort—for she was used to disciplining editors and castigating impertinent newspaper critics—had left her miserable adversary with not a leg to stand on. Sometimes these readings were interrupted by the sudden arrival of her two brothers. They did not remain with us for very long, and generally produced the impression of having descended from a different plane. Circling rapidly around the room, and as rapidly shaking hands, " How are *you* ? ", they would enquire, " And how are *you* ? ", placing the emphasis upon the last word, in a tone that, although kindly and courteous, did not suggest that they required an answer. Bayswater was not their natural habitat ; one associated them with a delightful house in Chelsea, with evenings at the Russian Ballet and supper parties at the " Eiffel Tower ". Soon they exhausted their store of greetings, in which *ave* conveyed a hint of *vale*, and by a series of swift, circuitous moves had swept back gracefully towards the door. Their fine heads, as they turned to vanish, recalled twin faces stamped on a single coin. Having embraced their sister and assumed their overcoats, they began to hurry down the stairs.

Edith, Osbert and Sacheverell Sitwell, at the period of which I am writing, formed a solid literary phalanx, always ready to charge headlong against the monstrous array of boors and boobies. But their literary method was as eclectic as their controversial strategy, if they had been sufficiently provoked, was bellicose and straightforward. They assembled the imagery of their poems from a dozen diverse sources—from the art and architecture of Southern Europe, from the ballet and the modern stage. They loved travelling and listening to music ; and their youth had been spent between an Edwardian seaside resort, from which

31

Osbert Sitwell drew the raw material of many of his short stories, a castle among the vineyards of Tuscany and an ancient English country house, islanded in the Derbyshire coal-fields, where smuts float down from the air like snow and a delicate film of soot darkens the tree-boles and gathers on the rims of the fountains and the white shoulders of Italian statues. With so broad and fruitful a province to command, they did not believe that poetic inspiration developed most prosperously beneath an English hedge ; and they were apt to laugh at the rustic Georgian Poets, who seemed to pass their time sauntering and botanising around the muddy landscape that enclosed their country cottages, picking a celandine here, and there, over a five-barred gate, holding despondent conversations " with a lonely lamb ".* The flora that the Sitwells admired could not be grown in a herbaceous border ; the fauna that peopled their verse was as odd as anything to be discovered in the mediæval bestiaries. Asked by his commanding officer at a wartime mess whether he were not fond of cats, Osbert Sitwell had returned a resolute negative, explaining that he preferred leopards.

With one of these rustic poets, nevertheless, I presently formed a stimulating friendship, not a friendship that was destined to last but, so long as it lasted, of unusual value. Robert Graves was then living at Islip, a stone-built village close to Oxford ; and when I went up to the University to sit for an examination at Balliol, I and my father, although he distrusted poets, whom he suspected of being drunken and promiscuous, left the grim outskirts of North Oxford and walked to Islip across the riverine fields. On our way, I remember, we were much troubled by the shameless conduct of a pair of lovers, who flung themselves on to the meadow grass and proceeded to engage in carnal love-making before we were fairly out of sight. " Couldn't they *wait ?* . . ." muttered my father furiously—he had naturally a very pure mind ; and their behaviour seemed a bad omen for our visit

* " I lingered at a gate and talked
  A little with a lonely lamb "
William Kerr : " Counting Sheep " : *Georgian Poetry* 1920–1922.

to an unknown bohemian poet, whom we might well discover living in concubinage, surrounded by an illegitimate brood. But, although the poet's manner struck him as " rough ", and his corduroy suit was rougher still, Robert Graves impressed my father as being probably a " decent sort of fellow ", with a fresh-cheeked and unaffected wife—curiously insistent, however, on being addressed by her maiden name : she turned out to be a passionate feminist who regarded the adoption of one's husband's name as a mark of matrimonial servitude—and a number of wholesome noisy children running wild around their small house. Neither of them " drank ", my father noticed ; the food they provided was plain and sensible ; and Graves appeared to love the country and take some interest in the local antiquities, a subject about which my father was always prepared to talk at length. Meanwhile I was studying the writer's appearance—a nose broken like that of Michelangelo, and thick dark hair that curled on his forehead like the locks of Michelangelo's *David*, together with a sallow skin and a mobile, slightly twisted mouth. It was clear that he was a remarkably affectionate parent, and he told us that a poet ought to write seated in the middle of his family, while he minded a fractious child or kept his eye upon a bubbling saucepan. His view of life, at the time, was still intensely puritanical ; and he even asserted that a " bad man " —bad in the accepted moral sense—could scarcely hope to be a good artist. This was a statement that my father found unexpectedly reassuring.

Once I had gone up to Oxford, I made a habit of revisiting Islip, and Robert Graves would pay me flying visits in my over-heated rooms at Balliol. Flying—for he arrived on a bicycle and was always hurried though always good-tempered, carrying a heavy knapsack full of groceries and vegetables, which, as soon as he had smoked a cigarette, he must immediately shoulder and trundle home. The cigarette came from a big expensive box —aromatic " Balkan Sobranies "—much more expensive than I could rightly afford, but bought on credit at the College stores.

The Sign of the Fish

I had already begun to develop a dangerous taste for worldly luxuries ; and the austerity of the poet's ideals and the honest bleakness of his domestic surroundings provided a useful corrective to the silliness and wanton frivolity of youth. Robert Graves also supplied some valuable ideas about the art of writing. His theories had not yet solidified into a dogmatic critical system. The fearsome White Goddess had yet to ascend her throne ; and his remarkable literary partnership with Laura Riding—a pale mop-headed young woman who reached London, while I still knew him, as Laura Riding Gottschalk—was not to be established and proclaimed until he and I had both left Oxford. At the moment, the influence he felt most strongly was that of the fabulous Lawrence of Arabia ; and Lawrence's opinions, often wildly erratic, he distributed broadcast to all who listened. There were only three French poets, he once informed me —Villon, Baudelaire—he had forgotten the name of the third. Where had he learned this, I cautiously asked him. Lawrence had said so, he replied, as he hoisted his knapsack between his shoulders.

On the other hand, if he spoke from his own experience, the advice that he gave was usually sound. The poet, he once remarked, must always be careful in his use of colour-adjectives. A mere versifier was apt to employ them lavishly—his productions blushed and beamed like a bad picture of a tropical sunset ; whereas the true poet rarely introduced a colour, and then only at a point where it greatly heightened and enriched an image. Did I remember two poems by Donne, each of which contained a single mention of a colour, so aptly and unexpectedly placed that it seemed to flash from the surrounding lines ?—the sixteenth *Elegie*, addressed to his youthful mistress—

> Nor in bed fright thy nurse
> With midnight's startings, crying out, Oh, Oh,
> Nurse, O my love is slain, I saw him go
> O'er the *white* Alps alone . . .

34

—and *Elegie V*, imagining his return to her arms after an adventurous voyage overseas—

> When weather-beaten I come back ; my hand
> Perhaps with rude oars torn, or sunbeams tann'd . . .
> My body a sack of bones, broken within,
> And powder's *blue* stains scatter'd on my skin . . .

Such were the conclusions of a modern who studied his art as thoroughly and diligently as a cabinet-maker or a master-mason ; but his point of view was already distinguished by a certain touch of genial crankiness, which he owed (his biographer may decide) to an interesting combination of ancestral strains. On his mother's side, for example, he was descended from erudite German stock : on his father's, related to a Cromwellian regicide and an eccentric eighteenth-century clergyman, author of *The Spiritual Quixote*. The seventeenth and the odder regions of the eighteenth century were, I have often thought, his proper background ; and I could imagine him producing one of those gigantic volumes, in the same tradition as the works of Browne, Burton or Henry More, the " Cambridge Platonist ", where a poetic will-o'-the-wisp flutters ahead of the reader's footsteps through an endless forest of curious learning, occasionally coming to rest on some fantastic branch or twig. Later, he was to publish a quantity of books, in which he revised the New Testament or cast strange sidelights on Classical mythology, and was to advocate a method of scholarly research entitled " analeptic thinking ", which, so far as I have been able to discover, encourages us first to decide what we wish to believe, then look around for scholarly evidence to give our intuitive convictions a decent measure of support. But at Islip the Quixotic man of learning had not yet definitely taken control. He was as vulnerable as he was easily impressionable, and still exhibited the wounded features of a shell-shocked public schoolboy, who had gone straight from Charterhouse to a line regiment, had been shot through the body on some Flemish battlefield and temporarily left for dead. In common with many survivors of the battle, he wore the strained and troubled expression of a young man who had lately emerged from an inferno.

Graves' devoted friend Siegfried Sassoon showed possibly even deeper scars. Like Wilfred Owen, his contemporary and companion-in-arms, he had proved in action that he possessed unusual courage ; and, when he denounced the filthiness and futility of modern warfare and proclaimed his support of a negotiated peace, he had displayed courage of a very different and, it may be, of a more exalted kind. But the crisis that he had undergone would appear, in some way, to have benumbed his faculties. He had become the poetic solitary, the poetic malcontent, an *El Desdichado* of twentieth-century verse, apt in conversation to make rather too much of his separate and unfriended plight. Melancholy, handsome, reserved—his hollow cheeks and noble brow suggested an imaginary portrait of a distinguished Hebrew Minor Prophet—he was inclined to compare the ascetic life he led with the worldly junketings enjoyed by other writers, and to describe his lonely dead-quiet evening hours, during which he listened to a recorded symphony concert and ate his modest dinner off a small tray. His unworldliness was evidently a matter of pride ; and, in a series of engaging autobiographical volumes, he would soon popularise the view of his character that he liked to enlarge in desultory talk—the inspired Muff who reaches his goal despite a fumbling deprecatory approach, who invades the enemy's lines or takes a difficult fence with the same disarming, undemonstrative ease. His pacifist war-poems were now behind him ; but, at least in the late 'twenties and early 'thirties, they had not lost their controversial fire ; and I used on occasions to read them aloud to my Japanese students, while, through the dusty classroom panes, I watched a squat goose-stepping drill-sergeant as he led his submissive charges backwards and forwards across the square below.

Most of the " Georgian Poets " were more or less obedient to the traditional verse forms. But a great iconoclast had already appeared ; and, before I had parted from Oxford, or Oxford had decided that, for some months at any rate, it would prefer to part with me, *The Waste Land*, in its blue-mottled boards, was to be seen carelessly deposited on the table of every literary undergraduate. Its impact was often explosive—not every reader, particularly in academic circles, had yet discerned its true value ; and there was a memorable summer afternoon when my friend Harold Acton, himself a well-known undergraduate poet and a celebrated Oxford figure of the day, having been asked to perform at a Conservative Garden Fête, decided that he could not do better than recite the entire poem from beginning to end. His audience's good manners were severely tested, as this dirge for a godless civilization, delivered in Harold Acton's rich, resounding voice, swept irresistibly above their heads ; and one or two old ladies, who were alarmed and horrified but thought that the reciter had such a " nice, kind face ", rather than hurt the young man's feelings by getting up and leaving openly, were obliged to sink to their knees and creep away on all fours. I had envisaged T. S. Eliot as a revolutionary poet—revolutionary, indeed, was the effect he produced ; and nothing in his verse had prepared me for the impression he made in real life. Mild, retiring, unfailingly courteous, he seemed impossible to associate with Prufrock or Sweeney, with Doris carrying a glass of brandy or Grishkin whose uncorseted bosom offers the prospect of " pneumatic bliss ": with the dark crowds hurrying across London Bridge, or with the wind that comes whining up from the Thames and sneaks along the City's back-streets . . .

Instead, I encountered a black-suited publisher who bore some resemblance to an Anglican bishop. Jules Laforgue was a poet he much esteemed ; and, just as Laforgue's Parisian acquaintances were often struck by his likeness to an English parson—he is said to have been " *un peu clergyman et correct* " both in his appearance and in his mode of speech—Eliot's admirers can never lose sight of his New England ancestry, and the long line of distinguished clerics and scholars who have helped to make him

37

what he is. So he smiled politely and benignly ; and, if he did not tap the ends of his fingers together, he executed some equally soothing movement. Now and then, half apologetically, he would emit a little pun, crossing black-trousered legs and revealing thick black socks, rumpled over black boots. Although I have heard him quote, no doubt for its psychological interest, a Rabelaisian limerick, believed to have been written by Alfred Tennyson, only once did I detect a personality—or, rather, traces of a personality—that *might* have had a remote reference to the origins of *The Waste Land*. That moment occurred in " The Poetry Bookshop ", the home and emporium of Harold Monro, from which he distributed modern books of verse, as well as poetic leaflets and illuminated broadsheets. Above the shop he kept his own rooms, equipped with wooden settles that imitated the furniture of an old-fashioned country inn, and hung with numerous wood-cuts designed and embellished by Lovat Fraser. In his youth, I believe, Monro had adopted some profession as improbable, and as unsuitable for a man of his tastes, as that of a Scottish land-agent. But he had given up all to follow Poetry ; and he was now established at his shop, in the middle of the poetic world, selling verse and writing it, advising, encouraging, deploring ; while over the shop he entertained his friends, among the massive settles and the hand-coloured prints, and poured out bottle after bottle from a rather curiously assorted cellar.

His eyes were fierce behind thick convex lenses ; his blunt features, barred by a black moustache, were burnished to a fiery copper hue. Because his eye-sight troubled him, he smoked pipe-fuls of pungent herb-tobacco ; and the odorous smoke-wreaths —rosemary-and lavender-scented, with an occasional whiff of smouldering rope—added to the mystery and obscurity of his surroundings and gave him somewhat the air of a mediæval sage, an alchemist bothered and exasperated by his constant failures to produce the Philosopher's Stone. In certain respects, I suppose, Harold Monro was a disappointed man ; but poetry is a marvellous preservative, for, although the poet is often disappointed,

hope perpetually comes flooding back ; and Monro was a poet
by vocation whose poetic task absorbed his whole existence.
Energy and enthusiasm irradiated him, whether he was discussing literature or playing host ; and he managed to transmit his
enthusiasm to the guests whom he received at dinner. Meanwhile bottles appeared and were opened in rapid but unpre-
dictable sequence—he had no use for the snobbish ceremony of
comparing vintages and smelling corks—and, as his guests'
spirits rose, their critical intelligence waned. Otherwise my
recollections of an evening with T. S. Eliot might be less fragmentary and less confused. But I remember that, as he talked of
his " dreams ", in a manner that vaguely recalled the haunted
landscape of his early verse, our host talked to us about his
" sins ", which seemed to weigh upon him darkly and heavily :
that neither Eliot nor I could quite discover what his sins were :
and that the problem was still unsolved when we at last descended
into the Bloomsbury streets and found ourselves face to face
with the Doric portico of the British Museum. Eliot, as always,
took a large and charitable view : he characterised the confession
as " Scottish mist ".

It was on Harold Monro's friendly recommendation, offered
to a credulous Eastern enquirer who happened to stray across his
threshold, that I was appointed, in 1930, Professor of English
Language and Literature at a Japanese government university—
a post for which I had no training and, as both I and my students
were soon aware, very little aptitude. When I returned to
England after eighteen exhausting months, the intellectual
climate had begun to change. Wystan Auden's poem *The Orators*
was published in 1932 ; and the works of Stephen Spender,
Cecil Day Lewis and Louis MacNeice were gradually becoming
known. *Georgian Poetry* was dead ; its contributors had vanished
or scattered. The new poets were partisans of the Left ; and
their sympathies, heightened by a sense of impending conflict,
coloured or clouded much of the verse they wrote. This is not
the place to discuss the political efforts of English and American

intellectuals during the third decade of the twentieth century, or that long sad courtship of the Russian Communist Party by Western Men of Good Will, which exposed the wooers to so many rebuffs, provoked such bitter heart-searchings and plunged some of them into a state of moral perturbation from which they have not yet recovered. But it is clear that the " Fight against Fascism ", notwithstanding the valour that a number of young poets displayed in the Spanish Civil War, and the eloquence displayed by an even larger number in support of democratic principles, was directly productive of no more genuine poetry than the struggle against Napoleon Bonaparte. Imaginative literature takes its raw material from private life ; and, although an artist may be admired if he feels passionately about public questions—to have remained indifferent, indeed, between 1930 and 1939 would have argued a very hard heart—he is not necessarily to be applauded if he attempts to mount the public stage. The main objection is purely practical—few artists have succeeded there ; while the majority of political artists are apt to do more harm than good. Secondly, the artist who aspires to be a political force seems completely to misunderstand the nature of the art he practises. The artist is essentially a secret agent, who wears numerous disguises and whose influence remains clandestine. Many of the young poets of the 'thirties were prone to write verse in the form of speeches—orations about the death of liberty or the bombardment of the Karl Marx House. Between writers who have helped to change the world and writers who have set out to change it, there exists a very sharp distinction. Every really gifted writer is, in some degree, a critic of his own age ; but his criticism is implied, hidden deep beneath the surface, inseparable from a larger view of the condition of humanity as a whole.* Proust, for instance, became a critic of society through

* " I am far from finding fault with you for not having written a point-blank socialist novel. . . . The more the opinions of the author remain hidden, the better for the work of art." Engels to Margaret Harkness, 1888. Three years earlier, writing to another feminine correspondent, Engels had declared that there was " no compulsion for the writer to put into the reader's hands the future historical resolution of the social conflicts which he is depicting ".

his preoccupation with the life of the emotions, which gradually involved him in a study of their social background. He depicts the decay of the Faubourg St. Germain, refers in passing to the trial of Dreyfus ; and the reader draws an irresistible inference from these reflections of national grandeur and decline.

In short, whether rightly or wrongly, the literary decade that was cut short by the Second World War seemed considerably less sympathetic than the decade that had preceded it. Nor did the war itself provoke any literary outburst comparable to the earlier explosion ; while the demand for poetry, although persistent, certainly showed signs of dwindling. Post-war poets were fewer, more inconspicuous and a good deal quieter. Then across my horizon whirled the dervish-shape of Dylan Thomas. The didactic and rhetorical mode of poetry is derived from its connection with Apollo ; and here at length was a poet who belonged unmistakably to the Dionysiac school. He was a word-intoxicated man—unlike the majority of his immediate predecessors who seemed to value language as a means of expression rather than as a field of discovery to be cultivated for its own sake. Dionysiac, too, were his habits and appearance—a snub-nosed satyr, a young Silenus and, if he had been drinking very deeply, now and then a drunken helot. I was luckier perhaps than many of his friends ; for, although during the late hours of the night and the early hours of the morning our paths were often bound to cross, I usually found him a friendly companion, indistinct but inoffensive, and admired the strange mixture he displayed of genuine simplicity and elemental guile. In this aspect, I think, he may have resembled Paul Verlaine, " *le pauvre Lélian* ", another passionate lover of words with an uninhibited thirst for pleasure. Both were capable of remorse ; but neither was much afflicted by shame. Dylan Thomas, at least, made no attempt to conceal or excuse the crapulous disorder of his daily life ; and I remember that he once advised me to use a barber's shop in Soho, adding that the barber was a sensible sort of person who did not at all object should a client succumb to morning nausea while in the midst of being shaved. He imparted this comforting information in a perfectly straightforward and unselfconscious way, as if such a mishap would almost certainly occur, and a wise man naturally took his precautions by going to the right establishment.

Yet a keen native intelligence lurked beneath the crapulous mask, glinting in the prominent eyes, twitching at the corners of the thick-lipped smile. With his love of words went an abundant verbal wit; and wit was accompanied by an inextinguishable sense of fun. Dylan Thomas was a comedian in the great tradition, whose gift of buffoonery recalled the art of that exquisite American mime, W. C. Fields. He had the same grandiloquence and rapid changes of tone, the same knack of making dignity absurd and giving absurdity a richly dignified air. He was in this mood when I last encountered him. The background of our meeting was Rome—that quarter of the city where its Classical and Baroque past meet and join forces with the most harmonious results, between the towering mass of the Pantheon and the airy palaces and fountains of the Piazza Navona. I was standing at the edge of the Piazza, thinking myself a thousand miles from England, when an elderly English personage came tiptoeing by, following his long nose through the sunlit square, and apparently bound on some mysterious quest, like M. de Charlus in one of the later volumes of *A la Recherche du Temps Perdu*. He was not very pleased to be recognised and, after a few words, quickly pressed ahead. No sooner had he vanished than Dylan Thomas suddenly appeared, as rumpled and red and bulbous as ever, with the remains of a damp cigarette adhering to his lower lip. He, on the contrary, seemed glad to see a familiar London face, explaining how he and his wife had come to Italy, lured by the promise of a " film-job ", how the job had failed to materialise and they were stranded and at large in Rome, without employment or hope of employment and with very little ready money. Meanwhile what they needed was the address of a really *low*, an indubitably disreputable, night-club. I could not supply the address; but we agreed that we must meet next day; and next morning I went to his hotel, a tall, narrow, ancient building wedged in somewhere just behind the Pantheon, entered a narrow dark hall and spoke to an amiable porter seated in a dusky crevice.

Most Italians have a certain respect for art ; and it was clear that Dylan's poetic character was already well-established. Mr. Thomas ? The English poet ? And the porter began to manipulate a jangling old-fashioned telephone. Yes, Mr. Thomas would descend in a moment ; and before long the noise of an explosive smoker's-cough came echoing down the uncarpeted stairs, and the poet shot into sight as if pursued by an invisible enemy. Brushing past me with extended hand, he stumbled and groped towards the threshold and hastened in speechless dismay across the cobble-stones and through the entrance of a bar. Here again he appeared to have made himself known ; he was warmly welcomed as the *signor poeta* ; and the barman, without waste of time, immediately poured a large glass of brandy and a larger glass of pale Italian beer. The order was at once repeated, and my companion slowly came to life. Certainly they had found the night-club they needed and a roostful of congenial night-birds, some of whom, when the night-club closed, had been enchanted to accompany them home. Vaguely solicitous and, no doubt, slightly pompous, I enquired about his wife's health. Dylan instantly caught my tone, which he proceeded to adopt and parody in his own stately and sonorous manner. His eyes grew extremely round and even more curiously protrusive than usual. " My late espousèd saint ", he intoned, and after a pause : " *my little chocolate drop*, when last I saw her lay extended . . ." But I forget in what despondent position he professed to have discovered Mrs. Thomas, though he added, I recollect, that, when he turned her over, so far as he could see she was still alive. I dare say he was merely embroidering the tale ; it was the solemn pause, followed by an abrupt transition of imagery, that gave the sentence a dramatic point. To labour an effect, however, was not his way ; and, with a nod to the attentive barman, he imperiously ordered another round. As it happened, we did not meet again ; and, seven or eight years later, I heard the horrid story of his collapse and death in New York. His closing period has been minutely—perhaps too minutely—chronicled. We have read of his growing fatigue and despair, and of a process of deliberate self-destruction which seems to have culminated in a kind of ritual suicide ; we have also watched the development of a popular literary legend that he himself, with his caustic and ribald sense of humour, might well have considered inordinately entertaining ; and this legend, like the legends of every age, has involved some misrepresentation of the human subject. If one remembers the " Artist as a Young Dog "—and as a dog no longer very young but still abounding with a doggish zest for life, ears pricked, tongue lolling, muddy paws sprawling over carpets and beds—it is often difficult to recognise his features in the sepulchral effigy of the Dead Lion.

*　　　*　　　*

Apart from the poets sketched above, I have known many less distinguished versifiers, nowadays almost entirely forgotten or remembered only for a few anthology-pieces. Should they appear to form a somewhat saddening procession, it is not because they lacked integrity or wanted the kind of dignity that goes with arduous labours and lofty hopes. What saddens one is the poignant contrast between those hopes and their actual poetic gifts, between the splendid objective they had set themselves and the meagre rewards they at length obtained. Every poet, in every literary period, embarks on a prodigious gamble ; in no other branch of art does the artist play for higher stakes ; in none has he so slight a chance of succeeding or will his failure seem more ridiculous. Whereas a poor novel may include some details that recommend the book to an intelligent reader—a scrap of original observation or two or three passages of well-reported dialogue—the badness of really bad verse has a negative quality that defies analysis. To criticize it is to attempt to describe a

44

vacuum ; it is nothing or a little less than nothing ; and yet this vacuum was evidently the product of genuine feeling and deep unselfish care. Always, just behind a poet, stands the Devil's Advocate, whose whispered doubts, loud or soft, fill the pauses of creative activity. * Sometimes he adopts a human form. Thus I remember meeting a distinguished classical scholar who had made a special study of the early Greek poets, and seemed to delight in reducing their fragmentary remains to a collection of unintelligible sounds. He had developed a particular dislike for Sappho, whom he styled " the Lesbian bitch ", and enjoyed pointing out that an especially famous line, hitherto translated as " I sleep alone ",† in the dialect that the poetess employed could only mean " I alone am asleep "; which, he concluded blithely, was utter nonsense and provoked the conclusion that the whole fragment must be corrupt and valueless. Similarly, he would turn his attention to the poetic achievements of the English nineteenth century, describing how he had just looked into a *variorum* edition of Tennyson's work, full of successive re-touches, each of them more preposterous than the version that had preceded it. He had memorised them and proceeded to quote them at length, accompanying his recital of absurdities with a high-pitched academic crow.

Now and then, the case against poetry has received vigorous expression in print. For the last thirty years, during which so many much more important books have unaccountably de-materialised, I have been carrying around a squat parchment-covered volume entitled *De Incertitudine & Vanitate omnium Scientarium & Artium Liber, lectu planè jucundus & elegans*, the work of Henry Cornelius Agrippa von Nettesheim, the " Great Agrippa " of the German cautionary tale, best known for his

* " *Alors, j'ai fait d'la littérature,*
  Mais le Démon de la Vérité.
  Sifflotait tout l'temps à mes côtés:
  ' *Pauvre! as-tu fini tes écritures . . .'* "
                          Jules Laforgue: *Des Fleurs de Bonne Volonté.*
  † " The Moon has sunk, and the Pleiads. It is midnight : time goes by. But I sleep alone."

hand-book to occult learning, *De Occulta Philosophia*. Like Erasmus, Cornelius Agrippa was a wandering humanist ; and his attack on the arts and sciences, first published in 1531, is a satirical disquisition of somewhat the same kind as Erasmus' celebrated *Praise of Folly*. He amuses his readers by hammering away at the contemporary exponents of every branch of knowledge—from philosophers, grammarians and historians to heralds, magicians and professors of astrology and magic—reserving some particularly severe gibes for those who dabble in the imaginative arts. Poetry he denounces with especial fervour—" *ars non in aliud inventa nisi ut lascivientibus rhythmis, syllabarum numeris ac ponderibus, nominumque inani stripitu, stultorum hominum aures demulceat . . .*" And then, besides cozening the ears of mankind by means of lascivious rhythms and the inane rehearsal of sonorous names, poetry encourages the propagation of deceptive and perverse ideas, being the " *architectrix mendaciorum & cultrix perversorum dogmatum* ", pandering to our inbred childishness, flattering our wrong-headedness and helping to kindle the unlawful passions that are the bane of any civilized society. It springs, in fact, from the darkest regions of the mind, where wisdom and judgment seldom shed their light—a relic of our race's primitive youth, unfit for serious consideration by the modern humanist.

Poetry, when Agrippa tilted against it, was a living part of social life ; and, since that time, not only has it lost the popular appeal that it continued to exercise until the death of Tennyson, but the territories that a poet commands have gradually grown more and more restricted. He was long ago obliged to retreat from the wide provinces over which his predecessors ruled. We have ceased to expect that he should instruct us on such subjects as morality or history ; and " philosophic " poems on the Lucretian scale are evidently foredoomed to failure. Meanwhile he has slowly drawn back towards the central massif of the Sacred Mountain ; and there his concern is not with writing good verse—which may or may not, thanks to skill and taste,

46

acquire incidentally a real poetic value—but with mustering all
his resources in some splendid flash of " pure poetry ". That
phrase—a recent coinage—seems already to have done considerable harm ; for it implies that any other kind of poetry is necessarily cheap and spurious. Yet English writers have often excelled
in the production of " occasional " poems, which we remember
and re-read after we have given up hope of their epics and their
blank-verse tragedies. By " occasional " poems, I do not, of
course, mean a rhyming " Address to a Young Lady " or even
Wordsworth's lines prompted by the contemplation of a harp-
shaped needle-case, but Matthew Prior's verses, for example—
probably the most enduring that he ever wrote—inscribed on
the fly-leaf of François de Mezeray's *Histoire de France*, in which
the poet compares the grandeur of human ambition with the
vanity of human wishes. Mezeray, Prior remarks, has raised a
magnificent monument to the resounding exploits of the French
people :

> " Yet for the fame of all these deeds,
> What beggar in the Invalides,
> With lameness broke, with blindness smitten,
> Wished ever decently to die,
> To have been either Mezeray,
> Or any monarch he has written ?

> " It strange, dear Author, yet it true is,
> That down from Pharamond to Louis,
> All covet life, yet call it pain ;
> All feel the ill, yet shun the cure :
> Can sense this paradox endure ?
> Resolve me, Cambray, or Fontaine.

> " The man in graver Tragic known,
> Tho' his best part long since was done,
> Still on the stage desires to tarry :

And he who play'd the harlequin,
After the jest still loads the scene,
Unwilling to retire, tho' weary." *

And then, there are those delightful verse-letters which Swift used to address *To Stella on her Birthday.* They may not be " poems " in the noblest meaning of the word ; but we should be wrong, I think, if we discounted them as mere ingenious literary exercises. They have a poetic content besides a poetic form— productions haunted by the genius of poetry, though we can point out no single line in which that genius makes a distinct appearance. Conversational verse, however, is beyond the average modern poet's scope ; and during the last two or three decades he has also retreated from the field of satire, the region in which Dryden and Pope established their poetic supremacy. Ours, after all, is an age of specialisation ; and just as science and literature are now completely separate, so literature itself has been sub-divided into many different and widely divergent branches. The poet's position is equally lofty and lonely ; alone and unsupported he must either succeed or fail.

Nevertheless, the nature of the art he practises is no better understood than it was a hundred years ago ; and, from every pronouncement on the subject issued since the birth of writing, it is clear that, despite their various theories as to the purpose that the art of poetry may serve, very few poets can explain clearly either why they are impelled to write or what are the exact processes by which a poem takes shape in the writer's mind. Compare, for example, W. H. Auden's inaugural discourse at Oxford, delivered in 1956, with A. E. Housman's Leslie Stephen Lecture, entitled *The Name and Nature of Poetry*, published in 1933. During the course of his penultimate paragraph, Housman describes how, " having drunk a pint of beer at luncheon—beer is

* *Poems on Several Occasions,* 1709. This is a poem for which Walter Scott is said to have had a deep affection.

48

a sedative to the brain . . .", he would go out for a walk of two or three hours, " thinking of nothing in particular, only looking at things around me and following the progress of the seasons." As he walked, " there would flow into my mind, with sudden and unaccountable emotion, sometimes a line or two of verse, sometimes a whole stanza at once, accompanied, not preceded, by a vague notion of the poem which they were destined to form a part of . . . The source of the suggestion thus proffered to the brain was an abyss " that Housman identified with the pit of the stomach. Sometimes " further inspiration " was vouchsafed on the following day ; " but sometimes the poem had to be taken in hand and completed by the brain, which was apt to be matter of trouble and anxiety involving trial and disappointment . . ."

In this account of his own creative method—considerably more explicit than anything provided by the modern poet—the author of *A Shropshire Lad* and *Last Poems* makes a number of interesting and important points. The suggestions that coalesce as a poem are said to arise from a mysterious abyss ; the emotion they stir is " unaccountable "; the poetic framework, reared by inspiration, is often "taken in hand" and completed by the brain —or, rather, by that section of the brain over which the poet exercises a conscious control. In W. H. Auden's lecture, on the other hand, the involuntary aspect of the poet's activities seems to receive comparatively little notice ; but he tells us that the writing of poetry is inspired by " awe ", and that " the impulse to produce a work of art is felt when, in certain persons, the passive awe provoked by sacred beings or events is transformed into a desire to express that awe into a rite of worship or homage, and to be fit homage this rite must be beautiful ". But then, what constitutes beauty, and why should some objects be sacred and others, poetically speaking, profane ? Turning to his own case, the poet informs us that, before he had begun to write verse, he had already recognised a class of " Sacred Objects " in books on mining and mineralogy : " A word like *pyrites*, for example, was for me, not simply an indicative sign ; it was the Proper Name of a Sacred Being . . ." No doubt every poet cherishes a private pantheon of the same kind—a group of associated images to which he attaches an especial value. Housman's favourite symbols included the Doomed Soldier and the Hanged Man. But we are still a long way from deciding why these symbols should first of all have acquired their ascendancy over the imagination of the individual poet. Some—like those which Auden mentions—have a distant origin in the poet's reading. It was a volume of old travels that helped to launch *The Ancient Mariner*. Yet it was Coleridge's personal experience of life— which had induced a passionate sense of guilt—that gave his verses their poetic unity. In fact, whenever a gifted verse-writer happens to have become a genuine poet, we seem to distinguish a fusion of reading and experience, of memory and passion, of personal and impersonal elements. Ideas that have been vaguely assembling in his mind suddenly fly together to form a poetic whole. A process of crystallisation occurs, precipitated by some unknown agent.

How or why that crystallisation occurs no literary critic has yet determined. Meanwhile we must always bear in mind the writer's indebtedness to his literary past. Whereas the untutored reader generally assumed that a poet derives " inspiration " from external nature—during my youth I was frequently recommended by my officious aunts and cousins to put away the book I was reading, and seek the stimulus they expected me to discover in a sunset or the springtime song of the birds—most adult poets, when we examine them at close range, prove to have been deeply bookish. Nor is this observation true of poets alone. If the artist's vision, announces André Malraux, differs from the common vision, it is because his view of life has been matured by his previous experiences among works of art : " *Il est révélateur que pas une mémoire de grand artiste ne retienne une vocation née d'autre chose que l'émotion ressentie devant une œuvre . . . L'homme bouleversé par un spectacle ou un drame, et soudain obsédé par la volonté de l'exprimer,*

on ne le recontre jamais."* The creative mood is also imitative—
though, even as a great artist imitates, he begins inevitably to
adapt and change ; and it is by considering the world through
the eyes of earlier artists that he may at length succeed in presenting us with a new heaven and a new earth. But poets—more
eclectic than painters—do not confine their borrowings to literary
sources. They are profoundly influenced by all the other arts,
particularly the art of painting ; and a critic has pointed out that
Keats' *Hyperion*—certainly the noblest of his long poems—would
appear to have been coloured throughout by a recollection of
one of Claude's works ; that not only has it the same atmosphere
of romantic melancholy and antique majesty, but that it is composed with the same exquisite feeling for natural background
and mythological detail, from the seated figure of the fallen Titan
himself—

> " Still as the silence round about his lair ;
> Forest on forest hung about his head
> Like cloud on cloud "

to the water-nymph, curious and apprehensive, who lies watching
him beside the river—

> " . . . The Naiad 'mid her reeds
> Press'd her cold finger closer to her lips."

The picture that Keats perhaps remembered may well have
been a work of genius. Yet it was not the quality of genius that
necessarily fired his imagination—writers are often apt to show
more enthusiasm than æsthetic taste ; and, indeed, the Grecian
Urn of his most celebrated ode has since been identified at the
British Museum and proves, in the light of common day, to be
a fairly trivial object. No less trivial are many of the other agents
that have brought about poetic crystallisation. Acting as cat-
alysts, they cannot do their work until the right conditions of
imaginative ferment have already been established ; and those

* *Les Voix du Silence.*

conditions may develop very slowly, throughout a period of weeks and even years. Then, almost unnoticed, some accidental stimulus happens to drop into the poet's mind, and a loose assemblage of ideas and emotions suddenly assumes a definite literary shape. At that moment, the poet himself will often appear to be losing control of the process that has been set on foot ; and various poets have gone so far as to suggest that their poems were either dictated to them or reached them from a dark and mysterious region—Housman's subliminal " abyss "—deep below the ordinary level of consciousness. Gérard de Nerval, for instance, declared that his marvellous sonnets were composed in a " state of supernatural reverie "; the pattern of *Kublai Khan* coalesced in a dream ; Blake would spring from his bed to transcribe the heavenly messages that he had received while he was lying half-asleep ; and his mood seems to have been particularly receptive during the aftermath of sexual pleasure ; for there is a design of his that shows the eagle of inspiration sweeping down on a recumbent man and woman, stretched out, relaxed and satisfied, along a rock above a stormy midnight ocean.

If, at this point, I write of my own experiences, it is not because I believe that the verses I wrote and published, between the ages of fifteen, say, and twenty-one, deserve to be treated as serious works of literature, but because writing them gave me a certain insight into the origins and growth of the poetic impulse. Although the results I achieved were inconsiderable, I felt the excitement shared by every poet ; and, until that excitement had gradually died away, the desire to produce poetry continued to dominate my lesser hopes and plans. At the age of fifteen, I distinctly recollect, I decided that if, by the time I was twenty-one, I had not yet written any poem that showed signs of true poetic genius, I should have no alternative but to commit suicide, since life on any other terms would evidently prove an insufferable burden. Luckily perhaps, I afterwards decided to extend the limit. Excuses for granting myself a reprieve were discovered in various works of literature. Were there not some famous lines

by Milton in which he writes of his frustrated youth ? * And
Milton's example was not unprecedented, as I learned from
reading literary biographies. Poetic Spring often arrived late ;
and the buds and blossoms of achievement had sometimes failed
to ripen until the approach of summer. I could allow myself,
I thought, at least a further half decade. And so I was induced
to temporise over my adolescent projects of self-destruction,
which, as the years went by, grew increasingly vague, to vanish
at length about the age of thirty.

Meanwhile I had ceased to write verse ; and even now I am
occasionally asked why I no longer publish poems, my juvenilia
having become a convenient stick, employed for castigatory purposes by good-natured friends. The answer is that I did not
abandon verse, but that the need to try to compose poems im-
perceptibly diminished in me. For it was a genuine inward need
that set me scribbling as much as a youthful desire to make my
mark ; and the need was less to convey my sensations—though
the desire to communicate underlies every form of creative
activity—than to release the tension that had been built up by
the secret pressure of many different feelings, which might
include both the pleasure I felt at the beauty of the world beneath
my eyes and the emotions derived from a book first opened
several days earlier. In combination, they had engendered a
state of excitement that could only be relieved if I attempted to
write a poem ; and, during the attempt, I sought to produce a
pattern of rhythmic and evocative words, through which the
tension that excited and troubled me might be accounted for and
exorcised. Writing verse, then, was a semi-magical manœuvre ;
and the result that I aimed at was not an exact description of
something I had felt or seen, but its symbolic equivalent, realised
by the mysterious powers of language. The poems I jotted
down were primarily spells. Once I had reached a more settled

---

* " How soon hath Time, the subtle thief of youth,
Stolen on his wing my three-and-twentieth year !
My hasting days fly on with full career,
But my late Spring no bud or blossom sheweth."

mode of existence—duller, no doubt, but calmer and quieter—
these incantations had outlived their use.

As in spells, a diversity of elements were combined to form a
single poem ; and, looking back through my juvenile productions, I notice that some of my borrowings can yet be traced.
A great many of them came from the visual arts ; a smaller
number, from my memories of travel abroad. In a poem entitled
Leviathan, for example, I was thinking of an early statue of the
dragon-god Typhon seen on the Acropolis, but elsewhere of a
Chinese sepulchral slab that depicted a group of heavenly beings.
A diving figure drawn by Blake provided me with an equally
compulsive hint ; and a picture by Carpaccio in Venice, which
illustrates the story of Samson and Delilah, also jolted my imagination. A poem, that happened to be written in Sicily, contains an
overt reference to the quarries at Syracuse, haunted by the ghosts
of the unhappy Athenian captives who were condemned to spend
the remainder of their lives amid that fantastic rock labyrinth ;
and some remembered scrap of history or legend reappears on
almost every page. The oddest combination of references, however, occurs in two succeeding lines, which I am encouraged to
quote since they were once picked out for praise by a distinguished
modern English poet. They concern the divinities of the past,
whom I imagined occasionally revisiting the landscapes of the
present day—

> " Whose passing fills calm nights with sudden wind,
> Whose spears still bar our twilight . . . "

Here the first line must have originated in my reading of a book
on Irish mythology, which describes how the Celtic " Invisible
People " could sometimes be recognised at night by the gust of
wind their passage raised ; while for the second I was indebted
to my recollections of one of Tintoretto's frescoes, of which a
photograph hung for many years on the wall over my parents'
bed. The subject of the picture is the Crucifixion ; and against
the twilight sky, behind the three crosses, stands a bristling

hedge of spears. I have a notion that I had always remembered this detail because, as a child, I had found it strangely enigmatic. Not until I had begun to grow up did I discover the mysterious hedge was, in fact, a rank of upright lances ; and meanwhile the impression it made had sunk into the depths of my subconscious memory.

Nevertheless, despite such jackdaw thefts, it was the unifying emotion that really counted—the emotion that related these haphazard *trouvailles* to the background of my own life. All the unsatisfied feelings of youth came together in a moment of crystallisation ; and, when I knew that the moment was approaching, I went through a period of acute anxiety. " Persons from Porlock " constantly threatened to intrude ; the smallest interruption might snap the thread of my reverie ; and I was often reduced to leaving the house, and hurrying out across the adjacent common, in the hope that I should be able to exploit the impulse before it had developed beyond its most productive stage. I had no lack of enthusiasm or energy ; what I then lacked was the gift of co-ordination, and the adult intelligence, governed by Apollo, that controls and rationalizes the Dionysiac mood. Clearly a poet must endeavour to hold the balance between the two powerful gods who were worshipped at Delphi, welcoming the " inspiration " that Dionysus supplies, but subjecting its uncoordinated flow to the precepts of moderation that his rival taught. Thus the greatest poems represent a temporary alliance of the writer's conscious and subconscious mind ; whereas secondary works either depend on suggestion—the magical effect of words and images—or rely, as in most Augustan poems, on the force of eloquent assertion alone. In a poet of Shakespearian calibre, neither mode of poetry predominates. His verse is a criticism of life—of the outward features of the unchanging " human condition "—but invokes the aid of demons and divinities that hide far below the surface of the mind. There results, now and then, a harmonious arrangement of syllables, in which, as Coleridge remarked of Shakespeare and Milton, " it would scarcely be more difficult to push a stone out from the pyramids with the bare hand, than to alter a word, or the position of a word . . . without making the author say something else, or something worse, than he does say." *   Such unforgettable poems have an air of oracular freshness, as if they reached us directly from another world ; yet, at the same time, they seem merely to confirm something we have always known and felt. The landscape they unfold is dazzlingly new, yet, on second thoughts, not wholly unfamiliar.   Just as exquisite as our sense of discovery is the accompanying shock of recognition.

* *Biographia Literaria,* Chapter I.

II

Storytellers

As soon as I had reached Japan and had taken possession of a new house, which smelt not of drying paint but of freshly sawn aromatic timber and of finely woven rush mats laid down while they were still green, one of my first constructive moves was to order a large writing desk. A local craftsman, produced by my servant, built me a piece of furniture in the traditional style, a knee-desk beautifully carpentered of silvery-grey paulownia wood, plain and broad and extremely close to the floor, but with just sufficient space for the user's limbs if he sat cross-legged upon a thin cushion. Here I immediately began to write a book, partly as a means of defence against my hostile surroundings, partly in fulfilment of a long-considered plan. During the winter months, my position opposite the screens, which were all that divided me from a wet or snow-bound landscape, was often invaded by icy draughts; but on hot days it was pleasant to sit there and look out across the narrow garden. Cicadas whirred in the branches of the dead tree; clogs pattered beyond the garden fence; strains of high-pitched *samisen* music tinkled from a distant radio; the electric fan kept up a gentle drone, and dissolving ice-cubes softly clinked as they settled into a glass of whisky.

The book that I was writing, however, bore not the smallest relation to my life in Japan. It had an entirely English subject, a novel about life in London, seen through the eyes of characters who very closely resembled myself and one or two carefully selected friends. Indeed, it was an autobiographical novel, of the kind that every inexperienced writer at some moment feels compelled to publish. But my intentions were good ; my aims were high ; and I had received a hint, which I found encouraging, from no less a source than Holy Writ. My authority was the mysterious prophet of Patmos. Students of *Revelation* will remember the " mighty angel " who offers him a little scroll. " Give me the little book ", the prophet exclaims. " And he said unto me, Take it, and eat it up ; and it shall make thy belly bitter, but it shall be in thy mouth sweet as honey." I had, of course, envisaged no comparison between my own capacities and those of the mighty angel ; but the novel that I hoped to write was to have followed the example of the " little book ", in so far as it was smooth on the palate and left behind it an astringent, even a sharply bitter, after-taste. Almost everyone is a cynic at twenty-five ; and my cynicism was all the more pronounced because it had been largely absorbed through reading. Among the French novelists I had recently read and admired was that phenomenal personage Raymond Radiguet ; and the explosive content of Radiguet's stories lay hidden beneath an inoffensive style, quiet, harmonious and decent, with never a libertine word or phrase. Very well then, my " little book " should practise a somewhat similar deception. Such acerbity as I managed to inject should be concealed by its bland and pleasing surface.

As I wrote, I felt occasional misgivings ; and they were certainly justified when the book appeared. I have long ceased to own a reference copy ; and, if I happen to catch sight of it among the volumes upon a friend's shelves, I am tempted to approach it by stealth and push it out of sight behind the row. Its title, *The Phœnix Kind*, stolen from Fulke Greville,* has a pleasantly

---

* " Love is of the phœnix kind,
And burns itself with self-made fire,
To breed still new birds in the mind,
From ashes of the old desire."

Storytellers

romantic ring. Otherwise, its chief attraction is that it demonstrates how a novel should *not* be written and, by contrast, what are the qualities that keep works of fiction living and moving. For the chief demerit of my novel was that it possessed no independent life ; the spirit that should have animated it had expired while it was being born ; and all that remained, once it had been brought to birth, was an elaborate piece of literary invention. Nor should this result have surprised me, considering the method I had adopted : I had imagined a situation and equipped it with characters, whereas (as I discovered too late) the characters whom a novelist presents ought, almost of their own accord, to produce a situation through which they grow and change. My characters failed to develop since they were schematic in the fashion of a child's drawing—heads, bodies and legs, linked together with a series of casual strokes. Two brothers bore the burden of the story ; and they had been evolved by a process of self-bisection. To manufacture them, I had cut myself in two, allowing to the older kinsman all my worthiest, dullest and prosiest traits, giving the younger the doubtful benefit of my looser, more anarchic impulses. The older envies the younger, who repays his loyalty and affection with grudging respect ; but, when my rakish hero acquires a mistress, she throws their joint household into sad confusion ; and, by a strange accident, my middle-aged alter ego temporarily usurps the lover's rôle . . .

No less artificial was the method I had chosen of situating my story in space and time. The background consisted of a succession of carefully executed landscape-studies, vignettes of London and its suburbs and a Mediterranean island I had recently visited, laid down side by side to form a continuous decorative frieze. I was not dissatisfied with such embellishments ; but I was well aware my novel lacked cohesion more damning, that it lacked substance, the density and solidity of a serious work of art. While I laboured, I sometimes amused myself by composing an imaginary review ; and, parodying Jane Austen's famous reference to

59

her " little bit (two inches wide) of ivory ", I observed that this new novel seemed to have been painted on ivory, or like Nicholas Hilliard's miniatures on the surface of a playing card, " with a finely pointed camel-hair brush dipped in a decoction of the weakest china tea ". Some of the notices that actually appeared, when they at length reached me, proved nearly as fanciful and high-flown. They were far more eulogistic than I had any right to hope; and Harold Nicolson gave me an avuncular pat on the head. But a Marxist reviewer acclaimed my opuscule as a minor masterpiece of the current Silver Age, showing the depths of despair and futility to which the literary bourgeoisie had now fallen; and a fellow critic, who wrote from the provinces, compared it to a tiny jewelled casket, beautifully designed and chased, containing only a pinch of poisonous dust.

In the meantime, four of my Oxford contemporaries were hard at work becoming successful novelists. Evelyn Waugh, Anthony Powell and the writer who prefers to be called Henry Green I knew best during their undergraduate period; but Graham Greene I had also known at school, the red-brick school where his father was headmaster, of which he has supplied so dramatic a description in a travel-book entitled *The Lawless Roads*. To see a place that one remembers vividly reflected on the screen of another writer's mind is an odd and disconcerting experience. I remember the school as dull, and the town as drab; but the undertones of evil that Graham Greene detected made no impression on my more unreceptive spirit, which often revolted against my humdrum surroundings but never associated my revolt with a sense of sin. After all, the town had a broad and pleasant High Street, which included some dignified ancient houses, though its late-Victorian periphery was certainly rather grim and squalid. Encompassed by the hideous school-buildings was a venerable Tudor hall; and most of the masters attached to the school struck me as respectable, if somewhat uninteresting, men. But

60

beyond the town, above the ruins of its castle, stretched an enormous tract of open common, where larks spun dizzily up from the turf and dark pine clumps stood islanded in acres of bracken and yellow-flowering gorse bushes. It was bordered by the palings of a park that extended for many miles along a ridge of the Chilterns, as far as a bold eminence named Ivinghoe Beacon, crowned with a small prehistoric barrow, which surveyed the placid Vale of Aylesbury. Through the park itself, around Wyatt's battlemented mansion, mysterious deserted rides ran between colonnades of massive beech trees; the gardens of the house, after its owner's death, had lapsed into a romantic jungle, a wilderness of tall grass, unclipped hedges and tumbled statues.

These same prospects I find strangely transmogrified in my distinguished contemporary's recollections. The school that we both attended proves to have been a place of almost unfathomable iniquity, haunted by adults and adolescents " who bore about them the genuine quality of evil. There was Callifax who practised torments with dividers, Mr. Cranden with pale bleached hair, a dusty gown, a kind of demoniac sensuality "; and from such heights " evil declined towards Parlow whose desk was filled with minute photographs—advertisements of art photos. Hell lay about them in their infancy." But I was conscious neither of the hellish atmosphere of the pedestrian life I lived at school, nor of the signs of spiritual degeneracy that I might have run to earth among the adjacent streets. I never glanced into the windows of the " shabby little shop " that sold second-hand copies of a fetishistic weekly paper; and I remained unaware of " Irish servant girls " (twice referred to by my friend the novelist) creeping from back doors in the early dark to make " their assignations for a ditch ". Perhaps I was unduly simple-minded, perhaps unusually self-centred; but the intimations of Evil that seem to have coloured Graham Greene's youth, and that since then have had so profound an effect on the shaping of his creative talents, failed somehow to enrich mine; with the result that my memories of the school and the town are much less valuable as a source of literary legend. It may be that they are slightly more accurate. But here we come face to face with the unending problem of how an imaginative artist should employ his material.

For the moment I must put aside that problem and return to the author of *The Lawless Roads*. Graham Greene was not, in those days, the careworn and hag-ridden personage whom one might possibly conjure up from a study of his recollections. Tall, lank and limp, with an extremely pallid skin but sharp, cheerfully observant eyes, he would have made an admirable Pierrot in the eighteenth-century Commedia dell'Arte, concealing under his rather woebegone mask a great capacity for cynical humour. He was often exuberant : he could be positively blithe. Nor have the exuberance and the blitheness vanished. And even at the present period, when I re-read his books—those sombre chronicles of sin and suffering, where every form of pleasure is naturally suspect, every love-affair inescapably doomed, and a breath of Evil mixes with the fog that swirls around the lonely street-lamps—I sometimes feel that I am confronting the spirited schoolboy in a more accomplished and more portentous guise. I cannot resist the suspicion that he gets a good deal of fun— light-hearted schoolboyish fun—from causing his own and his reader's flesh to creep, and that he half enjoys the sensations of disgust and horror that he arouses with such unusual artistry. But is his use of these sensations, regarded as the constituents of a work of art, always perfectly legitimate ? Are not the scales weighted against his characters a little too heavily and too deliberately ? His men and women drag a burden of guilt like prisoners dragging a ball-and-chain ; and it is a foregone conclusion that their experiences of physical love will turn out to be squalid and ignominious. No device is ever neglected that might help to rub the squalor in. Thus, when the hero and heroine of *The End of the Affair* wish to invent a private code-name for the act of love-making, one is not particularly surprised to learn that the word they choose is " onions ". He has caught us there ! One imagines the novelist exclaiming, with a delighted smile and a gleeful rubbing of the hands. No doubt we had had thoughts of Proust, of Swann and Odette in the same circumstances and their feebly romantic "*faire catleya*"? But then, Proust's lovers had a sofa and a bed : Graham Greene's are usually condemned to come to grips with passion upon the naked floor.

I must admit, then, that, much as I appreciate his ingenuity and virtuosity and the remarkable aptitude that he shows for plain straightforward storytelling—what could be more effective, to take a single instance, than the episode of the beleaguered watch tower in *The Quiet American* ?—I am often a little uneasy about the means he has adopted to achieve his ends, and am conscious of a touch of artificiality, even of artistic fraud. Yet, considered from a technical point of view, each of his more recent novels is an amazingly deft performance ; and the reader's enjoyment is only spoiled by an occasional journalistic trick, which provokes the suspicion that this extraordinary display of cleverness may conceal, at least in some passages, a certain lack of seriousness. Evelyn Waugh, on the other hand, with an equal degree of skill combines a primarily æsthetic gift. He has a journalist's flair but an artist's temperament ; and the journalist is always subordinated to the artist's sense of style. The devices he employs are seldom laboured ; and, although a favourite stratagem may be brought into play during the course of several different books—few novelists have made so ingenious a use of literary legerdemain and the element of surprise—the result has an air of novelty that accords with his fresh and lively writing. *Decline and Fall*, his explosive extravaganza, was first published in 1928, not long after he had left Oxford, at a time when Waugh the care-free bohemian, as distinct from Pinfold-Waugh the romantic reactionary, had not yet been completely submerged. Since that period, the artist and the conservative seem to have developed side by side.

Their association has helped to mould his style; but many of his early friends must regret the vanished bohemian. " All gentle and juvenile, curly and gay ", in the fashion recommended by the less conventional of the two more expensive Oxford tailors—a light-blue suit of rather hairy tweed, accompanied by a loose silk tie—with a thick stick, short and knotted, which he frequently thumped upon the pavement, Evelyn Waugh presented an engaging appearance as he crossed an Oxford quadrangle, very unlike the grave-faced man of the world, sheltered beneath a bowler hat that resembles a crash-helmet and armed with a tightly rolled umbrella, carried like a marshal's baton, nowadays sometimes to be observed pounding up St. James's Street. Of the shape he subsequently assumed I need not attempt to write here—Pinfold the literary recluse, Pinfold the tormented pachyderm, whose armour-plating is intersected by deep and painful crevices, has been acknowledged by the author as, in some respects, a self-portrait. Pinfold, as presented in the novel, is a staunch believer who does not enjoy the consolations of faith, but suffers from a spiritual condition that the mystics know as *accidie*. He has strong feelings, but they refuse to flow; the fount of emotion has been choked or dammed. " Why (asks Gilbert Pinfold, when he has been paying his mother a farewell visit) does everyone except me find it so easy to be nice ? " Similarly, the chief character of *Officers and Gentlemen* lives in a spiritual and emotional desert. Not so tired of life as the unhappy Pinfold, who, whenever he looks at his watch, finds that the hour it registers is considerably earlier than he had expected and hoped, and observes, " always with disappointment ", how much of his mortal existence still lies ahead of him, he is conscious of having exhausted his emotions before he has exhausted his energy. Both are characteristic products of the novelist's private Waste Land; and beside it Graham Greene's inferno, peopled by lewd demons and full of salacious sideshows, seems to belong to the picturesque mediæval past.

Storytellers

Although in an ideal condition of society, where every work of art formed a perfect self-contained organism, the critic might prefer to disregard a creative artist's human traits, it is still difficult to dissociate a book from the background of an individual character. On English fiction the writer's temperament often leaves a peculiarly definite mark; but, of the only two famous foreign novelists whom I have been lucky enough to examine at close range, both provided some rewarding personal clues, which led directly to a consideration of their style. The first was an eminent female writer, one of the greatest stylists and storytellers of her age. '*Vous verrez*', remarked my host who had invited me to meet her at luncheon, '*que c'est une femme très savoureuse*'. This was an adjective I had never before heard applied to any modern woman of letters—indeed, in my previous experience, few contemporary authoresses could be said to have deserved it; but, as soon as Madame Colette crossed the threshold, I had no doubt that it was well placed. For there was an unmistakable richness about her whole personality, even in the rough burr of her deep and resonant Burgundian voice. She was old and tired and already half-crippled; but her appearance was commanding, her air was gay; and, when we sat down to luncheon, she scrutinized the food and wine with lively interest. Mustering my small resources of conversational French, I inquired whether she had ever visited England. Once, she replied. She had spent two or three days at a château in the Thames Valley, and she remembered '*une assez aimable petite rivière*'—here her voice became lightly caressing—that wound its serpentine way across the park. Naturally the house was haunted —she believed that every English château had its family ghost; and, while she was staying there, an unfortunate *femme de chambre* —who, she added rather surprisingly, like all English maid-servants '*était vêtue tout en rose*'— had encountered the phantom on its nightly rounds and been discovered next morning, rigid and insensible, just outside the door of the bedroom that she herself had occupied. As for the English in general, she had supposed them to be silent and apathetic, and had been much struck by their capacity for displaying emotion and raising a tremendous hubbub. The London crowds had been wildly excited. Did she recollect, I asked, what had caused their change of mood ? Something, she seemed to remember, called ' *la prise de Mafeking* . . .'

Thus the visit to which she referred, and which had never been repeated, must have taken place in May, 1900, forty-six years earlier, when Colette was beginning her ' Claudine ' period and was still under the domination of the incorrigible M. Willy. After the lapse of a decade, in 1956, while I turned the pages of a book, *Près de Colette*, written by her third husband, Maurice Goudeket, I often thought of the great woman as she then appeared to me, with her broad cheekbones, her sharp nose and chin and her huge nimbus of grizzled grey hair. Talking of the amiable rivulet that wandered across an English park, she spoke of it in a tone of tender reminiscent affection and seemed to be describing a fellow creature. Maurice Goudeket's book contains many glimpses of the novelist's attitude towards the natural world. ' *C'est peu dire* (he writes) *qu'elle aimait les bêtes. Elle éprouvait devant toute manifestation de vie, animale ou végétale, un respect qui ressemblait à une ferveur religieuse*'. Colette was no literary outcast : she had her place in the world to which she was warmly attached ; and, like the cats whom she adored and with whom she felt so strong an affinity, she resented any infringement or invasion of what she regarded as her territorial rights. Such was her preoccupation with her immediate surroundings that her first thought when she woke up was to consult a large barometer ; while, if she occupied an unfamiliar room, she was never quite at her ease until she had ascertained how it was situated in relation to the points of the compass. She loved life both as a hedonist and as a naturally active and industrious woman who enjoyed the business of living for its own sake : ' *vivre lui était une occupation en soi suffisante* '. Thus, although she sometimes declared that she would never have begun to write if circumstances had not forced her hand, once she had adopted the habit of working it became a habit she could not relinquish. But she was exceedingly modest about her literary gifts—' *Il n'y avait pour elle d'occupation supérieure ou inférieure . . . Ecrire n'était pas une activité plus noble que, par exemple, fabriquer des sabots*'. She was content simply to do the best she could : ' *Elle a été comme un luthier de province qui, à son insu, fabriquerait des stradivarius*'.

There was, of course, another side to her temperament. ' *Elle était casanière et aventureuse, à la manière des chats, passionnément attachée à ce qu'elle possédait et prête à le risquer ou à le donner à tout moment*'. In her youth, after her escape from Willy, she had been just such a wandering bohemian actress as the heroine of *La Vagabonde* ; and it is to the combination of these two personages—the home-loving housekeeper and the adventurous wanderer—that we owe the peculiar quality of the novels that she wrote in middle age. Each personage contributed to the development of her splendid prose style ; and on the subject of literary style in general she held characteristically definite and modest views. She frequently employed the word, says Maurice Goudeket : ' *mais jamais pour signifier manière d'écrire. Elle parlait du style d'un homme, d'une bête, d'une chose pour désigner par quoi cet homme, cette bête, cette chose, dans son mouvement, son maintien, se conformait à une espèce*'. Her celebrated style, in fact, had been gradually evolved as a means of conveying, with the greatest possible accuracy and delicacy, the stylistic attributes and inborn charm of her natural and human subjects. Her appreciation of the world, moreover, besides being untroubled by a religious sense of sin, was almost completely unimpeded by the desire to theorise. ' *Je n'ai pas, je n'ai jamais eu d'idées générales*', she would inform the too-solemn or the too-inquisitive interviewer. She was glad to enjoy the universe as she found it, and not unduly perturbed by the problem of its ultimate ' meaning '.

Here a great gulf seems to have divided Colette, not only from many younger writers now flourishing in France and England, of whom it certainly cannot be said that they find the business

of being alive " *une occupation en soi suffisante* ", but from not a few
of her immediate contemporaries, for example, from the tormented André Gide. But Gide was always deeply curious about
any phenomenon he had failed to understand ; and not long
before his death he paid Colette an unexpected visit. It was the
first and last meeting of these two very different writers of genius;
and neither of them succeeded in crossing the gulf, though each
of them made strenuous efforts and threw out a series of friendly
signals. Colette, by that time bed-ridden, had filled her room
overlooking the *Palais-Royal*, where she worked beneath the
famous *fanal bleu*, with all the objects that she had loved and that
testified to her sensuous enjoyment of life—her collection of
Brazilian butterflies, her barometers, her watches and clocks, her
illustrated travel books and her Chinese crystal globes. This
poetic luxury, however, aroused no response in the embarrassed
guest ; but, evidently remembering Colette's love of animals, he
endeavoured to establish a bridgehead by describing his dog,
which, he said, had an appetite for the printed word and had got
into the habit of devouring his library. Colette did her best to
pursue the dog ; but its trail soon vanished and silence again
descended. Finally, they resorted to talking of health, and the
various infirmities from which they each of them suffered ; until
Gide could discover an excuse to go, and bade his dear colleague
a polite but unhappy farewell.

The effect of celebrity on celebrity is bound to be a trifle disconcerting. Yet, even with an obscure young man, Gide's
attitude in conversation revealed something of the same embarrassment. He was very bald, very angular, unnaturally rigid
and strangely reserved, with coat-collar carefully turned up—
whether to exclude draughts or discourage attention, his English
admirer found it impossible to decide—and the general look of
an elderly fallen angel travelling incognito. Under the shelter of
darkly beetling brows shone suspicious and inquisitive eyes,
which lurked spiderlike in their bony sockets, as brilliant and

penetrating as they were quick and wary. The background of these impressions was a small restaurant on the Quai Voltaire. Gide had been dining alone ; but, when a friend led me to his table and performed the usual ceremonies of introduction—" *un jeune écrivain anglais . . . critique . . . grand admirateur de vos livres* "— he politely suggested that I should sit down and, with many rapid interrogative glances, proceeded to question me in slow and somewhat clumsy English, phrase-book English which gave his remarks a doubly meaningful and diplomatic air, as if he were determined that I should understand always a little more than he was quite prepared to say. He was anxious to inform himself about the London literary world—what precisely was the critical position adopted by certain weekly papers ; how did their editors and contributors fit into the general scheme of things ? Those, at least, were the questions he asked—and the answers I produced were, no doubt, hesitating and deplorably vague, for the English literary landscape is almost impossible to portray in clear-cut continental terms ; but I had an odd impression that none of his queries exactly corresponded to the speaker's meaning. One interrogation mark concealed a second and a third ; in his talk, as in his novels and stories, he radiated an atmosphere of surmise and doubt.

He evoked at the same time a sense of *inquiétude*—to borrow the expressive word that he himself employed so often. All his protagonists suffer from a moral *malaise*, whether it is the deep-rooted perturbation of *L'Immoraliste* and *Les Faux Monnayeurs* or the ludicrous dismay of the middle-aged hero of *Les Caves du Vatican*. But nowhere is it more boldly depicted than in his autobiographical studies—*Si le grain ne meurt*, the tale of his youth, and *Et nunc manet in te*, the brief, poignant, yet curiously unsympathetic, account of his frustrated married life. In the achievement of every gifted writer traces of conflict here and there emerge. But in Gide the private conflict forms a recurrent underlying pattern. His puritanical inheritance provides, so to speak, the pattern's rectilinear background ; and, through it and across it, like a sinuous rampant vine, run the tendrils of pagan feeling and fantasy, which cover and embellish, yet never completely conceal, the geometric framework that lies beneath. Gide could neither renounce and deny his homosexual tendencies—at certain moments, indeed, they became a source of painful pride—nor could he quite forgive himself for entertaining them and following them. Hence the troubled front that he presented to the world, and continued to present until his death. My last meeting with him was in London, whither he had come on his way to Oxford, where he had been invited to accept an honorary degree. In his old age he seemed to have grown smaller ; and he wore a stiff, ill-fitting tweed suit, apparently a size too large for him that looked as if it had been made for Grock. Again his manner was evasive and diplomatic ; and I was flattered to hear him speak of an article, on an English translation of one of his books, that I had published in a weekly review several years earlier. Yes, he had read it and had approved of it. But now could I give him some information about the procedure of receiving a degree at Oxford ? Undergraduates, he had been told, filled the gallery of the Sheldonian Theatre. They were noisy, were they not, and apt to indulge in high-spirited public demonstrations ? What especially provoked them to shout or boo ? Well, I explained, it might be for political reasons, if a particularly unpopular statesman were honoured by the Vice-Chancellor. " Never for *moral* reasons ? " he responded quickly, throwing out from under his osseous brows a sudden sharp-edged interrogative glance.

At home, I had noticed a similar wariness, though its origins were plainly very different, in the conversation of Virginia Woolf. She, too, was very much on her guard ; and the air of mistrust, even of sharp suspicion, that she sometimes exhibited as soon as she began to speak, contrasted strangely with the sculptural elegance of her noble head and attenuated limbs, which recalled a thirteenth-century Gothic saint or the musing Bodhisatva portrayed by an early Chinese artist. In repose, her finely modelled features had an impassive, almost sexless charm; but, when she talked, the impassivity vanished, and a look of cautious enquiry took its place, as she threw off a series of pointed questions about her interlocutor's tastes and habits—questions that were often baffling, since they seemed to reach him from so very far away, from a claustral world of the imagination that she alone had ever entered. But her thirst for knowledge there was no denying. " Perhaps because Virginia lacked the novelist's sense for the dramatic properties of character and was more interested in the texture of people's minds (writes her old friend Gerald Brenan),* she was much given to drawing them out and documenting herself upon them ". Her most searching questions she addressed to the young—she was " intensely and uneasily aware (Gerald Brenan also tells us) of a younger generation who would one day rise and sit in judgment on her ". But her curiosity failed to conceal a certain want of human sympathy; for she appeared to regard her youthful acquaintances as members of an entirely separate race, born at an unlucky moment in the history of civilization and debarred, through no fault of their own, from many of the pleasures and privileges that she and her Cambridge friends had enjoyed.

No less enquiring, and no less detached, was the attitude she adopted towards life in general. " What is meant by reality? " she was fond of demanding both as a novelist and as a literary critic. " Something (she decided) very erratic, very undependable now to be found in a dusty road, now in a scrap of newspaper, now in a daffodil in the sun . . ." But one receives the impression that, wherever reality lay, she did not feel quite sure that she had fully grasped it, and that she was haunted by thoughts of the enormous realms of experience in which she herself could never hope to travel. Between the inquisitive novelist and the world she studied, temperament and upbringing had raised a glassy barrier. It was as though she inhabited a secluded room, high above a busy street, and were perpetually looking down at

* *South from Granada* by Gerald Brenan. Hamish Hamilton.

the passers-by and speculating eagerly about the lives they led
—an old man scavenging for cigarette-ends, the pretty girl arm-
in-arm with a soldier, the tired woman with a heavy parcel,
bound for a tea-shop or a public house—but were equally incapable either of descending to join them or of forgetting that
such mysterious characters existed. Thus the questions she so
determinedly asked were apt to suggest the impatient drumming
of fingers on a window-pane. Like Sterne's famous starling she
" couldn't get out "; and her efforts to inject her stories with
contemporary detail, and give a sympathetic account of modes
of existence she did not understand, are remarkably awkward
and unconvincing even in her earlier and less allusive books.
The small circle of friends she had known as a young woman
provided the subjects that suited her talents best—personages
who constantly re-emerge until, as a procession of faint romantic
wraiths, they make their final appearance in *The Waves* and *The
Years*.

About the portrait that my memory retains there is something
both aloof and eager. She sits leaning slightly forward, her
head bent a little to one side, her arms resting upon her knees
and her long fingers loosely interlaced. The dress she wears is
by no means fashionable but hangs around her in drooping pre-
Raphaelite folds ; and behind her is the plain chimney-piece of
a small Victorian London sitting-room, which her sister, Vanessa
Bell, had enriched with characteristic decorations—flowering
cornucopiæ, glimpses of Southern scenes, vague curlicues and
vegetable arabesques executed in clear and cheerful colours
according to the *avant garde* taste of the period. This portrait,
I imagine, must date from the latter 'twenties or the early 'thirties;
whereas my admiration for Virginia Woolf had begun in 1919
when I was still at school and read an appreciative notice of a
short story entitled *Kew Gardens*. It proved to be a somewhat
surprising pamphlet, bound in covers made of old wallpaper,
which had been embellished, evidently by hand, with splashes of
brightly hued paint distributed at random across a black field.

Storytellers

The contents were no less spirited—a brilliant impressionistic vision of Kew Gardens beneath a summer sun, built up (it seemed at the time) of a series of shimmering transparent layers, one transparency dissolving into the next as the incidents of the sunlit landscape change, to produce an enchanting effect of clarity and lyrical gaiety. My enthusiasm did not decline until I had reached her last novels. For there, in the attempt to escape from her prison and to capture and pin down " reality ", the novelist at length abandons all the conventional restraints of narrative art ; and the result is an extended prose-poem that forfeits much of the distinction of prose without quite achieving a true poetic impetus. Meanwhile she had her private tragedy—the ever-recurrent threat of mental breakdown. Again and again she was obliged to retire from the world, which pressed intolerably on her disordered nerves ; and, when the world itself appeared to be losing its reason, she adopted a desperate, self-destructive remedy. By then, she had left London, and the flat she used to inhabit had been demolished by the German bombardment. During those hideous days I happened to walk through Bloomsbury and found myself standing in Tavistock Square. A huge chasm divided the row of house fronts ; and high up on its lofty northern flank, neatly attached to an expanse of naked wall, I caught sight of Virginia Woolf's fireplace, now unsupported by hearth or floor, but still surrounded by a ghostly suggestion of garlands and fruit and horns of plenty. The pictures were already flaking ; and, when I next passed, they had completely vanished. All that remained was the sooty hole in the brick, with nothing to distinguish it from fireplace above and below.

*　　　*　　　*

Virginia Woolf was too thoughtful an artist not to speculate constantly about the mechanism of her art ; and in *Phases of Fiction,** an essay written thirty years ago, she was already con-

* Reprinted posthumously in *Granite and Rainbow.* Hogarth Press.

sidering the different methods adopted by various types of story-teller, and seeking to distinguish between the results they achieved from the standpoint of an artist-critic. Since those days a long succession of critics, for the most part far less highly qualified, have discussed the prospects of the modern novel and the rôle that the novelist plays, or ought to play, in relation to the twentieth-century world. Little apparently remains unsaid—except, perhaps, that the core, the æsthetic nucleus, of any work of fiction that regularly demands re-reading is not always where it seems to be, and that the emotion such a book arouses can often be traced back to some half-hidden source. As we review the impressions a novel has left behind, we may notice that we have begun to forget the story, while many of the characters portrayed are growing vague and insubstantial. What the memory cherishes is an isolated episode, a single scene or fragment of dialogue, which in a magical and mysterious fashion illuminates the whole narrative. Proust's celebrated novelist Bergotte, towards the end of his life, his creator tells us, carried this attitude to extreme lengths :

" *Sans doute . . . pour se séparer de la précédente génération, trop amie des abstractions, des grands lieux communs* (we read in *A l'Ombre des Jeunes Filles en Fleurs*) *quand Bergotte voulait dire du bien d'un livre, ce qu'il faisait valoir, ce qu'il citait, c'était toujours quelque scéne faisant image, quelque tableau sans signification rationelle. 'Ah! si!' disait-il, 'c'est bien! il y a une petite fille en châle orange, ah! c'est bien', ou encore: ' Oh! oui il y a un passage ou il y a un regiment qui traverse la ville, ah! oui, c'est bien' "*.

Was Virginia Woolf thinking of Bergotte as she contrasted the exquisite but irrelevant poetic passages that occur in Laurence Sterne's masterpiece with another kind of poetry " more natural to the novel, because it uses the material which the novelist provides . . . the poetry of situation rather than of language, the poetry which we perceive when Catherine in *Wuthering Heights* pulls the feathers from the pillow ; when Natasha in *War and Peace* looks out of the window at the stars." Here the novelist, she adds, " produces a feeling of deep and intense poetry without any disruption or that disquieting sense of a song being sung to people who listen ".* And, similarly, the most imaginative writers sometimes irradiate the material objects they describe, so that our memory reflects a detail of the background much more vividly than the incidents of the human drama being enacted in the foreground—a detail as memorable and precious as Elstir's " *petit pan de mur jaune* ". Even the greatest novels and short stories, despite the general impressiveness of the story-teller's theme, owe something of their literary effect to sudden flashes of poetic observation—to the author's record of a few words, to his sketch of an unrelated gesture or, not infrequently, to " *quelque tableau sans signification rationelle* ". For instance, one remembers the two rosy-lipped, sonorous conches, " *deux de ces coquilles roses où l'on entend la bruit de la mer* ", that Flaubert places on the chimney-piece of the apartment in which Madame Bovary meets her young lover : the green lining of Swann's top hat, which he is holding as he explains to the Duchesse de Guermantes that the doctors he has consulted have just pronounced a death sentence : the furniture of the *Lys dans la Vallée's* drawing-room : the gold beads around the neck of the child whom Moll Flanders is momentarily tempted to strangle : the slice of melon that Tchehov's hero devours when he rises from the arms of *The Lady with the Dog:* " There was a water-melon on the table. Gurov cut himself a slice and began eating it without haste."

These details are not mere fortunate accidents, but have the quality of true poetic feeling : in them is summed up the imag-

---

* The same idea was recently expressed, under a slightly different guise, in an article by Philip Toynbee : " I am more and more coming to believe that we do not judge novels by their structure, in spite of our constant effort to do so. It is the *texture* of a novel which really decides our reaction to it—the flow of the river rather than its course ".

inative quality of a tale, as the inward significance of a poem may be condensed into two or three images. The storyteller must strive for concentration no less energetically than a dramatist or a poet, whatever the scope of the subject he has undertaken, and whether he is composing an extended chronicle or has adopted the framework of the long short story. Now it is precisely in the gift of concentration that the average modern novelist would appear to be most deficient; and his failure can no doubt be attributed both to historical and to personal causes. Ours is a period of astonishing cleverness; and quite how clever are the innumerable men and women who nowadays write and publish novels may be gauged by referring to some of the well-known books that aroused a furore during the late Augustan period. When *Evelina* originally burst on London, it swept the reading public off their feet. In other respects usually severe critics, Johnson, Gibbon and Edmund Burke admitted that they had been completely overwhelmed—not only by the fact that the author was a modest, sensitive and well-brought-up young woman, who had had the courage to invade the literary field, but by her wide knowledge of contemporary social life and her fascinating grasp of human conduct. They were utterly unprepared for the peculiar brand of intelligence that they detected in their old friend's daughter; and perhaps, as they read, they may dimly have foreseen the eventual emergence of a strange new species—the novel-producing female of the nineteenth and the twentieth centuries.

Yet *Evelina*, when we read it today, appears a somewhat dull and prosy tale; and, compared with the flickering peep-show that Fanny Burney offers us, the panorama that a modern novelist provides is as extensive as the stage of a large theatre. Thousands of diverse personages throng the arena of contemporary fiction, skilfully delineated " straight from life ", wearing the appropriate costumes, speaking a language that we recognise. The social historian of the year two thousand will owe the modern storyteller an immense debt. Here, in popular novels of the age, he will be able to lay his hand upon a gigantic hoard of miscellaneous information, illustrating a vast range of mid-twentieth-century characters and scenes. But will the artist-critic feel equally satisfied ? Where he had hoped to find artistic concentration, may he not become aware of an extraordinary dispersion and diffusion of talent, among men and women who were often remarkably gifted yet somehow lacked the genuine creative impulse, who made of the novel, not a form of imaginative litera-ture, so much as an ingenious substitute for art ? In Japan, every literate citizen prides himself on his capacity to write a poem—from the Emperor, who salutes the New Year with a traditional three-line *haiku*, to the restaurant-keeper or the fishmonger, advertising his newly opened business. Almost as widespread in the countries of the West is the gift of manufacturing a novel ; with the result that novel-writing threatens to become less a vocation than a spare-time occupation, and that the apparatus and vocabulary of the novel is growing more and more stereo-typed. How difficult, for the twentieth-century novelist, to avoid slipping into " novelese "—the peculiar shop-worn jargon that he has inherited from his immediate predecessors ! On some it confers a damnable facility of expression ; but elsewhere it may act as a crushing deterrent. While he writes, the novelist may begin to see his book as a book that someone else has written, equipped with precisely the same set of adjectival and adverbial trimmings, in which the characters make their exits and entrances according to the same routine. " I have started *another novel* ", he reflects despairingly. " A thick veil is even now falling between my own mind and the subject I have chosen. I am in the grip of a literary convention that stifles my original impulse whichever way I turn."

Yet a new novelist may very soon emerge capable of brushing all these difficulties aside, a writer who will transform the methods of novel-writing as thoroughly as Proust transformed the con-vention that he had taken over from Bourget and Anatole France,

77

or hammer out a means of expression as strangely original as that of James Joyce. Meanwhile, until he has at length emerged, " the future of the novel " must remain a somewhat barren subject, on which no literary prophet can hope to pronounce with any certainty. Negative conclusions, of course, are a good deal easier to draw—for instance, that the great nineteenth-century tradition of the naturalistic novel is now unlikely to be resurrected. Fiction, it is true, remains a wonderfully elastic medium ; and " there is room in the novel (Virginia Woolf admits) for storytelling, for comedy, for tragedy, for criticism and information and philosophy. Something of its appeal lies in the width of its scope and the satisfaction it offers to so many different moods, desires, and instincts . . ." But just as important as the breadth of a novel's scope is the presence of a unifying spirit—the spirit that pervades *Anna Karenina*, but which Tolstoi failed quite to impose on the vast and complicated structure of *War and Peace*. In the latter book, we watch the dramatic movement of history and trace its chance connection with the development of individual men and women : in the former, we observe the slow, steady growth of individual characters, each bearing the unique burden of his own identity. We judge a great novel not by the verisimilitude of the impression it produces but by the heightened sense of the beauty and oddity of life that has filled the reader's mind before he puts it down. Nothing can replace that vivid sense of life, as Virginia Woolf was always well aware ; and, when she spoke of the " poetry of situation ", revealed in a series of unrelated episodes, she was referring to the element that distinguishes a work of art from a detailed survey of contemporary manners. The great novelist studies the individual through society, rather than society through the individual, and without disregarding the relationship of his personages to their fellow human beings, or their joint relationship to the social system under which they are doomed to live and die, illuminates those aspects of personality which give them their essential separateness. He may examine the social macrocosm, but plunges with even deeper zest into the secrets of the private microcosm. His works include both a description of society, considered with objective care, and an evocation of the rare moments that make our experience of life seem worth describing. Although society changes, and the forms of the novel change, such evocations cannot lose their value.

III

Stylists

STYLISTS ARE among the heroes of literature ; often they provide
its victims ; for, whereas the impetuous, naturally prolific writer
may be fascinated and uplifted by the spectacle of his own exuberance, and the visionary writer feels himself swept along by
the sheer urgency of what he has to say—neither Shakespeare nor
Blake, one imagines, spent much time on correction or revision
—these searchers after the truly expressive word and devotees of
the well-balanced paragraph are constantly at war with a problem
that grows more difficult as their knowledge and their taste
increase. The struggle allows them little respite. All day the
same unsatisfactory line continues to run through their distracted
heads ; and they may suddenly spring up from sleep with the
sense of a crime committed or a duty neglected, and plod down-
stairs to their unfinished manuscripts, to delete an adjective or
re-cast a faulty phrase. Like most artists, they are equally arro-
gant and humble. Did not George Moore once inform the
world that any critic might be sure of his unending gratitude if
he could help him to establish the correct punctuation of a single
sentence ? And, when I caught sight of the great man in Ebury
Street, I sometimes remembered his significant remark and
imagined the burden of literary cares that, even at that moment,
he must be carrying. His mind, evidently, was far away from
London as he ambled towards Victoria or Chelsea—an elderly
figure, neatly but baggily dressed, whose bent knees and slightly

shuffling gait, rounded back and loosely seated trousers, gave him the look of a venerable Belgian hare walking on its hind legs. Beneath his silvery moustache protruded a moist pink underlip. His pale blue eyes, prominent and globular, swept the passers-by with a blank unseeing gaze.

His vision was turned inwards—firmly focused upon the problems of his art. But just how deep his self-absorption was I did not quite understand until I had met him face to face. Having recently reviewed a book of his, I was invited to meet the novelist at dinner ; and, as soon as our hostess had left us alone, he began to talk about my appreciative article, slowly and very pleasantly, with many vague half-finished gestures, with elaborate modulations of the voice and occasional lapses into idiomatic French. He was glad to have seen it, he remarked, and glad to know that I had enjoyed his novel. But now there was a question he would like to ask me. As I read, had I noticed any passage that had struck me as particularly effective ? Was there any episode or individual portrait that appeared to stand out from the surrounding text ? This bland enquiry could not have been worse timed, and I was invaded by a feeling of helpless panic ; for, in fact, much as I had admired and enjoyed many of the great stylist's earlier volumes—for instance, *Hail and Farewell*, *Memoirs of my Dead Life* and his memorable collections of short stories—I had found his latest novel, *Aphrodite in Aulis*, a sadly over-written and uninspiring book and, rather than damn it with words of faint praise, I had devoted most of my article to a consideration of its predecessors. Indeed, I had purposely refrained from digging too deep into the Grecian narrative ; some of its pages still remained uncut; and my impressions of how the plot developed were as hazy as the recollections of last night's dream. But, luckily, in every printed book, there are places where it tends to fall open ; and a passage thus exposed, I seemed to remember, had had something to do with an adventurous gang of thieves rifling an Egyptian pyramid.* Not very hopefully, then, I replied

* See *Aphrodite in Aulis*. Chapter X.

that I thought his account of the tomb-robbery a particularly accomplished piece of storytelling, and was surprised and delighted to watch an expansive smile spread across George Moore's features. He was especially pleased, he told me, that I should have happened to select this incident, which had cost him a great deal of anxious thought and, before he was at all satisfied with it, had needed endless re-writing. Clearly, a weight had been removed from his mind, and for the rest of the evening he would be calm and easy. The pleasure he showed was entirely unselfconscious; nor did it, of course, depend on any exaggerated notion of my own importance as a critic. I interested him merely as a reader, ally or adversary of the dedicated writer, in his constant efforts to hammer out a style by which his experience of life will be worthily reflected. Once he had obtained the reassurance he sought, he sank comfortably back into his dining-room chair and proceeded—though with a good deal less attention—to interrogate me about my own existence, beaming at me from those pale glaucous eyes and gently waving a large Havana cigar. Did I write novels in addition to critical essays? Was my wife a *femme de lettres*? It was possible, he supposed benevolently, that we might practise literature " à *quatre mains* " . . .

When we parted, he issued an invitation to visit him in Ebury Street, explaining that he was usually at home there every Sunday afternoon. I must have misunderstood his invitation or taken it very much too literally; for, when I arrived on his doorstep one cold and cloudy autumn day, I was confronted, as the door opened, by a rather stern, old-fashioned parlourmaid, who regarded me with some suspicion and said that Mr. Moore never received visitors. But she agreed to take in my name and, at length, I was allowed to cross the threshold and entered a double room on the ground floor, behind a small bow-window looking out on the street. George Moore was seated by the fire, his knees covered by a heavy rug. He suffered, towards the end of his life, from a painful and humiliating infirmity; and the purpose of the rug, as I later discovered, was to conceal the apparatus that he was sometimes obliged to wear. Evidently, it irked and embarrassed him ; and altogether his mood was gloomy. The room itself was by no means cheerful, with dusk outside rapidly falling and shadows surrounding him as he sat at his hearth, amid furniture that recalled the equipment of a late-Victorian lodging-house parlour—a thick reddish cloth, displaying a bobble fringe, draped over a massive centre table, a black-leaded grate and a huge black coal-scuttle, such as only a well-trained Victorian servant would ever have consented to drag upstairs. A brown teapot on an ancient tin tray soon completed this sombre domestic background. But through the shadows Manet's *Etude* (which I was to meet again in a very different setting) glimmered from the dusky wall-paper ; while opposite me my host's face made a pallid, almost phosphorescent oval. Many of his most gifted contemporaries have attempted to describe his curious appearance—among others, his friend Max Beerbohm, who speaks of George Moore's " illusory look . . . the diaphanous, vaporous, wan look of an illusion conjured up for us, perhaps by means of mirrors and by a dishonourable spiritualist ".* At the best of times, he could be portentously silent, as he waited for a thought to break surface—he was a man of comparatively few ideas ; but, if an idea occurred, he welcomed it eagerly—and, on this occasion, he was feeling tired and ill and was troubled by an awkward, unwanted guest, with the result that he scarcely attempted to speak and, in the dim light of his crowded, comfortless room, seemed to be melting into an ectoplasmic blur.

Could I arouse him ? How should I justify my visit ? Well, I considered, it might amuse him to discuss the heroic figures of his youth ; and I plunged in with a random reference to Balzac who, I assumed, he must regard as a literary ancestor. I proved wrong ; the author of the *Comédie Humaine* was briefly examined and summarily dismissed. What a clumsy writer, what an im-

* *Mainly on the Air.*

perfect artist! Balzac, he declared, reminded him of a man who is determined at any cost to climb a difficult wall, who succeeds in climbing it, admittedly, and crashes down upon the opposite side, but does so by tearing his hands and clothes and outraging all the stylistic graces. Next I tried my luck with Guy de Maupassant; but here I elicited a note of personal resentment. He had met Maupassant during his Parisian apprenticeship; and the impressions he received had failed to please. " Such a *vulgar* fellow, my dear boy! Like a rich farmer's son "—a description that certainly accords with some of Maupassant's later photographs, which represent him as taurine and truculent, flaunting a wiry, aggressive moustache and wearing a diamond-studded horse-shoe pin affixed to a broad satin tie. Only at the mention of Turgenev's name did his voice soften and his expression light up. " Such a *gentleman*! " he murmured—a characterization of Turgenev's genius far less inadequate than one might at first suspect, though clearly it bore the imprint of the speaker's social prejudices. Turgenev was, indeed, *une âme bien née*, besides being an unusually gifted product of much the same social stratum as had produced Moore; and his style had that air of innate distinction, a blend of ease and simplicity and natural grace, after which the English storyteller had always hankered and which he had at last achieved by dint of agonizing efforts. In his admiration there may also have been a touch of envy; for, compared with Turgenev's, his literary life had been hard; no writer, he admitted himself, had had to work on more unpromising materials or had begun his laborious career with a more inadequate provision of taste and judgment.

Apart from Turgenev, however, there were not many novelists whom he seemed inclined to praise. For example, when I brought up Fromentin, feeling sure that he must admire *Dominique*—at least, the narrator's exquisite descriptions of the lonely manor house in which he passed his youth, of the romantic landscapes near La Rochelle and the great flocks of migratory birds that swept over the gardens and the woods—I found that my companion chose to regard him as a successful academic painter rather than as a writer. Fromentin, he observed, had been a clever draughtsman—he had seen a number of his Eastern sketches—whose chief distinction was that he had acquired the difficult knack of rendering the " kink in an Arab horse's tail ". Otherwise he had little good to say of nineteenth-century novelists, either French or English. He appeared to inhabit an intellectual solitude; and one was aware simultaneously of his deepening personal loneliness—the price that he paid for the unselfish egotism with which he had prosecuted his pursuit of truth and beauty. The effect was saddening; and yet it provoked thought. Already, during the early nineteen-thirties—*Aphrodite in Aulis*, his last completed book, was published in 1931—there had been talk among writers and critics on the subject of "engaged literature", the "engaged" artist being a man who identifies his existence with the current social struggle. Now Moore was supremely " disengaged "; he cared everything for art and almost nothing for the cause of humanity; to him men and women were always the same, and literary standards never varied —he had an unchanging view of artistic perfection that he cherished obstinately so long as he lived. And then, besides being disengaged—which may, or may not, have assisted his development in the field of art—he was also remarkably detached from the ordinary preoccupations of the human race. True, in *Esther Waters*, he had dealt with a social problem; and, at the time of the Boer War, he had uttered some vigorous protests against the policy of the British government. But, as a general rule, he preferred to remain aloof and had continued serenely to cultivate his own garden—a *hortus conclusus* of phrases and images which formed a separate, self-contained world.

" Engaged " writers, I suspect, have had their day; but they helped, no doubt, to enlarge our literary prospects; and an obsessive preoccupation with the use of words is apt to devitalize a writer's talent, unless that talent be rooted in a strong intellectual curiosity. Of such curiosity, however, George Moore had a surprisingly small allowance. He had mastered comparatively few books, though he enjoyed re-reading the books he had written himself—indeed, he once declared that he only wrote because he derived so little amusement from the *chefs d'œuvre* of his fellow novelists ; and, despite his habit of " conducting his education in public " (as Oscar Wilde had unkindly called it) and of imploring his good-natured friends to initiate him into the pleasures he had missed, his knowledge of painting and literature was neither deep nor comprehensive. Thus, in his old age, his spiritual resources were meagre ; while the solitude, imposed on him by his passionate sense of vocation, became more than ever burdensome. Here, I thought, as the twilight enveloped us, is a cautionary picture of the Perfectionist's end—the end of a single-minded life devoted to an unattainable object, in which the promise of a book had always begun to fade before its author reached the last paragraph, and his hopes were perpetually flitting ahead towards the majestic works he had not yet composed. How much wiser to emulate Balzac, who proclaimed that, for a really creative artist, " the important point is not to avoid mistakes but to have a quality that sweeps everything in front of it ", or some equally vigorous exponent of what Arnold Bennett entitled " the higher literary carelessness " ! Moore had announced that he was " *un esclave de l'art* ", which meant ultimately that he was the slave of words, and that his preoccupation with the problem of form had gradually taken the place of every other literary interest. As a true perfectionist, he would have counted the world well lost for half-a-dozen pages that completely satisfied his own judgment. But, alas, there is no sphere of human activity in which we can hope to escape from imperfection—a fact that artists greater than Moore have recognised and even turned to profit. By concentrating on the suppression of small vices— the dissonances, vulgarities and awkward tricks of style, that George Moore was constantly detecting and removing—a too-conscientious writer may eventually forfeit many of the most essential literary virtues.

Yet my admiration for Moore did not decline ; nor have I ceased to cherish a high regard for the ideals that he epitomised. Perfection of style is an absolute—unattainable, no doubt, but because it is impossible of achievement, and an over-strenuous attempt to achieve it sometimes produces disastrous results, from an artist's point of view none the less desirable. His style is the basis of his lifework ; it enters into every department of his career ; it is an expression of the relationship that he has done his best to establish with the alien surroundings amid which he has been born. An indication of how he looks at life, it also represents his constant efforts to reach a harmonious relationship with himself, by endeavouring to see his character clearly and co-ordinate his talents usefully. More authors learn to think and feel in the laborious process of learning to write than have ever mastered the art of writing under the pressure of urgent thoughts and violent emotions. Indeed, if I wished to divide the dedicated artists from the spare-time writers, I should suggest that the second category were apt to set to work with a clear conception of what they had to say, and that the first only discovered the full meaning of the subject they had undertaken as they gradually developed it. For, unlike the teachers and the propagandists, they are not interested in imposing an opinion or distributing a public message, so much as in re-creating a given subject through the medium of their own intelligence, allowing it insensibly to grow and change, assume new colours and unexpected shapes, until the finished product bears very little likeness to the original crude schematic plan. Here problems of style play an important part ; for the technical difficulties of writing help to determine an author's mode of expression ; and, while he is considering and trying to solve them, he may find that the theme he has selected discloses novel possibilities. Poets, Paul Valery tells us, often derive similar benefits from the employment of a traditional verse-pattern. " *Les exigences d'une stricte prosodie* (he remarks in his essay *Au Sujet d'Adonis*) *sont l'artifice qui confère au langage naturel les qualités d'une matière résistante, étrangère à notre âme, et comme sourde à nos désirs . . . On ne peut plus tout faire, une fois acceptées; on ne peut plus tout dire ; et pour dire quoi que ce soit, il ne suffit plus de le concevoir fortement, d'en être plein et enivré . . . A un dieu seulement est réservée l'ineffable indistinction de son acte et de sa pensée. Mais nous, il faut peiner; il faut connaître amèrement leur différence."* During his struggle to bridge this gulf, which becomes a struggle against the laws of prosody, the poet succeeds in crystallising a vision that might otherwise have been vague and fugitive. It owes its definition to the painful effort it cost him ; and some of its chief beauties may have originated in the varying accidents of the struggle, when the search for the necessary rhyme prompted a new conjunction of ideas, which by evoking a series of fresh images helped to enlarge and enrich his whole design.

Although the discipline of prose-writing is far less strict, the restrictive influence that it exerts is, in some ways, no less salutary, provided that the writer's ambition is to produce a book that has an æsthetic, rather than a commercial or purely propagandist, value. Every writer would prefer to write with ease, and now and then enjoys some intoxicating moments during which his pen races abreast of his thoughts ; but those are the moments when he should be most on his guard, for the advance that he appears to have made has often carried him far from his true objective, and he is obliged to return to his starting-point and resume his expedition at a snail-paced crawl. *" Pour bien écrire,* (announced Joseph Joubert, among his other coolly sagacious maxims) *il faut une facilité naturelle et une difficulté acquise "*; and that " acquired difficulty " is apt to be acquired through a concern with style, which acts as a brake on our natural facility and increases the impetus of a writer's attack by constantly restraining his impulsive flow. The case for style and the case against facility have been brilliantly argued by one of the most prolific and expansive of modern English novelists. Aldous Huxley begins by praising Flaubert, in whose books there is nothing—but had he forgotten *Salammbô* ?—" that remotely resembles a vulgarity ", and whose example, if we practise his religion, we must pray for strength to imitate :

" The strength is seldom vouchsafed. The temptations which Flaubert put aside are, by any man of lively fancy and active intellect, incredibly difficult to be resisted . . . A phrase, a situation, suggests a whole train of striking or amusing ideas that fly off at a tangent, so to speak, from the round world on which the creator is at work , what an opportunity for saying something witty or profound ! True, the ornament will be in the nature of a florid excrescence on the total work ; but never mind. In goes the tangent—or rather, out into artistic irrelevancy. And in goes the effective phrase that is too effective, too highly coloured for what it is to express ; in goes the too emphatic irony, the too tragical scene, the too pathetic tirade, the too poetical description." *

Thus speaks a gifted writer whose own immense facility has frequently outrun his sense of style, and who half despises, and yet half regrets, the artistic advantages that he has thereby forfeited. His books are remarkably personal—he is repeatedly flying off at a personal tangent embarking on ingenious digressions that allow him to exhibit the powers of an astonishingly active brain ; but his digressions have a journalistic charm that very soon shows signs of dating. To be personal in works of literature is not always to be individual ; and by giving us so much of himself, with such freedom and uninhibited gusto, he has given us far less of himself than perhaps he might have otherwise conveyed. The writer's task is to hold a careful balance between journalistic exuberance and æsthetic impersonality : to capture the essence of the self (in which he recognises a mysterious yet compelling relationship with the million selves by which the ego has been preceded, by which it is surrounded, by which during the course of time it will be followed), while he discards its more trivial and ephemeral aspects. If he is to do

* *Vulgarity in Literature: Digressions from a Theme.* Chatto & Windus.

so, he needs the help of style ; for the stylist is just as sensitive to vulgarities of thought and emotion as to superficial defects of language, and has noticed, indeed, that the latter have often a close connection with the former—that we write awkwardly and incorrectly because we think and feel loosely. A famous French critic declared that " the style is the man ". But might it not be more accurate to say that the style represents the super-man, what remains of the author's personality when he has removed the inessential residue ? Only a man of genius, however, succeeds in quite discovering his superior self, which permeates a whole book and, to a greater or less degree, leaves its stamp on everything he writes. Hence Joubert's announcement that " *tous les hommes d'esprit valent mieux que leur livres. Les hommes de génie valent moins* "; for they alone, the men of genius, have completely utilised and transcended their own characteristic virtues and failings. Elsewhere a book may be merely a partial reflection of the author's intelligence and taste and humour.

Style, then, is inseparable from self-knowledge ; and it is by way of self that we naturally approach the world. Having gained some understanding of the microcosm, we pass on to the macrocosm ; and again a love of literary form—the desire to shape a book as well as communicate an idea—generally speeds an imaginative writer's progress. H. G. Wells, who disliked and distrusted stylists and was particularly contemptuous of the efforts of Henry James, once published a sneering reference to the modern storyteller who puts his art first—" the artist who lives angrily in his stuffy little corner of pure technique." * Creators of this type, he seems to imply, are cut off by technique from the world of experience ; they lose all contact with their age and with the passions of ordinary men and women ; and their books come to resemble silent, beautifully-lit churches, "every light and line focused on the high altar. And on the altar, very reverently placed . . . is a dead kitten, an egg-shell, a bit of string . . ." † In fact, it is Wells' books that now appear to be dead, while Henry

* *Mind in the Making.*   † *Boon.*

90

James' retain a vital glow ; for the Lesson of the Master, patiently
though his old friend continued to instruct him, was one that he
could never learn ; and he persisted in his belief that a modern
novel should contain a direct transcript of the novelist's immediate
impressions, of the social theories and political prejudices provoked by a study of his own period. " Strange to me . . .", James
confessed, in 1912, after he had read *Marriage*, " the co-existence
of so much talent with so little art, so much life with (so to speak)
so little living ! " Earlier, when he wrote to Wells to con-
gratulate him on the publication of *Love and Mr. Lewisham*, he
expressed his appreciation of " your humour and your pathos—
your homely truth and your unquenchable fancy ", yet admitted
that he had failed to see " your *idea*—I mean your Subject . . . as
determined or constituted : but in short the thing is a bloody
little chunk of life, of no small substance." * To Bernard Shaw,
also an inveterate opponent, James delivered a similar admoni-
tion. Works of art, he then declared, were capable of saying
more to a man about himself " than any other ' works ' whatever
. . . and it's only by saying as much to him as possible . . . in as
many ways and on as many sides, and with a vividness of presen-
tation, that ' art ', and art alone, is an adequate mistress of, that
we enable him to pick and choose and compare and know,
enable him to arrive at any sort of synthesis that isn't . . . a base
and illusive humbug." *

Art, he told Wells, " *makes* life, makes interest, makes importance "; and just how he was accustomed to absorb and
transmute the raw material that life offered, giving it back again,
as a story or a novel, in a far more permanent and more coherent
form, is the theme of the prefatory essay with which he introduced
The Spoils of Poynton. Life, he said, was " all inclusion and confusion ", whereas art was " all discrimination and selection ";
and no sooner, amid the débris of experience, had the artist
unearthed the " tiny nugget " of gold, that he hoped to " ham-

* Quoted by Leon Edel and Gordon N. Ray in *Henry James and H. G. Wells:
A Record of their Friendship, their Debate on the Art of Fiction, and their Quarrel.*

mer into a sacred hardness ", than " clumsy Life " threatened to wreck his hopes by providing the wrong dénouement or adding superfluous details ; for it was what *ought* to have happened that concerned him, according to his private conception of the story, not the events that had actually occurred in a certain place and at a certain time. Until imagination has taken a hand, experience means very little. All experience must be raised by imagination to the height of literature ; but, in endeavouring to do so, the artist does not lose touch with the human society from which his material is drawn. Once he has developed a method of regarding the world, his aim is to increase our awareness of living. " For myself (wrote James), I live, live intensely and am fed by life, and my value, whatever it be, is in my own kind of expression of that." Indeed, his readers may feel that he loved life—though he had moments, presumably, of hatred and instinctive fear ; while his popular rival, author of the " honest and inimitable " *Kipps* and *Love and Mr. Lewisham*, was not so much a genuine lover of life and of his fellow human beings as a doctrinaire enthusiast, who preferred types to individuals, and the opportunity of prosecuting a cause to the privilege of observing human nature. Conrad, like James, had disputed with Wells on the rôle that art should play in life ; and, like James, he at length abandoned the struggle, pointing out the very different attitude that each of them adopted towards humanity : " The difference between us, Wells, is fundamental. You don't care for humanity but think they are to be improved. I love humanity but know they are not ! " *

Incidentally, the writer should love language ; for he will fail to express either his sense of living or his appreciation of humanity if he treats language as a convenient means to an end. His ways of thought and feeling, I have suggested in an earlier paragraph, are insensibly developed during the process of learning how to write, and he only establishes his personal response to existence when he attacks the problem of putting it into words. He enjoys the problem, which is always with him,

* Quoted by Leon Edel and Gordon N. Ray in *Henry James and H. G. Wells.*

no less than the occasional solution ; and the difficulties of his native tongue become no less attractive than its capabilities and its natural beauties. Why, then, should he be expected to use words merely as a series of convenient symbols, deliberately restricting his range and disregarding the luminous effect that words, carefully arrayed and balanced, may produce in combination ? A large mind needs an ample vocabulary—Shakespeare's, for example, was unusually large according to the standards of his own, or any later, period ; and, in so far as literary style should be an image of life, it is difficult to see how the colourless and colloquial style, that some novelists and critics assure us they prefer, can do justice to the bewildering variety of the world they deal with. The dryness of Stendhal's prose—often recommended as the ideal form of modern narrative—though well suited to passages of psychological analysis, is unsuitable to undertakings of a more graphic order ; as when he attempts to show us the effects of passion, having previously delved deep into its hidden causes. *Le Rouge et le Noir* is an extraordinarily uneven book ; and there comes a stage when even the most devoted reader's attention may perhaps begin to flag, so rapid and so unequal is the flow of the narrative, so abrupt are the transitions from analysis to plain straightforward storytelling. In *L'Education Sentimentale*, on the other hand, one notices how careful Flaubert was to establish an equipoise between passages of cold matter-of-fact narrative and his rare moments of lyrical expansion : how the interest of the story (like the interest of life itself) seems to rise and decline : how delineation of character and description of background combine in a possibly limited, but certainly harmonious, whole.

Twenty years ago, Cyril Connolly published a fascinating critical-autobiographical volume entitled *Enemies of Promise*, which exerted a considerable effect on the taste of his contemporaries. Here he distinguished between the " Mandarin Style ", employed by the majority of English nineteenth-century prose-writers, and the " vernacular " style widely used by the writers who succeeded them, and who endeavoured to break up the Mandarin dialect into "something simpler, and terser, destroying its ornamentation, attacking its rhythms and giving us instead the idiom of today." He quotes, not entirely without approval, from a pronouncement issued by Samuel Butler :

> " I never knew a writer who took the smallest pains with his style and was at the same time readable . . . Men like Newman and R. L. Stevenson seem to have taken pains to acquire what they called a style as a preliminary measure—as something that they had to form before their writings could be of any value. I should like to put it on record that I never took the smallest pains with my style, have never thought about it, and do not know or want to know whether it is a style at all . . ."

Butler added that " a man's style in any art should be like his dress—it should attract as little attention as possible ". But his point of view appears to reflect two obvious popular misconceptions : first, the belief that a style is developed merely in order to lend additional value to the author's work : secondly, the notion that his style may be compared to his clothes, which he can assume and again remove at will, rather than to his skin or the muscles beneath the skin, which have become an irremovable part of his existence. Butler was a puritan in literature, though in life a philosophic pagan ; and his puritanical creed has now been inherited by many writers of the present age, whose habit it is to approach the reader with an air of self-important *gaucherie*, as if determined to disarm the suspicions that any display of art would inevitably arouse. Hence those long, clumsy disjointed sentences which set out to reproduce the rhythms of the spoken language, or to reflect the rambling parade of thoughts supposed to stray through an imaginary character's mind. The " stream of consciousness " technique, however, is just as artificial as the machinery of a Greek play—the Messenger's explanatory speech or the interventions of the Chorus. We think in pictures as well as in words—a fact of which even Mrs. Bloom's

famous monologue clearly fails to take account; while the
language we speak is far too rough a medium to afford the sim-
plest of writers the scope he requires. Were the dramatis personæ
of a work of fiction to talk as loosely and vaguely as their author
talks, his novel would soon degenerate into a maze of broken
sentences.

Thus a work of literature is necessarily artificial; and we
should not forget that the adjective "artificial", when first
introduced, was definitely a term of praise. To be ashamed of
artifice is generally a sign of the type of literary puritanism I have
already mentioned, which regards the cultivation of an artificial
style as a form of sinful aristocratic pride, quite out of keeping
with the temper of our present righteous democratic society.
Whether in personal or in literary conduct, undue asceticism is
always blighting; and as important as a capacity to resist tempta-
tion is an ability, displayed at the correct juncture, to succumb
with grace and gusto; for, in every prose style that gives us
genuine delight, an element of restraint and reserve is accompanied by occasional touches of exuberance, where the literary
artist emulates the musician skilfully enlarging on and embellish-
ing his theme. The sonority and rotundity of Gibbon's periods,
the endless qualifications indulged in Henry James, would be
defects were they not counter-balanced by so vigorous a sense of
style and did they not correspond very closely to the artist's
peculiar vision of the world. It is only if the correspondence
ceases that style becomes a matter of virtuosity and, having out-
lasted the underlying talent, continues to emit the same mech-
anical tunes, like a clock chiming the hours through the rooms of
a dead, deserted house. Such is the sound that often reaches us
from a celebrated author's later volumes. I thought that it
reached me from *Aphrodite in Aulis*; but it did not lessen the
admiration I felt for *Aphrodite's* predecessors, and in no way
diminished my respect for the aged Perfectionist of Ebury Street,
seated alone, as I left him that evening amid the shadows of his
gloomy Victorian parlour, at the end of a long life entirely

dedicated to the cause of art. By the time I said goodbye, he seemed to have forgotten that his visitor existed and had sunk back into the silent reverie from which I had aroused him when I crossed his threshold, pondering, no doubt, over the books he had written—how could they be re-written and improved ?—but even more deeply and anxiously over the books that he still hoped to write. There was nothing devotional about George Moore's temperament except his pious devotion to the art he practised ; but at that moment, brooding and remote, the pagan storyteller had an almost saintly air.

IV

The Traveller

I HAVE suggested elsewhere that, unlike French writers, who are almost always centripetal, the average modern English writer exhibits a centrifugal tendency. In other words, the Gallic poet or novelist, once he has begun to make a name, usually abandons his native province and sets forth along the road to Paris ; but no sooner has a literary Englishman read the notices of his first successful book than, if he is already established there, he lays his plans for leaving London and, having perhaps tried a house in the country, next considers leaving England and is presently heard of among the Greek islands or as the lonely inhabitant of a Mediterranean village. Frenchmen travel with some definite end in view ; Childe Harold and Waring are peculiarly Anglo-Saxon types ; and at no period have romantic wanderers, who travel for the sake of travelling, been so numerous as during the restless period that preceded the outbreak of the last war. English writers scattered across Europe ; some followed D. H. Lawrence and pushed their explorations very much farther afield. Many of my own contemporaries took to travel as they might have taken to a drug, finding it a substitute for mystical or sensual experience, the palliative of every woe, the solution of every private problem, and wrote home from the mountains of Abyssinia or the jungles and savannahs of British Guiana. A drug it frequently became, no less insidious and deleterious. Rightly employed, however, it is also a powerful stimulant ; for, though

97

the only changes that encourage a writer's growth are the changes
that occur within, they may be accelerated, if not provoked, by
the sudden sense of personal solitude, when one is cast headlong
into an alien world and obliged to sink or swim amid unfamiliar
faces.

Not all expeditions, of course, produce the same imaginative
reward ; and, just as at home the most enjoyable experiences are
apt to be experiences we have not sought, so the most stimulating
and rewarding journeys are often embarked on in the least
romantic spirit, and develop with the brilliant unexpectedness of
a happy love affair. I returned to England by the trans-Siberian
railway during the summer of 1931 because I had already made
the sea-voyage, and was anxious to revisit Peking—a city that
I loved and admired no less than I detested Tokyo—before
London and its literary-journalistic life had finally dragged me
down again. So, towards the end of a sultry summer evening,
I drove in a rickshaw to an odd little railway station hidden
beneath an ancient rampart and entered the wagon-lit train that
would carry me as far north as the Manchurian capital. To
Peking I had paid my last homage—Peking in its summer robes,
a forest-city, if one surveyed it from the artificial slope of Coal
Hill. A torrent of vegetation flooded every family courtyard
and besieged the " peacock roofs " of the Manchu Palace, glittering cubes of polychrome tilework, their iridescence bloomed
or dimmed by a film of feathery wind-sown grass ; and trees
crowded the gardens and waste places that hid behind the
outer walls. Beyond the walls, through the towered gates,
stretched endless fields of verdant maize which had submerged
the whole extent of the plain to a depth of some six or seven
feet.

Now darkness had fallen ; the station was hot and noisy ; and
in the glare of harsh electric lights, illuminating prominent cheek-
bones and shaven skulls, a talkative Chinese crowd milled up
and down the narrow platform. There were loutish soldiers, who
wore grey-green uniforms, attached presumably to the forces of

the " Young Marshal " or some other successful war lord of the time : handsome large-bellied gentlemen, all in sober blue silk, ponderously processing backwards and forwards at a measured, dignified, duck-like pace : and a number of thin, elegant, highly painted, rather diabolic-looking Chinese ladies, arguing shrilly with a ragged peasant who was offering them apricots and small woolly-coated green almonds. But at last the train pulled out into the dark, and I rediscovered the mysterious universe of the solitary nocturnal traveller. I slept, but awoke as day was breaking. Dawn is never so pure, the early morning sky never so lofty, so transparent and so cold, as when it is seen from the window of a railway carriage in which one has passed a hot and restive night. We were crossing a bridge ; and, along the broad bed of the river below, pools gleamed with a pallid nacreous lustre. But, above the precipices that enclosed the stream, a stronger light had begun to fill the sky ; and against this trans-lucent background the winged eaves of some fortress or hill-top shrine appeared in inky silhouette.

Somehow I missed the Great Wall ; no doubt it had already dropped behind ; and, when I had dressed and breakfasted, we were evidently in Manchuria. A queer spiky range of volcanic hills, which had sprung up on the right-hand side, were replaced by a rolling country of downs and hillocks, channelled through by water-courses and traversed by deep-sunk rutted paths. Everywhere the landscape was patched with fields of tall green maize, and I was reminded, now and then, of the central Sicilian plateau from which the Romans stocked their granaries. At Mukden I had to change trains ; and, there, in the Japanese Leased Territory, I recognised the pretentious concrete office-blocks, the telegraph poles, the taxicabs and the straw-hatted businessmen of twentieth-century Tokyo ; while, overlooking them like a cynical opponent, steeped in the grey decrepitude of China, old and dirty but still commanding, stood the grey-walled Manchu city. Then, at Changchun, the ghost of Imperial Russia re-emerged from the pre-revolutionary past. On the pavements one saw Russian bootblacks and threadbare uniforms of the Imperial army ; in the beer-garden, where I spent an hour or two before a second change of trains, the tables were served by blonde sulky Russian waitresses. Otherwise Changchun seemed empty and desolate, a haunted place of no return. As if their course had been set for infinity, its muddy streets rambled off into the void between low house-fronts of drab-coloured brick, with an occasional Chinese grocer's shop displaying Japanese or American tinned goods.

Here Slavonic officials took charge of the line, and the attendant who unlocked my sleeping-car had the silver pince-nez and the fan-shaped beard of an old-fashioned Russian intellectual. Arrived at Harbin, I noticed him again ; but his buttoned tunic had been exchanged for a silk embroidered blouse, and a middle-aged woman, with a market-basket and a little curly white dog, had joined him at the station and was accompanying him as he walked home. It was Sunday, a whole holiday ; and groups of fair-haired girls, their arms linked, hurried past him on their way to the river. The river that flows through Harbin is the Sungari, itself a tributary of the gigantic Amur, which after some thousands of miles finds an outlet in the Gulf of Tartary. Even at this stage of its progress, it is far more massive than most European streams ; but not until I had left its banks did I become fully acquainted with its sweep and grandeur. My motor-boat had an uncommonly shallow draught ; and, from where I sat, deep in the stern, close to the broken surface of the water, the Sungari unfolded as a majestic horizontal landscape, scalloped with miniature waves, clouded and corrugated by downward puffs of winds, ploughed into hollows and troughs by the wash of distant vessels, valleys and mountains and glassy plains, perpetually subsiding and perpetually renewed. Across the flood slanted a procession of sails. There were sailing dinghies piloted by young men, stretched out almost naked, the sheet wrapped around one careless hand, and larger boats which wallowed slowly forward under a huge spread of bellying and blustering canvas. Sometimes, near the launch's prow, shone the head and burnished shoulder-muscles of a particularly strong and adventurous swimmer, who glanced up at us from the crest of a swell as he shook the wet hair off his forehead ; and crowds of less determined swimmers peopled the shallows beneath the green-fledged shores, which were lined with house-boats and rafts and topped with untidy wooden cottages. The citizens of Harbin evidently adored the sun ; and, in the dazzling reflected light of the river, their sun-burnt bodies had a golden effulgence. Their faces I could seldom distinguish clearly ; but, pinnacled on the green bank or poised to dive, they formed a long frieze of radiant featureless statues, all of them beautiful and all desirable, like the gilt-bronze masterpieces described by Baudelaire in his vision of mankind's naked youth.* Doubly disturbing were the emotions they roused after eighteen months among the Japanese, whose ideas of physical grace rarely approximate to Western standards.

At the statues' feet, the broad expanse of the river glittered a sharp metallic blue ; behind them, the edge of a grassy steppe and the whitish margin of a heat-discoloured sky quivered and undulated through the summer haze. Yet the inhabitants of this torrid paradise must look forward to a bleak future. Exiles or the children of exiles, washed up in Harbin by the revolution, they lived on sufferance, from day to day, caught between three unfriendly powers. The Japanese ignored them : the Chinese exploited them : the Soviet government regarded them as dangerous relics of the old régime. To Tsarist Russia they certainly belonged—those handsome strapping young men and attractive young women in their flimsy cotton dresses, whose skin was burned a darker shade than their hair, and who might have stepped straight out of a story by Tchehov or a novel by

* *J'aime le souvenir de ces époques nues,*
Dont Phœbus se plaisait à dorer les statues.
Alors l'homme et la femme en leur agilité
Jouissaient sans mensonge et sans anxiété,
Et, le ciel amoureux leur caressant l'échine,
Exerçaient la santé de leur noble machine.

Turgenev. Some of them would probably drift southwards to staff the restaurants and cabarets of Shanghai ; and pretty White Russian girls often found their way into the harems of luxurious Chinese warlords ; while others would remain in Harbin and scrape up a living there as best they could. Westwards and southwards, the Soviet Union barred escape ; and, when next day I arrived at Manchouli and rather hesitantly crossed the Russian frontier, I was conscious at once of the almost impassable gulf separating old and new worlds. Overhead in the crowded customs house, a large crudely printed poster advertised the Triumph of the Masses—a colossal workman trampling to death a Lilliputian horde of capitalists, kings and mitred bishops. Stalin's sardonic mask stared down from a second poster. Even in their physical appearance, the Russians at Manchouli, compared with the long-limbed nostalgic exiles of Harbin, seemed to belong to an entirely different race. Small and squat and unsmiling, as they probed packages and wrenched open trunks, they were enveloped in an air of determined grimness that suited their revolvers and belts and the numerous official badges they wore. A cold draught blew from the gulf that divided us. It was pleasant to leave the customs house and join an old-fashioned broad-gauge Russian train, a drab-grey reptilian monster basking and hissing in the fierce sunlight.

Long railway journeys produce a dream-like impression, which grows more dream-like with every mile we travel. Now clouds of red dust were whistling beside the track—dust from the Outer Mongolian desert, which silted into the carriage, covering books and clothes. A hot wind scourged the dry steppe, flat and naked to a blurred horizon ; and, cantering against the gritty blast, a solitary horseman pursued his cattle ; while in the far distance crouched a fortified village, guarded by low mud walls and solid quadrangular towers, the same dusty reddish-brown as the bare beaten earth from which they sprang. Woods and meadows followed the Mongolian waste ; and the bright immensity of Lake Baikal, a wave-fretted inland sea, shone through a grove of silver birches. Those birches, their polished boles and the deep meadow-grass between the trees, are all that I can now remember of the vast lake and its forested southern end, where the line leaves the country of the Buriat Mongols and swings north-west towards the Siberian forests. For, at that point, an enjoyable dream became a continuous hallucination, strengthened by the reverberant pounding of the wheels, the cumulative effects of bodily fatigue and the endless movement of an interminable landscape that seemed to flow past the eyes of a stationary observer. I received a painful jar if the movement suddenly ceased; and once, when I awoke in the middle of the night and discovered that the train was at a standstill, I jerked up the blind of the carriage-window with sensations that were close to panic. A mysterious hush surrounded and buried us. Opposite the window, sharply bristling upon a patch of dark-blue midnight sky, a stunted fir-tree was standing sentinel, and above its black crest floated a single star. Through the dust-screen that protected the window I caught a smell of earth and fir-cones. A few rain drops pattered from the sky; otherwise an inutterable silence. All the outside-doors of the coach were locked. And, before far-away voices were heard and a glimmer of lantern-light touched the branches of a tree, I had begun to experience the pang of unreasoning fear that is seldom felt except in childhood, so much stronger and more poignant than the fears and anxieties of adult life.

Later, as our journey progressed, the train would frequently halt in broad day. When an obstruction was reported on the line ahead, we lay quiet for nearly twenty-four hours, immobilised next to a forest siding where a miserable peasant family had taken up their quarters in a decrepit goods-van. Throughout our stay there, heavy rain descended, and the father of the family, a gaunt red-bearded man, and his pale-faced skeletonious wife often emerged on the threshold to study their extraordinary neighbours, while their thin children crawled from the van to relieve themselves between its wheels. More pleasing were the apparently purposeless halts in some wide clearing rimmed around with firs. The clearings were always full of flowers, notably vetches, meadowsweet, wild snapdragon and willow-herb or rosebay, the tall, graceful, beautifully-named plant that makes a habit of following the wood-cutter's axe. Among the passengers bound for Moscow, besides a party of German engineers —stout, assertive, noisy Teutons, great eaters and expert house-keepers, who loudly delighted in one another's company—and three slender young delegates from a Central-Asian Soviet Republic, wearing little embroidered skull-caps and long belted knee-length coats, we carried a detachment of soldiers from one of the garrison-towns of the Far East. They were cavalrymen, but passionate flower-collectors ; and, as often as the train had announced its departure and his fellow passengers had climbed aboard, a military botanist, absorbed in his hobby, was almost certain to be left behind and would be seen chasing the last carriage with top-booted giant-strides, encouraged by a chorus of friends half-dependent from the open window.

The flowers that grew in these forest-clearings had a look of paradisal freshness ; and just as fresh and uncontaminated was the whole enormous Siberian landscape—meadows that might never have been trodden, with not a path or a sign of a grazing animal, and broad rivers that wandered into the distance with no trace of human activity visible on either bank ; though close to a bridge we crossed I saw the remains of sand-bagged trenches, an outpost that had perhaps been fought over during one of the battles of the Civil War. After that, image succeeded image with dreamlike monotony and dreamlike rapidity : when we were approaching Omsk, where Dostoievsky served his term as a political prisoner, the white walls and flashing domes of a monastery built on a riverside bluff : in European Russia, when we had crossed the Urals, which somehow eluded me under the cover of night, a small manor-house, infinitely forlorn and remote, perched half-way up a wooded hill. But the dream dissolved as we entered the suburbs of Moscow. That clamorous, dishevelled

city jolted the dreamer wide awake, battering his senses with its
heat and noise, bewildering him with glimpses of old and new—
Palladian façades from which the stucco had crumbled, unfinished
offices and public palaces swathed in clumsy wooden splints.
Over the tramlines marched young Komsomols, rifles slung
behind their shoulders, boys and girls keeping step and singing
deep-throated revolutionary songs. The famous collection of
French Impressionist pictures happened to have shut its doors
that day; the interior of the Kremlin could not be visited,
though I admired the lofty circuit of red-brick ramparts, built,
I believe, by an Italian architect; while the oddly entitled " Park
of Culture and Rest " proved to be a torrid wilderness, dotted
with gimcrack pavilions housing displays of propagandist
pictures, among flower-beds representing aircraft or designed
to commemorate favourite slogans, such as *Equal and Out-
strip the Capitalist Countries!* inscribed in a pattern of scarlet
begonias.

Next the discouraged guide suggested a visit to Lenin's tomb,
and inserted me at the head of a queue that stretched across the
Red Square. Slowly, in solemn, silent file, between walls lined
with slabs of polished red and black basalt—the black stone had
crystalline reflections like the blue wings of imprisoned butterflies
—we made our shuffling descent towards the central tomb-
chamber. Heine speaks of seeing Napoleon as he rode along
" that very great avenue of the Court Garden at Düsseldorf " in
his " invisible-green uniform and the little world-renowned hat ";
he rode " carelessly, almost lazily . . . holding his reins with one
hand, and with the other patting the horse's neck. It was a sunny,
marble hand . . ." For the author of *Reisebilder* this was one of
two or three occasions—an equally impressive moment was his
meeting with the aged Goethe, whose air of Augustan majesty so
confounded him that all he could do was babble distractedly
about the wild plums he had picked and eaten on his way—from
which he gained a sudden sense of confronting History personified. In Lenin's tomb-chamber I had the same impression,

although what I saw was not a man but a mummy, a carefully restored, brightly lighted corpse, laid out in a shining glass case, tall sentries stationed at either end with reversed arms and reverently lowered eyes. We entered the chamber behind the head of the coffin ; and the first detail, I remember, to catch my attention was a diagonal groove across the dead man's skull. Then we were shepherded along the side of the body and could peer down momentarily on an illuminated mask. The skin had a curiously waxen texture, and its colouring seemed unnaturally harsh and vivid. Some years earlier, when the flooded sewers of the Kremlin had overflowed into the adjacent tomb, the sacred relic they swamped was said to have suffered heavy damage. But its mishaps had not yet impaired the living quality of those sunken features—less substantial perhaps than in life and now protected no doubt by a layer of pigment, but still expressive and authoritative under the bright electric bulbs. A finely marked, ascetic face, with the high cheek-bones and large domed forehead of an early ikon-picture. Propaganda portraits of Lenin give him a brutally determined frown, and show a powerful proletarian fist firmly clenched as he prepares to strike the table. But it was a small right hand, the fingers slightly contracted, that lay at rest against his thigh ; and the tapering fingers themselves were delicate and well-shaped. His left hand was placed on the breast of his jacket—a drab-hued uniform jacket closely buttoned up to a plain collar ; while over his knees was spread a plum-coloured dressing-gown, evidently worn and old.

Between coffin and polished walls drifted an unending silent procession, past the diminutive central figure, caught in a flood of brilliance like an insect trapped in a block of amber, past the massive, motionless sentries, and up towards the Red Square. I was being carried along by the quietly shuffling crowd, when a burst of loud voices reverberated down the steps. Ahead of me was the German party who had cooked such good meals, and enjoyed so many vociferous private jokes, on the journey across Siberia. Now they were expressing their contempt for the ridiculous wax-work they had just seen. They knew a wax-work if they saw one ! Nobody could tell *them*, they reiterated. And, with a stiff, rolling, short-legged gait, they marched off in pursuit of fresh absurdities. Some hours later, we had all entrained, bound for Poland—where peasant reapers were cutting the corn, attentively followed by a patrician red-legged stork—and Berlin, then in the last stages of its riotous pre-Hitlerian carnival. London, by comparison, was both dull and sad ; and some of my friends seemed almost unaware that I had ever left the country. I was apt to receive dark looks as often as I described my impressions of Russia. It was, in his opinion, perfectly right and natural, said an ambitious Left Wing politician to whom I spoke of Lenin's tomb, that the modern Communist leaders, although they had dethroned God, should exploit, for their own far-sighted ends, the relic-worshipping enthusiasm of the uneducated Russian masses. I was no less severely handled by the editor of a Socialist weekly magazine, an arbiter of enlightened opinion, who for several years had been paying resolute court to the sternly implacable Red Siren, but later, at the Wroclaw Congress, was to hear himself denounced as a bourgeois opportunist—a " dancer on an inclined plane "—guilty of having discharged " poisoned arrows " against the forces of democracy. His sorrowfully prophetic eyes burned in a haggard, handsome face. So I thought, did I, that existence in Soviet Russia appeared ugly and discordant and raw ? That human life had been ruthlessly stripped of its protective outer covering ? Well, I must not forget (he pointed out) that the leaders of Soviet Russia had very little time to spare for vagrant dilettanti like myself. " After all," he reminded me, speaking apparently more in sorrow than in anger, " you are a *cultured individualist* "; and his fine voice lent a tragic weight to the last two damning words.

*   *   *

Part of the charm of the journey I have just described was a sense of travelling in several dimensions—of hurrying in space across the convexity of the globe from the Far East to the hypoborean West, and by the same route moving in time from the Middle Ages to the twentieth century. Simultaneously, my pilgrimage had unfolded within the mind; and its reward was a series of imaginative impressions memorable and valuable for their own sake. Each evoked, not its immediate surroundings, but some similar and equally vivid experience. Thus my recollections of Harbin, and of the range of sunlit statues found their place beside an earlier vision, which had had almost as disturbing an effect and had left behind as luminous a memory. Both were glimpses of physical beauty and freedom; and the first had been enjoyed while crossing a river in Indo-China, on a motor-drive after night-fall from Saigon to Pnom-Penh. As we slid down on to the ferry boat, our headlights breached the wall of darkness and scooped a deep mysterious cavern peopled with slender shining figures. Some peasants were washing at the ford; and the light played over their wet naked bodies, over thin shoulders and narrow classical flanks, golden breasts and delicate feminine arms lifted to wring out coils of blue-black hair. Around their knees, the surface of the water gleamed like a pavement of antique marble; and beyond, shutting them in, rose the raw earth of the hollow bank. The vision lasted only a few seconds; but during those few seconds none of them spoke or moved; even the glimmering drops that a woman pressed from her hair seemed to have been caught and frozen before they fell. Then, as our headlights changed direction, the roof of the cavern suddenly collapsed and its golden inhabitants disappeared.

My impressions of the Siberian waste-lands also brought back an earlier stage of the journey, when our ship had entered the Tropics and we were threading the Straits of Malacca or passing near the coast of Borneo. In Siberia, we had breathed the rich damp smell of a shaggy bristling Northern forest. English poets have often responded to the idea of an unconquered, unlimited desolation:

108

The Traveller

Oh for a lodge in some vast wilderness,
Some boundless contiguity of shade . . .*

wrote Cowper, who usually advocates the mild amusements of
civilised domestic life, but shows an occasional touch of darker
and more disorderly feelings. On board ship, it was a very
different wilderness that stirred the traveller's imagination—an
unknown, invisible forest, from which he was separated by miles
of sea. Starlight outlined a low wooded horizon, dividing dusky
sea and dusky sky ; and through the decks, which smelt of plank-
ing and tar and oil, blew a wave of some curious earthy fragrance,
the scent of sweet bark and ripening fruit, of rank vegetation and
rotten leaves, mixed with the elusive, ineffable scent of the
blossoms that grow only in the highest branches and form a
flowery aerial plateau stretching over the tree-tops for many
hundreds of miles. Seen from its roots, the jungle is dim and
dishevelled, a regiment of coarse grey shafts planted in a squelchy
pestiferous floor ; and this scent brought with it an image of the
Tropics as vivid as any real landscape—the literary Tropics
beloved since the eighteenth century by generations of European
writers.

Who created the tropical legend ? No doubt the author of
Paul et Virginie. But a whole volume could be written about its
influence on verse and prose. Baudelaire himself, though a poet
of modern cities, never forgot the Indian Ocean and the two or
three weeks that, as a rebellious young man of twenty, shipped
off in disgrace by his mother and his step-father, he had spent
between the islands of Mauritius and Réunion, where he had
known the enchanting *Dame Créole*, Madame Autard de Bragard,
and her servant " *La Belle Dorothée* ", a velvet-eyed child of the
Malabar Coast. Throughout *Les Fleurs du Mal*, his memories of
exotic splendour provide a contrapuntal theme. They haunted
him as they haunt the negress whom he describes dragging her
way along the pavements of a foggy Parisian street. By contrast,

* *The Timepiece.*

they sharpen his taste for the pallid sunshine of a Northern autumn—" *de l'arrière-saison le rayon jaune et doux* ". They are woven into the amatory symbolism of such poems as *La Chevelure*, *Parfum Exotique* and *Sed Non Satiata*. The favourite he presently chose, and in whose cruel service he squandered his health and hopes, was a coloured actress, Jeanne Duval ; and the fantasies with which he surrounded his idol were all dreams of escape to a fiercer, more voluptuous climate *—*au delà du possible, au delà du connu!* a form of imaginative gratification that far transcended sexual pleasure.

Few writers can expect to make so much of a single interrupted journey—it is significant perhaps that Baudelaire should have disembarked as soon as he reached Mauritius, abandoned his passage to India and returned to confront his destiny at home ; but for almost every artist there is something to be gained from a voyage across the Tropic of Cancer. His expedition will be particularly valuable if he loves the natural world. The flowers of the Tropics it may be hard to enjoy—huge papery, obtrusive blossoms that often suggest the showy merchandise of some prodigious bargain-basement. But the population of the sea and the heavens no literary traveller would find disappointing ; and today he can reach the Tropics within the space of twenty-four hours. True, the aeroplane he has boarded will probably develop engine-trouble ; and then sudden miraculous bursts of speed will be cut short by long pauses at desolate and featureless airports, even duller than railway stations and enveloped in the

* " Je plongerai ma tête amoureuse d'ivresse
Dans ce noir océan où l'autre est enfermé ;
Et mon esprit subtil que le roulis caresse
Saura vous retrouver, ô féconde paresse,
Infinis bercements du loisir embaumé !

Cheveux bleus, pavillon de ténèbres tendues,
Vous me rendez l'azur du ciel immense et rond ;
Sur les bords duvetés de vos mèches tordues
Je m'enivre ardemment des senteurs confondues
De l'huile de coco, du musc et du goudron."
La Chevelure

same atmosphere of suffocating, impersonal ennui. My own aeroplane was often delayed ; and I did not set foot on the promised island until I had given up hope of ever arriving. Midnight had passed ; dawn was still far off ; the friends who expected me had left instructions that I should hire a taxi-cab and go ahead alone. But I had forgotten, or possibly failed to ask, just how many miles the journey covered.

Uncertainty heightened the feeling of suspense ; and at that hour, under a dark and rainy sky, the tattered outskirts of a tropical pleasure-resort wore a peculiarly grim and ghostly expression. We stopped at a corner to take in petrol, opposite a pair of tall thin women, whom I afterwards discovered to be municipal street-cleaners, each wearing a white turban over her black indistinguishable face, and each, with a diminutive feathery broom, lightly scratching or caressing a small area of broken concrete pavement. They would chase a morsel of débris hither and thither, as if it absorbed their whole interest ; then carefully restore it to the centre of the path and, with soporific unhurried gestures, turn their attention to some new quarry. The faint sibilant noise of their brooms, unnaturally loud in the deserted street, recalled the evocative opening pages of *Le Rideau Cramoisi*, where Barbey d'Aurevilly describes how he halts at midnight between the shuttered house-fronts of a French provincial town, sees a square of red curtain glowing from a house above and hears the sound of a broom—" *coup de balai, monotone et lassé* "—wielded by an invisible hand in the shadows beyond a courtyard door. While I waited, the sweepers held their ground as tenaciously as a pair of Eastern dancers ; and they were still dreamily stroking and scratching when my taxi-cab at length drove off. " Is it a long journey ? " I asked the good-natured driver, who seemed puzzled by such an irrelevant question and pulled his baseball cap, with a coloured Celluloid peak, further down towards his eyes. " *Some waay* ", he responded cautiously ; and, although from time to time I repeated the question, I could never persuade him to give me a more definite answer. Our journey took us for seventy miles, across the hills and through the thickets of a dark and unknown country.

When I arrived, dawn had risen; dew was glittering on my friends' garden; and the immense arch of a nearly perfect rainbow spanned the Caribbean Sea. Against a background of big expansive flowers, a humming bird perched by the kitchen-door; and at the end of the garden, below a rocky cliff, tufted with palms and festooned with pendulous tree-roots, the trans-parent wind-ruffled lagoon thrust up gentle glassy waves, which lapped into the rosy mouth of a conch lying half-buried at the edge of the water. Derelict conches are scattered broadcast on every Caribbean beach. The living molluscs crawl through the shallows, with the help of a muscular limb that resembles a grotesque thumb, completed by a horny shield that horribly suggests a pointed finger-nail; and native fishermen throw them ashore and pound them to pieces for their tough flesh, until only the innermost convolutions remain and hundreds of broken conches litter the rocks like so many fossilised scrolls of music. But no fishermen visited this beach; and a single shell lay drying and fading in the sun, among round skeletons of delicate sea-urchins and spiky twigs of dead coral. The crescent of coarse white sand looked beautifully smooth and hard, sheltered from the storms of the Rainy Season behind a guardian barrier-reef.

The placid lagoon is a country in itself; and, indeed, it appears to have its own sky, if one assumes an ordinary rubber swimming-mask and paddles seaward over the rock-fringed pools. As one lies face down on the warm resilient water and turns one's glass-fronted helmet from side to side, the surface, viewed from below, becomes a sheet of wrinkled quicksilver, shedding a silvery-soft light that ripples and trembles across the sandy floor. Large fish move like planets; shoals hang like constellations, suspended in the blue-grey distance; while, about the weedy flanks of a submerged rock, pass in procession the small bril-liantly coloured fish who live close to the shore and hunt through the forests of coral and weed—immature Angel Fish, orange and heliotrope : youthful Parrot Fish, blue and grass-green, with wavering rosy touches around their scales : Butterfly Fish striped black and yellow ; and a fish that, having a large peacock's eye near the tail-fin, seems perpetually to be swimming backwards. There are other, more menacing presences—a miniature Barracuda, pencil-thin and torpedo-straight, which hovers alongside the swimmer and fixes him with its flat malevolent gaze, and, now and then, the speckled ribbon of a fierce Moray Eel, nosing and undulating through a bed of sea-grass. Pools grow deeper as one approaches the reef ; and those of them which neighbour the reef have an air of almost Gothic gloom—dark precipitous defiles in which the timid and inexperienced swimmer, although the nape of his neck is exposed to the sun, may feel that he is submerged beyond recovery. From the deepest, rock-framed windows look out into the depths of the Caribbean ; and here, clinging to the jamb of the casement, the unusually intrepid mask-swimmer has sometimes watched a shark sail by.

The lagoon comes to an end at the reef : and, where the rock-barrier is solid and undivided, the powerful Caribbean swell rushes in against its rugged edge, smothering the coral-branches with an intricate pattern of foam and, as the broken wave begins to recede, leaving them salt-glistening and miraculously bright. Jagged flakes of coral, prickly antlers of coral, Brain Coral in enormous circular bosses and leaves of the lacy Fan Coral that rise and subside with the current's ebb and flow. The colours of a Caribbean coral reef can only be compared to the colour-scheme of a Holbein state-portrait. Velvet was a material that the Tudors loved ; and a slimy living velvet clothes the white bones of the coral organism, vivid fungus yellow, tawny orange or a rich and lustrous brown. Dark-red and wine-purple are accompanied by a soft sage green ; and this embroidery gleams in the sun, or glows with a confused radiance beneath sheet upon sheet of sliding crystal. But the coral-garden does not welcome intruders. Many species are poisonous ; all can inflict a savage scratch ; and no less ferocious are the big sea-urchins that lie in wait on innumerable ledges, clusters of blue-black stars slowly rotating their needle-point rays. After the glitter and turmoil of the reef, the world of the shallows seems doubly quiet. Some of its population are almost invisible, the colour of wet sand or a scrap of desiccated weed. Tiny high-stepping, nearly translucent crabs dance ecstatically along the margin of the water; and at night, if one takes a step into the lagoon and shines the beam of a torch around one's feet, one discovers that the sea-floor has thrown up a mysterious harvest of swaying, thin-stemmed, opaline flowers—sea-worms that hide in the sand and raise their ghostly tentacles as soon as dusk has fallen.

During the hours of daylight, a warm Trade Wind usually blows landwards across the face of the lagoon, which shimmers with all the iridescent reflections of a dying mackerel—or, in these latitudes it might be more appropriate to say, with some of the green and blue variations of a living Parrot Fish. Meanwhile, high overhead, wide-winged sea-birds cut the air—Tropic Birds and Frigate Birds, both with graceful sharply forked tails, the former snowy white, having the quick, staccato movements of an English Oyster Catcher, the latter inky black, spreading the narrow, angular, elbowed wings of a primæval Pterodactyl. Smaller birds peopled the thickets of the half-tamed garden beyond the cliff, not only elegant grey Mocking Birds and a charming family of wild canaries—far more orange in hue than the domesticated English breed—but a bevy of noisy blackbirds, whom native Jamaicans have prettily nicknamed *Kling-klings*, and an odd melancholy visitor, the mysterious Clucking Hen. This peculiar bird seems to be one of nature's jokes and, incidentally, a living disproof of orthodox Darwinian theories, since, although by a process of natural selection it has managed to evolve a nearly perfect camouflage, it has also developed a trick of immediately giving its presence away. A sudden glimpse of its human enemy impels it to produce a nervous cluck, followed by a bobbing movement of its ibis-like head; after which it stalks off in its shabby pepper-and-salt suit, with the gait of an embarrassed and irritable old gentleman, short-sightedly at a loss among the arm-chairs of a London club.

By far the loveliest birds, however, were the smallest and the speediest. Vervain humming-birds, with golden-green backs and speckled stone-coloured breasts, flitted through the garden borders ; and every evening, about half past five, a minute but distinctly audible *chink-chink-chinking* noise would be heard from the summit of a tree, entirely covered with the leaves and pale-blue trumpet-shaped blossoms of an immense parasitic creeper, that rose twenty or thirty feet above the strip of coral beach. The Doctor was beginning his seaward rounds ; and soon he would make his appearance amid the dependent swags of foliage, darting obliquely from side to side in the style of an intrepid skier who descends an almost vertical mountain-slope, vaulting from cluster to cluster of flowers, until he had reached the low prickly hedge planted on the sea-wall. The Doctor is his local name—in the view of the negro inhabitants, his garb suggests a tail-coat ; by ornithologists he is known as *Trochilus Polytmus* ; while less scientific admirers call him the Jamaican Long-tailed Humming-bird. First his voice sounded from the heights of the tree ; then the powerful whirr of his wings—extraordinarily loud and im-pressive considering the flyer's bulk. At last he would drop down on to the hedge in a celestial spark of metallic brilliance.

The head and body of the male Doctor measure just over two inches ; but they are completed by spreading tail-feathers which may extend to nearly eight. Head, back and tail are a glossy sable ; his throat and breast flash with a vivid shimmering emerald-green. The bill, delicate as the spine of a moss rose, is a translucent coral pink ; and from the tip flickers a hair-thin tongue, apparently longer than the bill itself. Yet within this Lilliputian mechanism throbs a dynamo of hot-blooded energy. Indeed, the word " mechanism " is at once misleading : every movement a humming-bird makes is expressive of purpose and passionate life. By comparison, larger birds are dawdling, half-hearted creatures—for example, the black-and-yellow finches with whom, as with the fragile spidery wasps, the Doctor keeps up a constant chinking and chattering dispute among his favourite garden shrubs. The finches hop and pause and indulge in periods of aimless leisure. The Doctor darts straight to his goal, quivering with inward vitality, intoxicated by his own speed.

In the presence of human beings, he is surprisingly bold. Perhaps the human body is too vast and formless to produce very much effect on those microscopic powers of vision. Remain moderately quiet under the shadow of the bushes, and he will flit past over your head almost within arm's reach, pivoting around a diadem of blossoms, stabbing each of its calices straight to the heart, leaping on and on with a rapidity that dazzles and defeats the eye. Meanwhile the *vrrrp-vrrrp-vrrrp* of his wing-strokes swells to an infinitesimal roar; and at every turn, every down-beat of the wings, his burnished emerald breastplate flames in the sun. His wings themselves move much too fast to be visible; so that the human sight registers only a haze—a darkish nimbus, amid which the humming-bird's body, as he springs vertically upward and leans backward against the pressure of the air, seems at first to be hovering unsupported. Simultaneously, the two slender, out-curving black tail-feathers are in perpetual agitation. They whip behind him as he scuds through a tree, flirt and flourish and undulate as he goes hurrying along the crest of a hedge. Now and then the sea-breeze catches them; and they float up like the twin streamers of some fantastic antique head-dress.

Her dreams must be peopled with humming-birds, wrote Baudelaire of Madame Autard de Bragard's beautiful Indian handmaiden :

> . . . *Quand descend le soir au manteau d'écarlate,*
> *Tu poses doucement ton corps sur une natte,*
> *Où tes rêves flottants sont pleins de colibris* . . .

And, in the garden of a Jamaican house, the Doctor, though its smallest inhabitant, seemed the presiding genius of the place.

But his visit to the coral beach usually lasted less than half an hour ; and, having watched him as he explored the flowers of the hedge and followed his lightning departure when he soared up again into the summit of the tree, I would climb the steps that led to the garden and pursue him to a flowering thicket, draped with an intricate curtain of the parasitic creeper named Heavenly Blue, where most of his species appeared to have their home-ground. Nowhere else could the Doctor be observed in repose. Generally silhouetted on the same twig, he would go through all the customary actions of a bird preparing to retire for the night. While day declined and a lurid sunset died behind the palm groves, he would preen his plumage, whet his beak, repeatedly vibrate his wings as if he felt that, even now, they still required some exercise and, in a final spasm of wakefulness, vigorously scratch his ear. One eye shone—a pin-head fragment of jet. In profile, the feathers on the nape of his neck flowed up to form a curling fringe. Occasionally he would utter a strident *chink*. Then the darkness silenced and blotted him out, as a drum-fire of frog- and insect-noises began to sweep across the garden. The Caribbean night falls with a weight and density from which it is difficult to believe that day will ever re-emerge.

V

Camp-Followers

ALTHOUGH HUBERT ROBERT was an artist who loved scenes of
desolate autumnal grandeur, landscapes with ancient trees, fallen
columns and broken urns, and perhaps a marble Pegasus rearing
against a stormy sky, he sometimes turned his attention to a
homelier and more familiar subject. For example, he produced
a delightful conversation piece, entitled *Le Petit Déjeuner de
Madame Geoffrin*. There the famous woman sits in her arm-chair,
flanked by a fire-screen of blue and gold ; a comfortable wood-
fire burns on the hearth ; and above her head, just below a circular
medallion representing the Goddess Athene, hangs a large
romantic canvas—presumably the artist's own work—which
portrays rugged Alpine crags and the cascades of a mountain
stream. She is dipping a *croissant* into her cup ; while just behind
her stands a smart young footman, a dandified Parisian Joseph
Andrews, whose powdered mane flows down his back. He is
girt with an apron but has put aside his broom, which now leans
against another chair. Evidently he is a favourite attendant ;
and she has instructed him to read aloud.

That blend of dignity and informality was characteristic of the
artist's period, and seems particularly appropriate in a portrait-
study of Madame Geoffrin. Although she lived surrounded by
esprits forts, witty atheists and daring philosophers, discretion and
moderation were social virtues that she greatly prized ; and, if
the talk around her became too wild and rash, with a firm " *voilà*

qui est bien! "—as it were, " we've had enough of that ! "—she would arrest her friends' dangerous exuberance and direct the conversation along a smoother course. Yet her salon was a centre of intellect that drew even such travelling adventurers as the exiled John Wilkes ; and, with her fellow *salonnières* Madame du Deffand and Mademoiselle de Lespinasse, she occupies a small but important position in the history of eighteenth-century Europe. The *salon*, however, has remained a peculiarly French growth, which has had no exact equivalent upon the opposite shores of the English Channel—possibly because general conversation is antipathetic to the English spirit, or it may be because the pattern of English social life is very much more vague and fluid, and our men of letters are apt to be centrifugal, whereas their French colleagues are resolutely centripetal. Yet here, too, the creative arts attract men and women who are not themselves creative, but find a vicarious pleasure in collecting and encouraging artists ; for which the irritable artist sometimes rewards them with a display of fierce ingratitude.

During my own life-time I have met several of these distinguished camp-followers, each in his or her own way a curious and striking personage. Edward Marsh I have already mentioned as the founder and editor of *Georgian Poetry*. But then, he possessed himself certain executive, if not creative, talents ; and I must deal first with a group of *vivandières*—providers and entertainers by vocation and taste—whose activities helped for many years to brighten and diversify the English scene. As soon as I had gone up to Oxford, I heard discussions of Lady Ottoline Morrell and of the Renaissance court she held at Garsington Manor four or five miles beyond the city's limits. Among her friends had been such very different celebrities as Bertrand Russell, Augustus John, D. H. Lawrence, Aldous Huxley, Lytton Strachey and Virginia Woolf. But her friendships, I gathered, had not always stood the test of years. Lawrence and Huxley, at least, had broken away some time before I reached Garsington ; and each had published a book that seemed to portray her in an extremely critical and unkindly light. Huxley's alleged portrait was the more diverting of the two : Lawrence's, naturally, the more alarming. She had been recognised by some of its readers as Priscilla Wimbush, eccentric châtelaine of Crome, in that brilliant first novel *Crome Yellow*—and both the person and the place described unmistakably owed a good deal to Lady Ottoline and her Garsington household ; while *Women in Love* presented a fantastic character whom the novelist named Hermione Roddice, one of those " free women who have emancipated themselves from the aristocracy ", strange, impressive, malevolent, " her eyes heavy and full of sepulchral darkness ", apparelled in stiff antique brocades which make her look " tall and rather terrible " as she listens " with a drugged attention " to the table-talk of her intellectual guests. Lawrence's admirers will recollect that Hermione loves Rupert Birkin : that her passion for him is twisted and thwarted, and that she achieves a " voluptuous consummation " by crashing a large lapis-lazuli paper-weight down on to his unprotected skull : after which she confronts him, " tall, livid and attentive ", hoping to repeat the blow, and Birkin prudently backs through the door, muttering : " No you don't, Hermione . . ."

To equate an " imaginary " with a " real " character is always dangerous and often foolish ; and Hermione Roddice is not a portrait so much as a distorted and enlarged reflection. Nevertheless, Lawrence's former friend seems to have been deeply wounded ; and, since he was a sensitive and affectionate man at heart, when he heard that she was ill and out of spirits, during the spring of 1928, he wrote her a generous reconciliatory letter. Nor was he pretending to a gratitude he did not feel ; for simultaneously, in a letter to Mark Gertler, another previous member of the Garsington circle, he declared that " after all, she's a queen, among the mass of women ". To Lady Ottoline herself he paid an even more explicit tribute : " After all, there's only one Ottoline. And she has moved one's imagination . . . The so-called portraits of Ottoline can't possibly be Ottoline—

no-one knows that better than an artist. But Ottoline has moved men's imagination, deeply, and that's perhaps the most a woman can do ".* It is unfortunate that the subject of so many literary sketches—which include a sheaf of savagely amusing caricatures executed by Osbert Sitwell—should have left behind her no self-portrait, none at any rate that has yet been published. Her creative ambitions remained unsatisfied ; and the only specimen of her prose style that appears to have emerged from manuscript is to be found embedded in a huge and solemn book, entitled *Men, Women and Things*, given to the world a year before her death by her half-brother, the sixth Duke of Portland. Here is a description, written with considerable spirit, of how she had accompanied her brother to Welbeck Abbey, the vast unfinished house he had just inherited but until that day had never entered. Privacy, of course, had been the old Duke's mania ; he had been, indeed, a maniac of a peculiarly exalted and extraordinary type ; and his reputation, while he lived, had spread beyond his own country, reaching Villiers de l'Isle-Adam in Paris, who made him the hero of a characteristic tale. But no detail supplied by the storyteller could have been more astonishing and unnerving than the actual state of Welbeck. Except for the rooms that the Duke had inhabited, and which had brass letter-boxes, inside and out, fastened upon every door, all its apartments were bare and empty ; but all of them were painted a festive pink, and almost all had a water-closet placed conspicuously in an un-screened corner. Beneath the house and the surrounding park ran a labyrinth of prodigious tunnels. One gave access to an ancient riding-school, which the tunnel-builder, in a sudden short-lived mood of gaiety, had decided to transform into a ball-room, panelled with lofty looking glasses and hung with as many crystal chandeliers as could be suspended from the roseate ceiling. Another led to the gigantic kitchens, where a capon perpetually turned on the spit, so that the Duke, whenever he rang, need never fail to find a meal ready. Yet another, which

* *Letters of D. H. Lawrence*, edited by Aldous Huxley.

was over a mile long and dipped down under a shallow lake,
enclosed a carriage drive that stretched to the gates of the park
and was sufficiently spacious to admit two carriages abreast. In
these passages and in his echoing house itself, the lonely magni-
fico, who shunned the human face and preferred to exist behind
drawn curtains or paced his London garden protected by screens
of frosted glass, had gradually accumulated a rich fantastic
squirrel's hoard. Unframed family-pictures were stacked, forgotten, against the walls; and immense cupboards were filled
with tin boxes containing a large array of dark-brown wigs, and
with white silk handkerchiefs, each about a yard across, neatly
distinguished by sets of hem-stitched initials—those marked *T.* to
be worn when travelling: *W.A.* if they were to be used at
Welbeck: *H.H.* for Harcourt House, his shuttered residence in
Cavendish Square.

Such was one of the episodes of Lady Ottoline's youth; and,
although she was not closely connected with the tunnelling
master of Welbeck Abbey—her half-brother, to be exact, had
been his first cousin once removed—it seemed clear that she
must have inherited some distinctive and original strain. The
eccentric Duke had made his own world—a world of private
lonely grandeur; and she, too, aimed at an existence modelled
according to her own taste. At Garsington, she had for a time
succeeded. A small manor house, built of Cotswold stone, with
a steep-pitched roof and mullioned windows, it looked down
from the crest of a slope over a green and silvery-grey garden,
bordered by dark yew hedges, which descended towards a narrow
leaf-scattered pool, where, just as in *Crome Yellow*, favourite
guests were occasionally emboldened to swim. Garden-statues
lined the terraces; ancient trees surrounded the house. From
under the dusty shadow of an ilex would come wandering a
dishevelled peacock—like all peacocks, except when they are in
love and the quills of the tail, stiffly extended, rattle together
with a staccato vibration, it appeared despondent and a little
lost; and, after the trailing bird, the hostess might herself

emerge. She seemed to trail, as did the bird she followed—in a dress of bottle-green velvet that swept the lawn, trimmed with bands of thick white swansdown bordering the square-cut neck. The large feathered hat that she often assumed was both regal and pleasantly proletarian ; for it suggested a portrait of Queen Henrietta Maria but also recalled an Edwardian photograph of a Cockney *élégante* on Hampstead Heath. About her throat, which was lengthy and sinewy, she had cast a triple rope of pearls —big, irregular, antique pearls that often reminded me of childish molars.

The effect was Baroque and yet somehow Gothic ; for the lines of her features had a mediæval strength, a boldly baronial, high-arched nose being accompanied by a prominent prognathous jaw. Her hair, arranged in seventeenth-century curls, was darkened to a deep mahogany red, which the pallor of her face and neck made at first sight all the more surprising ; and from this strangely impressive mask proceeded a sonorous nasal voice, which drawled and rumbled, and rustily hummed and hawed, but might subside, if she were amused or curious, to an insinuating confidential murmur. No woman could have shown less regard for the conventions of English country-life ; but, at least when she walked in the garden, and the dejected, magnificent peacocks trailed around her buckled shoes, she had an air of genuinely belonging to the landscape, or to that corner of the Oxfordshire landscape which lay beneath the windows of Garsington. Crossing its threshold, however, one really penetrated her sphere of influence. The rooms on the ground floor were low and panelled ; and, instead of pickling the Elizabethan wood or treating it with some dismal stain, she had covered the walls with lively coats of paint, green and blue and Chinese scarlet, and hung from the central beam of her scarlet drawing-room a cardinal bird in a lacquer cage. Today her schemes of interior decoration might seem as self-conscious and out-moded as a room designed by William Morris ; and some of her pictures, extremely "modern" at the time, would have an historical

rather than a pictorial charm. But, combined with her voice
and her clothes and the fragrance of the numerous pomanders
that she kept on shelves and ledges, they helped to produce
an atmosphere of romantic other-worldliness, as though ordinary
life had come to a standstill the moment that one stepped
indoors.

Those, at all events, were the impressions of a somewhat
ingenuous and inexperienced observer. I have an unlucky way
of reaching the theatre just before the last act; and the Garsington
I knew was a beautifully lighted stage from which many of the
protagonists had already withdrawn. True, I once sighted
Lytton Strachey and questioned him, in petulant undergraduate
fashion, about his recent essay on William Blake : to which he
replied in a reedy falsetto, civilly and very patiently, stroking his
dense russet beard and gazing at me through large spectacles.
He supposed he must have thought that he was being *clever*—with
this disarming admission he brought my impertinent protests to
an end. From a letter published not long ago,* I observe that
Virginia Woolf continued to visit Garsington as late as 1923 ;
but she had never liked Lady Ottoline, who elicited all her latent
spleen, and complained of the artificiality of rustic surroundings
where she imagined that " even the sky is done up in pale yellow
silk ". Otherwise, the majority of celebrated names now associated with the legend of Bloomsbury had vanished from the
Garsington record ; and usually their departure was said to have
been preceded by some furious row. Echoes of disputes and
dissensions had not completely died away ; one heard of intrigues
and conspiracies, violent altercations and broken love-affairs. But
either the hostess had been much maligned or she was then
entering a calmer period of her life ; for to me she always
extended an amiably expansive welcome and would, now and
then, beckon me upstairs towards her private sitting-room off the
main staircase. There she kept several big jars of brightly

* Virginia Woolf to Barbara Bagenal. June 24th 1923. Quoted by Clive Bell in
Old Friends, Chatto & Windus, 1956.

coloured " boiled sweets "; and while she enquired into one's literary and personal progress—" *M-m-m*—Are you writing much poetry nowadays ? *M-m-m-m*—Do you often fall in love ? "—she would crunch them between strong equine teeth with an expression of sympathetic interest. She was accustomed to the vagaries of the young ; but " Doesn't that seem rather a *pity* perhaps ? " she would sometimes murmur thoughtfully.

That she was a deeply intelligent woman, I would not assert ; nor would I describe her as an intellectual. But she had a genuine respect for intelligence and a gift for promoting intelligence in others. Perhaps she hankered after a more distinguished rôle ; and it may have been her reluctant recognition that she could not share, as intimately as she would have liked, in the public activities of her intellectual friends that had once caused her to meddle in the adventure of their private lives. Her only monument was Garsington ; and such a monument is insubstantial. A time came when she deserted Oxfordshire and set up house in a London street ; and, removed from the décor that she had built around herself, she appeared to lose a good deal of her impressive, or demonic, quality. By comparison with her life at Garsington, the salon she maintained in Gower Street seemed somewhat characterless and overcrowded. Nonentities outnumbered celebrities ; among its most zealous frequenters was an opinionated little Irish poet, talkative, baldish and beetle-browed, one of those professional Celtic spell-binders who are constantly engaged in charming an imaginary bird from the branches of an invisible bush ; and even the presence of W. B. Yeats—with grey coat-tails and wide-ribboned pince-nez that recalled an old-fashioned American politician—could not quite dissipate the impression of circumambient mediocrity. For the hostess was ageing ; her fire was declining ; her extravagances were becoming a legend ; and the legend and the creator of the legend had begun gradually to drift apart.

Entirely different were the two remarkable women whose

portraits I must now attempt. The first was Lady Cunard : the second I will call Lady Thaxted. Emerald Cunard's conduct of her life was essentially wayward and instinctive ; while Mabel Thaxted's management of her career was founded on careful calculation, and she lived according to rigid rules, although they were not rules, I dare say, that she had ever clearly formulated. Admittedly she was attracted by fame, and did not seek the company of obscure persons. But, if the men and women she collected were, with very few exceptions, famous or fashionable, that (I have an impression she argued) was primarily a matter of sheer good luck. They were her dearest friends, cherished for their own sakes : by an odd and gratifying coincidence they happened also to be public luminaries. Having earned her regard and entered the ranks of her friends—under a Christian name or a playful nickname which the bearers of similar names would scarcely fail to recognise—the new arrival was treated with an affection often far beyond his real deserts. She was genuinely affectionate, thoughtful, solicitous ; for it would be wholly misleading to allege that she had a cold and shallow nature, or that the series of friendships which made up her life lacked any true emotional basis. On the other hand, not to have entered the ranks—not to be of a stature that could possibly command entry—was automatically to be excluded from the smallest pretence of consideration. She had a terrible eye, dark and narrow and penetrating, in which a sharp light would suddenly spring up, and as rapidly blink off again, should the person whom it surveyed reveal no immediate point of interest. The examination was quick and ruthless. Yet, with the passage of years, her glance might change. Books had been published : the name had been mentioned : cherished friends had spoken favourably. The rejected postulant became a friend and a guest, a member of the innermost friendly circle. It was difficult to believe—and Lady Thaxted seemed long ago to have forgotten —that he had not always had a place there.

Every human activity is apt to command respect if prosecuted

with sufficient zeal, so that the feelings brought into play take
on the character of disinterested passion ; and the form of
activity adopted by Mabel Thaxted must have involved both a
Puritanical single-mindedness and heroic self-discipline. In the
pursuit she had chosen she rarely faltered or flagged ; she was
one of those harassed-looking but dynamic women who seldom
permit themselves an unoccupied hour. Thus, if she were
staying with friends in the country, she would remain in her
room until half past twelve. But she was not resting ; she did
not dream or dawdle ; she wrote an interminable series of letters,
issuing urgent invitations or strengthening some important
link. I have occasionally seen them on a hall table—ten or
fifteen scribbled envelopes, addressed in a barely legible hand,
but never quite so illegibly that they could fail to reach their
destination. When she finally descended the stairs, she would
be carrying a sheaf of newspapers and weekly magazines and
perhaps a couple of recently published books ; and she had
already found time to turn over their pages and had made at
least a provisional survey of any treasures that lay concealed
within.

Yet she must have had moments of merely human weakness ;
and one such moment I happened to surprise in a crowded and
noisy London restaurant. She was sitting between two young
men, a well-known actor and a famous producer ; and I noticed
that their conversation, largely directed by Mabel Thaxted, was
even more fluent and animated than the conversations all around
them. She did not see me, but presently got up to telephone ;
and, when she passed, I became aware of an extraordinary
change. It had overtaken her within a few seconds, as soon as
she moved out of her companions' orbit. Alone and surrounded
by unknown faces, she appeared to have lost not only her vivacity
but several inches of her physical stature. She stooped ; she had
contracted and shrivelled ; she moved with slow uncertain steps.
Yet I have no doubt that, had she suddenly caught sight of a
party of accredited friends, another transformation, no less rapid

and thorough, would have revitalised her whole appearance, and that she would have joined them and settled down among them with an air of undiminished energy, again the most fortunate of women, blessed in the affection she always elicited, magnificently impervious to age and fatigue.

She had one consolation, moreover, that extremely masterful women very often lack : she was able to combine her taste for society with a firm grasp of the domestic virtues. She possessed children and a devoted husband, to whom she had never failed to do her duty ; and Sir Hugo Thaxted, a pillar of the English law, used to haunt his wife's festivities like a benevolent unobtrusive ghost. In this, as in so much else, she bore little resemblance to my next sitter. Mabel Thaxted was a middle-class Englishwoman, well-educated and well-brought-up, who retained many of the conventions and prejudices of late-Victorian social life. Emerald Cunard, on the other hand, was an adventuress who had framed her own laws. I use the word " adventuress " both in its widest and in its kindliest meaning ; and I can think of none that does equal justice to her peculiar blend of qualities. Mabel Thaxted may have had passion ; but she had passion without a trace of temperament : Emerald Cunard united strong feelings to an adventurous and romantic view of life. When Mabel Thaxted talked of the past, she told a plain, straightforward tale ; in Emerald Cunard's occasional descriptions of her youth, unexpected confidences alternated with mysterious reticences ; and there were many episodes of the story that, one soon discovered, she preferred to leave obscure. She remembered only what she enjoyed remembering ; and parentage and childhood she had always considered tiresome subjects. Nor did she care to think of marriage, since marriage was the inveterate foe of love, and getting married was something that happened, but by no means the kind of happening on which a sensitive person would choose to dwell. Her romantic nature found the scope it demanded among the experiences of the present day ; and her daily observations provoked an endless flow of comment in

Dame Edith Sitwell. Painting by Pavel Tchelitchew

Courtesy I. R. Tuckey, Esq.

Colette in youth

George Moore. Painting by Edouard Manet
Metropolitan Museum of Art

Jamaican long-tailed humming-bird. Illustration from
John Gould's *Monograph of the Trochilidae* (1861)
British Museum

Madame Geoffrin at breakfast. Painting by Hubert Robert

Photographie Giraudon, Paris

Lady Ottoline Morrell. An unfinished portrait by Augustus John

Courtesy Augustus John, O.M.

Lord Byron. Pencil portrait by Count Alfred D'Orsay

Courtesy Sir John Murray

The Artist Contemplates His Work. Woodcut by Hokusai

British Museum

which fact and fantasy were merged into a highly individual pattern.

Yet this enthusiastic lover of the present had had an interesting past history. Born " of wealthy parents " in San Francisco on August 31st 1872, Maud Alice Burke had been married in New York on April 17th 1895, to Sir Bache Cunard, a fox-hunting English baronet, who brought her home with him from his travels and introduced her to Victorian London, where at the outset, I believe, she received a rather chilly welcome—so much so that, many years later, Maurice Baring (as reported by his old friend Edward Marsh) said that he felt the time had at last come when he could decently take his name off the books of the " Society for the Prevention of Cruelty to Lady Cunard ". Sir Bache himself, according to his relict, had been a somewhat stern mentor, and she had constantly annoyed or offended him by her ingenuous social mis-steps. For instance, she had looked up at his club while he was standing in the bow window, and had stopped her carriage in Piccadilly to speak to a young man whom she was anxious to invite to luncheon. Just as unsophisticated was her manner of dealing with servants. She must on no account, her husband warned her, ever address a footman personally, but should always ring for the butler and transmit her instructions at second hand. I imagine that she may have sometimes regretted the comparative freedom of her transatlantic youth. Her bed-room (she once remarked), during the early stages of her married life, could only be approached by going through Sir Bache's dressing-room.

Sir Bache, however, had gradually receded, just as London had been slowly conquered. Nevill Holt, the house they occupied in Leicestershire, was a huge, rambling, ancient building, with a long range of mediæval battlements and a " tame church on the lawn " tethered behind it like a ship's dinghy. The baronet was a master of foxhounds ; and his American wife had learned to hunt. But she did not particularly enjoy hunting—in later life she developed an almost Gallic aversion from the open air ; and

before long their Leicestershire hunting neighbours were submerged by a very different set of friends—a renowned novelist, a
meteoric conductor and other gifted, entertaining and more or
less bohemian personages. The novelist, of course, was George
Moore, tolerated by Sir Bache because he had ridden to hounds
and, as a member of the Irish squirearchy, could claim to know
a horse's points. It was then that a strange one-sided love affair
first took possession of the writer's mind, an absorbing attachment to an ideal woman—" Very few men (he declared) have
seen their ideal as close to them as I have seen mine "—formed
by a lover who in most of his amatory relationships seems to
have been anything but idealistic. Although the object of his
cult appreciated her friend's devotion, there appear to have been
moments when she found it irksome. She may at times have
wished to be idealised—but not, she hinted, by so odd a votary.

Moore was the type of Irish enthusiast whose romantic propensities are often concealed beneath a superficial cynicism. He
continued to love her for more than three decades, until he died
in 1933; and during that period he sent her a host of letters,
constantly expressing the same devotion and uttering the same
plaints. Alas, his handwriting was often difficult to read; and
the recipient, busy or gay or tired, did not always consider that
they were worth deciphering. Still, she preserved them throughout the course of years; and, now and then, she would speak of
the hoard and wonder what she ought to do with it. After all,
she supposed, they were valuable documents; she had been
fond of " dear G. M.", if not quite so fond as he would perhaps
have liked. On whom could she rely to assist and advise her ?
Taking my cue from such an enquiry, I one day offered her my
own help, to my great surprise heard the offer accepted, and
received instructions to visit her about five o'clock on a summer
evening, when we could go through the correspondence together
and discuss the problem of its literary value.* A good many of

---

* This correspondence has now been published in *George Moore: Letters to Lady
Cunard* 1895-1933, edited by Rupert Hart-Davis 1956.

the letters, she added, she hadn't looked at since they were first delivered . . .

As I entered her sitting-room at the stroke of five, I was unfortunate enough to discover my hostess asleep, innocently disposed along a small French sofa, with her silvery-blonde head at rest against a heap of cushions, presenting an appearance both of extreme age and of timeless undefeated youth, like the virginal occupant of an ancient tomb on whom a shaft of daylight had suddenly descended. But she was too feminine not to resent my intrusion and, while a tea-tray was being brought, remained unusually cross and nervous. There could be no question of examining letters today : she didn't remember making the suggestion : in any case, she had a headache ; and the sun had begun to sink before she could be coaxed back into a better mood. But at last she relented, rose from the sofa and, with the youthful lightness that always distinguished her movements, tripped off to the adjacent bedroom, re-emerging with a white oblong box of the sort that usually contains shoes. The manuscripts that it now enclosed had been bundled in without regard for sequence, most of them still clad in their original envelopes, scribbled, post-marked, travel-worn, covered with the fine film of dirt that invariably collects on old papers. She handed me the box, returned to the sofa and gently relaxed among her outspread plumage. I was to remove one or two letters at random, and read aloud any portions of the text that struck me as sufficiently arresting.

I obeyed ; but it was not an easy task ; for George Moore had crammed each page to the margin with his rather hasty and untidy script ; and nearly every letter I unfolded seemed to have been written in the heat of passion. Stricken by love, the great stylist had abandoned all his literary defences. Nor, as year succeeded year, did the quality of his feelings change. That a decade separated two letters, now packed away within the same bundle, only became clear when they included some reference to men and women of completely different periods ; the movement of time was entirely unmarked by any alteration in his manner of writing. He was still so vehement as to be almost schoolboyish and, after twenty years, still poured out his feelings with effortless, unselfconscious ardour—*blurted them out*, indeed, as if they defied control and the impatient, exasperated lover had never been a literary craftsman, who would spend hours polishing a sentence or meditating on the choice of a single phrase.

The story unfolded in these letters had, of course, a comic side; but its comic aspects did not preclude an occasional tragic undertone. All journeys into the past are bound to be a little sad; and one personage who frequently reappeared—the heroine's closest relation from whom she had parted some ten or fifteen years earlier—I thought it wise to omit, pretending, when I was obliged to do so, that I could not read the next sentence. I would pass on quickly to some expression of undying, undiminished love; and now and then, if I happened to look up from the page, I would notice that my companion, as she lay opposite me along her brocaded sofa with the light of the large window gradually changing colour behind her head, had lifted a diminutive scrap of handkerchief and was dabbing delicately at the corners of her eyes. But the Comic Spirit presently returned; for soon we reached a celebrated incident that concerned her assumption of a second Christian name. " Maud " she had never much liked; and, emeralds being her favourite stone, she had decided at a certain stage of her progress to re-christen herself " Emerald ". She was in Switzerland at the time, and, although she did not always answer his letters, had had some occasion to write to George Moore. The signature she attached was " Maud Emerald ", merely adding, within brackets, that Emerald was her new name, but giving him no kind of hint as to why or how she had adopted it.

Since the patient Sir Bache was now dead, Moore had at once concluded that his idol had elected to re-marry, appointing as Sir Bache's successor a mysterious " Mr. Emerald ". But who could his sinister rival be ? How had he entered the beloved's life ? Moore, it seemed, had immediately taken wing from his lonely house in Ebury Street, sought out his faithful ally Tonks and exhibited the disturbing signature. ". . . His words were ' Is she married ? ' I answered ' I can put no other meaning on it' . . . After searching the telephone book he declared the name to be a mere whimsy, no more serious than a new plume in a hat. But I don't feel sure . . ." * The unhappy novelist had then returned home, again consulted the telephone book and plunged into a couple of London directories. " Emerald " is an uncommon surname ; and his researches had been laborious and futile, until at length an " Emerald " was run to earth who proved to be a manufacturer of paint. The deduction this discovery offered was clearly irresistible ; and an impassioned letter, pleading for reassurance, was followed by an urgent telegram. " You cannot fail to understand (he wrote) that it is unfair to leave a man who has loved you dearly more than thirty years in doubt "; and, while he awaited a reply, he paced his room " like a caged animal ". Another letter, from Lady Cunard's old friend Sir Joseph Duveen, had slipped into the same envelope. It described a recent visit to Ebury Street, where he had found George Moore, with the directories still open before him, still debating his intolerable problem. " He certainly looked quite ill " and, as he talked, " began to cry . . ." †

My companion smiled at the episode ; but, I think, she sympathised. Love was an emotion she understood ; I have no doubt she understood jealousy ; the longest love affair of her life was said to have ended in bitter disillusionment ; and, while she was growing old, her romantic affection for a gifted young *protégé*, very much younger and less experienced than herself— just such an affection as the elderly Madame du Deffand had once felt for the young and attractive Horace Walpole—took sudden command of her heart and involved her in acute suffering. But her natural resilience remained unbroken ; and, during the years when I enjoyed her friendship, it was her gaiety that most im-

* Op. cit.   † Op. cit.

pressed me. It was not a gaiety imposed from without; her vitality, unlike Mabel Thaxted's, did not depend upon an effort of will; but her high spirits appeared to arise from regions far beneath the surface, irradiating her whole demeanour, lending an electric quality to her smallest gestures, giving her flow of talk, however inconsequent, a curious prismatic sparkle. The noise of a shallow ice-brook, the springtime song of a delighted canary—both are images one is tempted to employ; but neither seems entirely adequate; for what held her listeners' attention, besides the trilling cadences that entertained the ear, was the strange diversity of subjects among which her fancy glanced and roved. Sense and nonsense were oddly interwoven; prejudices, paradoxes and personal whims were flung in with a defiantly dogmatic air; but one never quite lost sight of the speaker's underlying shrewdness. Even her absurdity—and her statements were sometimes extravagantly absurd—served its purpose in the conversational scheme : it jolted her company wide awake if she had noticed that they were becoming unduly solemn. And, although she was a woman of many serious interests—she had a lifelong passion for music, an unexpectedly wide knowledge of French and English literature—there was nothing she disliked and dreaded so much as gravity in its most sententious guise, personal solemnity if it were manifested at the wrong moment.

I have already suggested that she had a deeply romantic view of life ; but romanticism was accompanied by an inextinguishable vein of fantasy. Whereas Mabel Thaxted was a professional dealer in what she considered to be human masterpieces, and ranged them, so to speak, on her shelves with a sharp eye for their respective values, Lady Cunard resembled a capricious collector who loves his collection for its own sake and cherishes fragments of trifling bric-à-brac no less affectionately than his real treasures. She enjoyed mixing parties, just as Lady Thaxted enjoyed marshalling and combining them ; and the more incongruous the result, the higher did her spirits soar. Lady Thaxted

134

usually played for safety : Lady Cunard undoubtedly welcomed danger—a sense of impending crisis, of social catastrophe narrowly averted, seemed to bring out all her blithest traits. Then she would assume an expression of big-eyed astonishment, of half-horrified yet half-enchanted surprise. " Dear me, what is the Ambassador *saying* ? . . ." The Ambassador, bemused by the heat of the candles and flushed by his second glass of brandy, was explaining that every human being had some *alter ego* in the animal creation, and that his neighbour, although renowned for her Dresden China prettiness, was evidently related to a fruit-eating bat. Somebody else, on the other hand, was as obviously related to a seal. Now in his part of Scotland (he continued) the Gaelic-speaking fishermen's wives, when their husbands were far out at sea, used to go down to the shore and make love to the seals who lay basking there among the rocks . . . This uncalled-for glimpse of Scottish natural history threw his bewildered hostess into a kind of transport, in which perturbation appeared to struggle with delight : " Archie, you must please stop ! I've never known the Ambassador talk in such a way before. To what do you suppose he is referring ? Can it be something—something they call *bestiality* ? "

On an earlier or a later occasion, she might herself have taken up the theme, providing bizarre supplementary details from her personal experience ; and not being sure precisely " where one was "—whether the tone of the conversation was to emulate that of a seventeenth-century comedy of manners, or whether the presiding genius would suddenly swoop down with the pronouncement that " subjects of that sort are not discussed at *my* table ! "—added to the charm of her entertainments and kept her guests' intelligence constantly aroused. As I have said, she welcomed danger ; but seldom had it confronted her in a more dramatic form than when she decided, during the nineteen-thirties, that the impressionable Heir to the Throne really ought to meet some famous writers, and invited the author of *The Apes of God* to a royal luncheon party in Grosvenor Square. Wyndham Lewis

135

accepted the invitation, contrary to his usual practice; but he was taciturn and pensive and self-absorbed, and, as soon as they had sat down to luncheon, produced from his pocket a small pearl-handled revolver, which he placed beside his wine-glasses. Did he mean to assassinate the Prince? Was it his intention to commit suicide? At all events, a crisis threatened; and, disengaging herself from the guest of honour, she turned her attention at the first opportunity to Mr. Wyndham Lewis' " pretty little pistol ", admiring its workmanship and the elegance of the design, handling it as if it had been a Fabergé Easter Egg or an enamelled Georgian snuff-box, at length with an absent-minded smile dropping the weapon into the bag she carried; after which she turned back to the Prince and resumed her social duties.

Her love of fantasy was also revealed in the romantic nicknames she bestowed on her friends—honorary titles that had no obvious link with the recipient's real character. Thus " The Idealist " seemed never to have recovered from his surprise at having been picked out for so odd a rôle: " The Great Lover " looked pleased but startled: " Lord Paramour " accepted the designation but clearly did not welcome it. In the personal Wonderland she created, every visitor must assume the shape she chose; and her manner of welcoming her guests was often strangely unexpected. Then she adopted the method of a Greek Chorus, introducing a new protagonist whose arrival they alone have noticed. " Here comes *Little* Grace ", she would exclaim, announcing the tall, stately, decorative relict of a renowned Edwardian proconsul; and all the guests who followed were greeted with the same enthusiasm and explained to the company assembled in a highly coloured dramatic aside. Most of them submitted; a few would blush and mumble; only Lady Oxford, I remember, once struck back like an indignant asp, called her hostess "Maud" —an unforgivable insult—and enquired loudly about her departure from England at the beginning of the Second World War; after which a silence descended and the contestants stood poised in breathless fury, until Lady Oxford decided to relinquish the field and, her sharp tricorne set at a menacing angle, seized an acquaintance by his wrist and drew off gradually towards a corner of the room.

Her pointed fingernails left a painful impression ; but such disastrous scenes were fortunately rare. On the whole, any embarrassment one suffered was soon forgotten in the pleasure one received. The hostess' personal appearance was itself a source of pleasure. At the time when I knew her best, she was in her late sixties and her early seventies ; but her hair, which George Moore had described as " fair as the hair in an eighteenth-century pastel ", was still a silky ash-blonde ; and, although her skin, if one examined it closely, proved to be puckered and scored with innumerable tiny wrinkles, it had kept the fineness and the softness that customarily vanish during middle age. As to her features, they could never have been beautiful—the delicate high-bridged nose was accompanied by a slightly receding chin; but even in profile they had a curious bird like charm that matched her trilling song-bird's voice. Her eyes were more difficult to depict. Either she painted them in the Eastern fashion or enlarged the pupils with drops of belladonna ; for, just as in miniature portraits of Persian beauties, a dark line encircled the inner margin of the eyelids, and the white of the eyeballs had acquired a faintly greyish tinge. But, if her appearance was the product of art—or of a harmonious collaboration between art and nature—its artificiality did not detract from a beguiling air of spontaneity. She seemed to look and dress as she did, not in a deliberate effort to defeat the years, but because the passage of time had had little real effect upon her thoughts and feelings. The colours she wore were always light and youthful—candid blues or pale ingenuous pinks ; and she had an affection for the kind of puffed sleeve that came into vogue in the eighteen-thirties, the period of *Hernani* and the French Romantic Revolution. She had reminded George Moore of a " Gavarni drawing "; and Gavarni and Devéria, assisted perhaps by some hints from

Fragonard or Watteau, were the artists one would have selected to render her especial quality. A lithograph in the pages of *La Mode*, showing her as a celebrated *lionne* of the day, would have been a far more faithful representation than any modern photograph.

Yet she was very much a part of her own period, and delighted in the spectacle of contemporary life, although its democratic manifestations often startled and offended her. Her snobbism was naïve and unashamed ; but to that too, as to her other foibles, she gave a remarkably individual turn. Thus, on right conduct among " ladies and gentlemen " she held strong and idiosyncratic views. " Ladies and gentlemen " (she once informed me—I suppose that I must have been complaining of a cold) " *never* blow their noses ! " And there were a good many other things that ladies and gentlemen did not do, according to the speaker's mood, whether she was happy and quite at her ease, or had been temporarily ruffled by some disconcerting or un-toward incident. But her snobbish principles were certainly not exclusive, and never stood in her way if she wished to make a new friend ; for her spontaneous, unforced friendliness was an important aspect of her character. There was no question of dividing her friends into separate social categories, entertaining princes and ambassadors upon one day, writers and painters upon the next. Hence her parties were usually stimulating, however exhausting and bewildering ; and a young novelist whom she invited to her table would have been foolish indeed if he had failed to go away without a sheaf of material for his private notebooks. She encouraged indiscretion at the proper moment ; and it is a significant fact that distinguished public personages (who frequently have somewhat weak heads) are apt to grow more, rather than less, indiscreet as they mount the rungs of the official ladder. At Lady Cunard's crowded dinner table, they sometimes unbent to an alarming degree ; and one reflected with amazement that the talkative So-and-so had just come from representing his sovereign in such-and-such a foreign country, notorious for its distrust of Great Britain and its elaborate system of domestic espionage.

The hostess liked to remain at table long after the coffee and the brandy had been served, particularly if she could persuade a poetic nobleman to launch into a recitation of Shakespeare's *Sonnets* or a literary statesman, with appropriate gestures, would interpret Browning's *A Light Woman*, choosing a suitable feminine companion to " stand in " for the poet's mistress. Meanwhile the warmth of the candle-flames beat upon the guests' faces ; and the gilt-bronze dish in the centre of the table-cloth seemed now to be approaching and now receding. It was supported by three naked figures, three couchant eighteenth-century nymphs ; and the smoothly dimpled back and flanks of the naiad lying opposite me recalled Paul Valéry's glimpse of Eve tempted by *Le Serpent* in the Biblical orchard.* Around the walls hung Impressionist pictures—notably Manet's *Etude pour ' Le Linge'* inherited from George Moore ; and beneath the pictures stood a bust by Houdon, more bronzes, one or two small statues and a various assemblage of books and golden or enamelled trinkets. When she re-established herself in London at the end of the Second World War, Lady Cunard had not returned to her house, which remained desolate and empty until she died, but had moved to a big cosmopolitan hotel overlooking Hyde Park. Here she occupied a couple of rooms, furnished with her own possessions ; but, although she soon built up the setting she needed, she continued to fret against an hotel existence, and the servants, whom she constantly reproved, wore a haggard and exasperated mien—elderly, crumpled, large-footed Italians, perpetually spilling the wine or ministering to her guests in the wrong order.

Yet her parties were generally high-spirited ; and the shadows did not begin to encroach until her friends showed signs of

---

* " O follement que je m'offrais
Cette infertile jouissance :
Voir le long pur d'un dos si frais
Frémir la désobéissance ! . . ."

leaving. She detested solitude : she dreaded the hours of the night : insomnia was an old and fearful enemy. And when the last guest had been allowed to say goodbye, and loneliness had entered and recaptured her rooms, she settled down to read, and read on and on throughout the small hours. Unless it had been patiently explained to her that some of her acquaintances had perforce to rise early, she would occasionally telephone from her bed to describe at considerable length the book that she had just finished. She read endlessly, indefatigably—novels, memoirs, works of criticism. Her taste was sound, her knowledge of literature wide ; her appetite for new experiences had never lost its pristine edge ; but she would never accept a contemporary " masterpiece " merely at its current value. I think she was lonelier than any of her friends suspected ; and that the loneliness she refused to show was accompanied by anxieties she kept persistently hidden. Her large private fortune was coming to an end ; many of her possessions had already been mortgaged; even the famous emeralds had returned to the jeweller, and towards the close of her life she was wearing paste copies. At one of her last dinner parties, I am told by a friend, she suddenly raised her glass and drank a toast to Death. But on other occasions she displayed her habitual ebullience and, although troubled by an exasperating cough, refused to admit that she might be seriously ill.

So dissimilar in their way of life, she and Lady Thaxted took their leave in a very different fashion. According to a devoted friend who watched beside her bed, Emerald Cunard, as her thoughts wandered, imagined that she was attending a party, greeted the delightful people who surrounded her and expressed the pleasure she felt at seeing them again. Mabel Thaxted, during the same crisis, returned in imagination to the circle of her family. She had been a widow for several years ; but about midnight, she is said to have called her nurse and explained that she had heard the doorbell ring. Mr. Thaxted must have forgotten his key—her memory had slipped back into the period before Sir Hugo had received a knighthood : she supposed that he had been working late and had walked home from his chambers in the Temple. The nurse humoured her by going to a window, and reported that there was nobody at the door. But a second, and then a third, time, Lady Thaxted protested that the bell was ringing, and insisted that the nurse should pull back the curtains ; and only a sedative injection eventually lulled her mind to rest. I am no believer in phantoms or *revenants* ; but this is an episode that encourages credulity. One would like to imagine that, by some inexplicable disruption of the normal time-sequence, Sir Hugo may have momentarily reappeared, and that the nurse, if she had looked more closely, might have caught a glimpse of the expectant figure below—a grave young lawyer home from the Temple, his old-fashioned brief-case stuffed with important papers—and seen the lamplight shining on the glossy crown of a well-brushed Edwardian top hat.

*   +   +

Edward Marsh numbered both Lady Cunard and Lady Thaxted in his interminable catalogue of valued friends, which included, as well as the great and famous, and men and women of acknowledged gifts, a vast accompanying throng of persons who were still obscure but whose gifts he thought he had recognised and hoped one day to see triumphant. Few kindlier critics have ever cherished false hopes, or settled down on a china egg in the sanguine expectation of hatching out a phœnix or a swan. To his *protégés* he was constantly doing good ; and he did good all the more effectively because he was an unselfish hedonist, and benefaction was a form of exercise from which he derived a lasting pleasure. Not that the occasion was necessarily pleasurable : his fortitude was often severely tried. If the consort of a well-known writer fell, in circumstances unexplained, from the window of a top-storey flat, it was Eddie who must have a private word with a colleague at the Home Office and thus avert any embarrassment that might have been caused by police enquiries.

If a young painter shot his unfaithful mistress and then turned his gun upon himself, again it was Eddie who hurried to the rescue, visited the hospital and sat beside the dying man. But, despite his natural affection for writers and painters, whom he supported in moments of crisis and subsidised in their hours of need, he did sometimes wish—and would have been the last to deny the fact—that they would pay rather more attention to the ordinary usages of civilized social life. He was ruffled by the bohemian discomfort amid which many artists chose to live, and pained by the shocking untidiness they often manifested in their hair and clothes, particularly when it spoiled the effect of an otherwise noble and attractive appearance. Thus one handsome poet had crossed the threshold of his office, wearing hobnailed shoes secured with string. What must the office-messengers have thought, as he shouldered his way down the red-carpeted passage ? Corduroy trousers were no doubt excusable. But even a Georgian poet could surely afford to acquire a pair of shoe-laces ?

In his own existence he was completely conventional—a distinguished civil servant who had been the private secretary of a long succession of cabinet ministers, a party-goer and a diner-out, prominent in the crowd at every successful first night. Above all else he was a " man of the world "; and this was a status that he greatly prized. A story, for instance, that I have heard him tell, and which he afterwards recorded, I think, among his published reminiscences, concerned a loquacious coster-monger who had ventured to approach him in a London street with the loud-voiced and impertinent suggestion : " As one man of the world to another, Sir, why not buy a calceolaria ? " Eddie was so deeply annoyed that he felt obliged to make a sharp reply, pointing out that an authentic man of the world would never have fallen into such a ridiculous error, but would have known that a calceolaria was the kind of plant men of the world did not purchase. Both his worldly pretensions and his essential innocence appeared in Eddie's telling of the story ; and both were reflected in the appearance and manner that he had developed during middle age. He was small and neat and decorously elegant ; and from beneath the shade of a mephistophelean eyebrow glittered an impressive eye-glass, which usually remained in its place but sometimes tinkled against the buttons of his waistcoat at the end of a thin silken cord. With the pointed enquiring eyebrows went a high and fluting voice. Even higher and thinner than Lytton Strachey's, if he were surprised or perturbed it rose to an almost childish treble ; and, whereas Strachey's astonished squeak seemed a deliberate conversational mannerism, often employed for the purpose of underlining a subtle snub, Eddie's was obviously wrung from him by an irresistible pressure of feeling and had a tone of plangent sincerity that at once excited the hearer's protective instincts.

When his sense of justice was outraged, his indignation grew particularly shrill, as, for example, during a heated discussion that he engaged in with a fellow secretary who denied that he had received an important paper and accused his colleague of having mislaid the document. " But I gave it to you ! I know I did ! *I remember the gesture!* " exclaimed Eddie in a high-pitched crescendo of dismay, illustrating the gesture he remembered so well and no doubt allowing his eye-glass to tinkle down to the farthest extent of its cord. His sense of dignity was as quickly ruffled ; and malicious acquaintances found him easy game. Thus, in the foyer of a theatre, he decided to turn his back on Ronald Firbank, since he had been informed that that fantastic novelist had spoken irreverently of Rupert Brooke. But Firbank, entirely unabashed, refused to accept the dignified reprimand and, approaching him with a sinuous, stealthy pace, removed Eddie's right hand from the pocket into which he had taken care to thrust it, shook it lengthily and ceremoniously and, having completed his salutation, politely put it back again. Describing the incident, Eddie remarked that he had been altogether at a loss for words. He may have attempted to speak ; but the protest that he emitted must have soared far beyond the range of audibility. He compromised by beating an abrupt retreat. " I executed the manœuvre (he explained) known as 'turning on one's heel . . .' "

It was to this aspect of his character—the element of lovable absurdity—that many of his friends referred in the composition of their posthumous tributes. They made too much of the man of the world—the owner of the eye-glass and the voice, the intensely gregarious and sociable personage whose private life appeared to be lived in public—and paid considerably too little attention to the scholar and the man of letters. Yet his scholarship, although it might have gone almost unnoticed in the days of Burke and Fox, when classical quotations were bandied to and fro across the House of Commons, and the orator who produced a false quantity aroused an immediate storm of ridicule, was conspicuous for its breadth and depth in our present slipshod age. Every year, as a matter of course, he would re-read part of the Homeric poems, refresh his memory of Horace and Virgil, and revisit the familiar landscapes of French and English literature. He read for enjoyment, but steadily and thoroughly, making numerous marginal notes ; and, unlike the average modern reader, if he opened a Greek or Latin text, he had no use for those convenient editions which print an English rendering upon the opposite page. At the same time he was almost always busy with the proof sheets of a friend's book, improving the syntax and punctuation, scattering a shower of queries, plaintively demanding in his clear and shapely script what the author thought he meant. Simultaneously, he would be translating La Fontaine ; and his translations, though sometimes prosaic, displayed uncommon ingenuity. At a rather desperate period of my early life, I frequently stayed with him in his large and comfortable flat overlooking Gray's Inn ; and thither he would return about midnight, having attended a diplomatic party. His evening had been full of interest ; mine—for youth is not invariably the season of joy, and the gift of enjoyment may be acquired only with advancing years—had often been dull and despondent, shadowed by loneliness or lack of money. I would have returned home an hour ago and be sleepily reading an indifferent novel. Eddie would enter, brisk and good humoured, remove his collar and his white tie, but not the enamelled order with its broad red ribbon that gently knocked his gleaming shirtfront, then pour a generous whisky-and-soda, clench a cigarette-holder between his teeth and, substituting horn-rimmed spectacles for his eye-glass, settle down blithely to La Fontaine's *Fables*. Later, when he had retired to his bedroom, I would catch the murmurous rhythm of an unbroken monologue. My host was talking to himself, as most elderly unmarried people do. Now and then, he recited a scrap of poetry or, at the recollection of some diverting anecdote, burst into a loud laugh.

Next morning we would breakfast together in his green-panelled dining-room. The tree-tops of the Benchers' Garden rose opposite the broad window ; and their colours and the light of the sky glimmered on a range of photographs, a portrait-gallery of especially favoured friends arranged along an old-fashioned side-board—a beautiful American actress whom he had known and admired and who, he told me, had eventually died of drugs : an English duke under whom he had served and who much resembled a ruminative elephant-seal : an Edwardian lady, who suggested Oriane de Guermantes, in a pearl-grey tailored suit : Ivor Novello displaying his faultless profile : Rupert Brooke, wearing a silk shirt and a loosely knotted foulard tie. Elsewhere, the walls were lined with pictures ; and pictures were hung even on the doors of his flat. They included a wash-drawing by William Blake and water-colours by Gainsborough and Romney, as well as a painting by Richard Wilson of a rocky landscape among the Welsh hills. But the great majority of the pictures were modern ; for, although his tastes in literature were conservative and he did not pretend to enjoy a poem unless he was sure that he had understood its meaning, while his judgment of plays was apt to be coloured by his personal affection for some popular star—with the result that he might sit through an imbecile melodrama as often as half-a-dozen times, shedding tears until they clouded his eye-glass at a particularly moving passage —he was very much more adventurous in his appreciation of the visual arts. He admired Post-Impressionists, Vorticists, bold experimentalists of every kind ; and their progeny, with huge glassy orbs, big wooden features and thick distorted limbs, competed for a measure of living space against the work of respectably orthodox painters. Surrounded by his collection of Anglo-Saxon *fauves*, the connoisseur looked doubly decorous, like the modest proprietor of an exotic menagerie, inspecting the cages on his Sunday morning walk.

Nearly all the painters were personal friends, since friendship was his dominant passion ; and he rarely bought the work of foreign artists because he was seldom attracted by the talent of an artist whom he did not know. In his attitude towards contemporary writers, he was similarly inspired or similarly prejudiced. When the occasion demanded it, he did not refrain from stern reproof, pointing out a " gross solecism " or an unpardonably obscure phrase ; for, once he had put on his spectacles, there was something of the pedagogue in Eddie's nature. But his admiration of a poem or a novel was closely connected with his knowledge of the poet or the novelist ; and, as soon as he had read a book that he admired, he would hasten to arrange a meeting, either at breakfast before he left his flat or at luncheon in his club near Whitehall, from which the author came away, flattered and uplifted and well-advised, having already fallen into the habit of calling his new admirer " Eddie ". None of the later protégés, however, though each of them was welcomed with fresh applause, quite effaced the memory of Rupert Brooke, in Eddie's mind the poet *par excellence*, a golden personification of genius and charm. He, too, had stayed at Raymond Buildings ; and his name, pencilled by himself but now half-obliterated by errand-boy scribblings, could still be distinguished beneath that of Eddie amid the occupants listed at the bottom of the stairs. To say that Eddie had been " in love " with Brooke would be to oversimplify the character of his feelings, and might perhaps give an entirely wrong impression of his emotional and moral temperament. But he found it difficult to admire without liking, and almost impossible to like and admire without experiencing some of the emotions of love. Women he pleased and amused rather than attracted ; and no woman, so far as I can learn, ever took him very seriously. Once, I believe, he had received a proposal from a young woman whose hand he solemnly accepted; but the following day she was obliged to inform him that her overtures had originated in a bet ; at which Eddie seemed both hurt and relieved—he had never, as he afterwards explained, been sufficiently rich to think of marriage and shuddered at the prospect of a threadbare debt-haunted middle-class life. Thus he remained a celibate—yet a romantic celibate, exercising his gift for affection in friendships that were much akin to love. No hint of personal frustration cast a shade on his placid and guileless demeanour.

Yet, so long as I knew him, he was always in love, according to his own conception of the state, as Socrates loved Alcibiades, and Plato may have loved Agathon. Like Socrates, he did not ask for any definite physical return ; and I doubt whether he ever expected to see his emotional largesse repaid in kind. The only reward he appeared to seek was the gratifying, heart-filling sensation of being allowed to render homage ; and his whole life passed in a series of love-affairs which succeeded one another without interruption until he had reached his eightieth birthday. Ingratitude he may sometimes have experienced ; but it had left behind it no perceptible scar. He considered himself a fortunate man and, with more reason than William Hazlitt, announced that he had had a happy life, even though the German bombardment finally blasted him out of Raymond Buildings and, once he had been pensioned off by the Civil Service, he was obliged to exist on a comparatively small income, part of which, curiously enough, he owed to his mother's link with Spencer Perceval, the unlucky Prime Minister murdered by a lunatic in the Lobby of

147

the House of Commons, whose descendants still enjoyed a consolatory grant made by an early nineteenth-century government. True, his Introduction to the poems of Rupert Brooke had at one time brought him regular royalties ; but these earnings he refused to touch ; and they were carefully put aside, to be distributed among needy writers. Despite his preference for assisting his friends, he was capable of looking beyond the claims of friendship ; and it was Eddie who had suggested to Mr. Asquith that a promising novelist named James Joyce, at that moment the little-known author of *A Portrait of the Artist as a Young Man*, deserved some official recognition and should be remembered in the Civil List.

Thus Joyce was awarded a stipend, which, meagre as it was, may have helped him to produce *Ulysses* ; and his gargantuan brain-child, when it emerged from the womb, caused Eddie deep distress and embarrassment. Worse than his failure to understand the novel was the effect that it made on Mr. Asquith, who, in the midst of a family luncheon-party, publicly reproached him for the advice he had given, which, he said, had induced a Minister of the Crown to sponsor the production of a pornographic book. Mr. Asquith was probably teasing his guest—none of his critics has ever described him as a prude ; but it is not difficult to imagine his victim's dismay, the fluttering movement of Eddie's hands, the agitated flash of his eye-glass and the flustered yet resolute manner in which he rallied his forces to withstand the attack. On other occasions so mild and courteous, he could be positively bellicose if his feelings of loyalty were aroused ; and he was all the more loyal to the artists he admired because he admired them at a certain distance and did not hope to share their privileges. He accepted the rôle of camp-follower without regret and without envy ; and, should a work of art exceed his comprehension, he merely sighed and shrugged his shoulders, supposing that he had been overtaken by age since he could no longer understand the young, but almost immediately setting forth again in the pursuit of undiscovered talent. Towards the end, he began to grow infirm ; his progress through gallery or book-shop was accompanied by sibilant puffings and blowings; but his glance remained sharp and inquisitive, and the air of romantic expectancy never faded. He parted from the world happy in the conviction that he had recognised a great new modern master.

VI

The Mighty Dead

MY INVOLVEMENT with Byron, like so many happy adventures, began more or less fortuitously. What I had at first hoped to do was to write a half-length book on Balzac, as part of a series of short biographies then being issued by a London publisher ; but my reception in the publisher's dark little office proved remarkably discouraging. A tall, lank, oldish young man, who, while he talked, kept winding his long thin legs amid the intricate substructure of a fine mahogany arm-chair, he explained that to the best of his knowledge and belief very few modern English readers had ever heard of Balzac, and that to include such a book in his series would, he imagined, be a suicidal plan. Challenged to produce a Romantic novelist or poet of whom every English reader must undoubtedly have heard, I next suggested I should attempt Byron. There, I felt sure, I was bound to arouse an echo ; but again the long-suffering businessman registered deep embarrassment and merely groaned or sighed. It was in a mood of obstinacy then, if not in the spirit of hope, that I presently submitted the same ideas to one of his commercial rivals ; and on this occasion I was much more cheerfully received ; for the second publisher, although he demurred at Balzac, happened to have made a study of that eccentric artist " Mad Martin ", was familiar with the English Romantic Movement, and agreed that the author of *Childe Harold* deserved descrip-

tion and re-examination. After some delay, he commissioned
me to attempt a portrait in a booklet of about a hundred
pages.

Writing a booklet, however, is just as onerous a business as
organizing and completing a full-length book ; and by the time
I had revised my typescript, handed it to the publisher and
accepted my fee, I saw that my unused notes contained material
for another study, and that in my text there was a succession of
important hints that I had lacked the space to follow up. The
writer being a person who abhors waste, my after-thoughts subsequently overflowed into a couple of less restricted volumes, each
dealing with a separate manifestation of Byron's life and personality. Thus I " commenced biographer ", to use a characteristic
eighteenth-century phrase ; and a biographer I remained for
many interesting, though sometimes exhausting years, during
which I ranged to and fro between the Augustan Age and the
end of the post-Romantic epoch, from Boswell, Gibbon, Sterne
and Wilkes—presently succeeded by William Hogarth—to John
Ruskin, the tragic prophet, saddest and strangest of all the great
Victorians. But it was with Byron I had begun ; and Byron was
an extremely fortunate choice, not only because very few human
beings have left behind them more abundant records—and he
himself was always acutely aware of the surpassing interest of the
life he led—but because there is something about his character
that soon establishes a decisive hold over every mind that comes
in contact with him. True, his influence was often alarmingly
strong. " Ah me, what perils do environ the man that meddles
with Lord Byron ! ", once protested an aggrieved contemporary ;
and there was always the danger of becoming so involved that
I lost the right degree of critical reserve. Byron appeared to be
drawing far too close, gradually crossing the delicate borderline
that should divide a writer from his theme, and presenting simultaneously too many aspects of his multiple nature. He himself
was never detached or aloof; he lived intensely through whatever part he played ; and his personal vitality was still so ebullient

that it seemed, now and then, almost impossible to contain and circumscribe.

These difficulties, nevertheless, heightened the interest of my undertaking. There are dull passages in Byron's poetic works —the blank verse tragedies to which he attached so much importance put a severe strain upon the reader's piety—but there is none in his private letters and none in the story of his life they tell. And then, Byron—a revelatory trait—was an omnivorous collector of his own relics. He seldom threw away a sentimental token or destroyed a scrap of written paper ; love-messages, cheque-books, restaurant bills eventually passed into his secret archives, which were carried around with him and carefully guarded until they reached his literary heirs. The whole hoard that he left behind reveals the imprint of his personal character. Even notes signed by another hand could have been addressed, one thinks, to him alone ; for Byron had inherited a dangerous power of drawing out his correspondents' gifts, of enabling them, through his magnetic example, to discover and realise an unsuspected identity. From the strangest acquaintances he elicited devotion ; in the oddest quarters he aroused passion ; and the passions he excited, though they stirred his senses, frequently warred against his peace of mind. Nobody, he used to grumble, was so enamoured of a quiet domestic existence ; he was a " facetious personage " ; he dearly loved to laugh. Yet he could not escape from the unaccountable vagaries of those who surrounded him and plagued him, appealed for his love or clamoured for a share of sympathy. His critics might talk of seductions and abductions, of hearts that had been broken and virginities despoiled ; he had been more ravished himself, he would like to point out, than any human being since the Trojan War. Byron, however, was an extraordinarily candid, yet, as his biographer soon perceives, not an entirely honest, man—his brain operated, that is to say, along a number of largely independent levels ; he had a feminine knack of remembering or forgetting in obedience to his rapidly changing moods ; and it is clear that he enjoyed the sense of danger that accompanied each new relation. To confer pleasure or pain was a hazardous privilege;* a single moment of mortal happiness might be paid off in destructive misery, when the feelings he had uncovered and brought to the surface mounted at length into a consuming blaze.

One method of approaching Byron, therefore, was through the influence he had exercised, by following the trail—often a charred trail—that marked his impulsive progress across society. Here I depended on the help of a mass of miscellaneous evidence : not only the letters he had written but the letters he had received and kept—some of these forlorn missives were blotted and heavily blistered with tears—as well as other tributes that he had picked up at various stages of his sentimental journey. Suddenly I encountered a scrap of verse, contributed by his autumnal mistress Lady Oxford, and near it I saw Aspasia's portrait carved on a circular fragment of white shell. During the eighteenth and nineteenth centuries, lovers were inclined to exchange ringlets ; and among Byron's collection of locks and tresses, neighbouring a dark-red braided tress cut from the Maid of Athens' head, was a childish faint-gold curl that had belonged to Lady Charlotte Harley, Lady Oxford's thirteen-year-old daughter, commemorated as " Ianthe " in his lyrical dedicatory lines—

> " Love's image upon earth without his wing,
> And guileless beyond Hope's imagining "

whose beauty and innocence Byron revered, but whom, if we can accept his wife's assertion, he afterwards hinted that he had attempted to seduce. Almost all these pathetic tokens retained the fragrance and gloss of living hair ; and all had been carefully

---

* " Alas ! they were so young, so beautiful,
So lonely, loving, helpless, and the hour
Was that in which the heart is always full,
And, having o'er itself no farther power,
Prompts deeds Eternity can not annul,
But pays off moments in an endless shower
Of hell-fire—all prepared for people giving
Pleasure or pain to one another living."
Don Juan. Canto II.

hidden away in neatly folded paper packets, distinguished by scribbled names or initials—except for the packet that, when I opened it, revealed a fragile-looking soft-brown strand, and bore an inscription briefly informing us that the recipient could not recall the donor. " Whose this was (he writes) I don't recollect but it is of 1812."

Even where initials were added, they very seldom evoked a face or a name ; and, as I burrowed through the contents of the square tin box in which these dustily fragrant packets lie, I seemed to become aware of the presence of a crowd of voiceless, unknown figures—women whose relationship with Byron, however transitory and however vague, had been their only connection with the life of deep feeling and of creative action. Some, I knew, must have been expelled from his orbit ; some, of their own accord, had probably retreated in alarm. Byron was an easy-going man ; but, if annoyed or hard-pressed, he might turn sharply cruel. And then, of course, there was his love of shocking and surprising, as manifested in his curious treatment of his wife, and of many other women whose folly and gullibility tried his irritable nerves beyond endurance. Both his kindness and his capacity for harshness were illustrated by certain of the letters he had received. Apart from the silent tokens he had methodically stored away, his archives contained numerous reminders of devotees who had refused to hold their tongues but, shrilly, poignantly, tiresomely, invoked his aid, or sought his recognition. Henry de Montherlant, in *Les Jeunes Filles*, has described the relationship between a famous novelist and his infatuated women readers ; but Byron's post-bag was very much more surprising than Pierre Costals' comparatively prosaic haul. Out of it, like distracted *revenants*, rose a mad peeress and a starving actress, a lovelorn Swiss governess and an ill-conducted Welsh housemaid ; and on their heels came a young woman whose letters, written in a fine slanting copper-plate script, had been summarily labelled ' H. Dubochet '. At first I did not recognise the name ; but then I remembered that it had belonged to an obscure clock-seller of Huguenot descent, whose three daughters had all entered the world as fashionable London courtesans. H. Dubochet, I discovered, was Harriette Wilson, authoress of the celebrated volume of reminiscences that begins with so bold and resounding a flourish.* The letters she addressed to Byron, however, reveal her in a very different light; for, besides suggesting that he should accept her love—a suggestion he quickly and politely declined—and afterwards soliciting a small gift of money—an appeal he almost immediately answered—she dashed off a highly unfavourable criticism of his latest poem *Don Juan*, imploring him not to debase his genius by the publication of such cynical and vulgar stuff. " Dear *Adorable* Lord Byron ", she begs, " *don't* make a mere *coarse* old libertine of yourself . . . *Don't*, dearest Lord Byron, keep . . . mistaking mere false pride and *temper* for a *bad heart* . . ." She too, despite her cheerful paganism, was a true child of the Romantic age; and she had been horrified by the perverse ingenuity with which her favourite modern poet now appeared to be bent on demolishing his own legend.

Though her protests can scarcely have interested Byron, they did not take him unawares. All the women he knew, including the Countess Guiccioli, abused his downright Spanish hero, since his poem (he said) depicted the " comedy of the passions " and made light of the sentimental credo that every modern woman cherished. Himself he found room in his nature both for the romantic and for the sensual cynic; and these two personages, throughout his existence, continued to alternate with astonishing rapidity and ease. At times, the transition was abrupt, as his Swiss admirer once noted, when she wheedled her way into his quiet Albany chambers, and Childe Harold dropped his romantic mask to exhibit Don Juan's saturnine smile. Among Byron's involuntary conquests, Henrietta d'Ussières is perhaps the most

* " I shall not say why and how I became, at the age of fifteen, the mistress of the Earl of Craven. Whether it was love, or the severity of my father, the depravity of my own heart, or the winning arts of the noble Lord, does not now much signify . . ." For the letters quoted from here (now in the collection of Sir John Murray), see " *To Lord Byron* " by George Paston and Peter Quennell.

touching. An intelligent middle-class girl in flight from a tyrannous, eccentric father, who had brought up his children according to Rousseau's doctrines, but then determined that his adolescent daughter should become the wife of a superannuated rake, she launched her first attack on her hero's privacy during the early part of 1814; and by June she had broken down his resistance and was hastening towards Albany heavily veiled. It is to Mademoiselle d'Ussières that Byron's biographer owes an odd and significant piece of information. Having entered his Albany sitting-room, she looked around her with reverent, dazzled eyes—at his bad-tempered parrot, or macaw, which he alone knew how to manage : his screen, his writing-desk, his bookcase : the pair of silver funerary urns that commemorated his visit to an ancient Grecian battle-field. But she also noted the presence of a crucifix conspicuously hung upon the wall. Byron, one remembers, was a speculative free-thinker who retained a home-sick regard for the idea of faith. Walter Scott remarked his religious leanings ; and Byron himself was afterwards to declare that, if he ever experienced a change of heart, the discipline he accepted would probably be that of Rome.

Meanwhile he existed from day to day, casually taking what the moment offered ; and today it offered an engaging young woman, who, although one understands that she was not very pretty—she had already thought it right to warn him that she was tall and dark and awkward—possessed presumably sufficient juvenile charm to stimulate Don Juan's predatory instincts. During the early stages of their interview he had been kinder and gentler than she could have ever hoped ; but now he came down to earth with a cynical suddenness that she found alarming and intensely disconcerting. The dream was cut short, her enjoyment ruined. " Why did you spoil my joy ? " she expostulated as soon as she had reached safety, in handwriting that reflects the per-turbation of her spirits. " The first half hour I was so happy ! I did not conceal it because this joy was pure and harmless . . . but for the remainder of the evening it was no longer Lord Byron

—indeed it was not ... I shall ask you one question—This Henrietta that you saw yesterday—do you think she deserves the end that would be hers were she to follow your advice ? I made a sad mistake. I thought that when once you were acquainted with my history you would only pity me and be my most zealous protector. Instead of that—oh ! Lord Byron, is it thus that you would repay so much admiration—so much esteem ? " *

Whether an apology followed we do not know ; Henrietta, at all events, declined to accept her dismissal ; and before long she was hurrying back to Albany, this time apparently uninvited. Nor had she chosen a particularly propitious day : Piccadilly was filled with a dense and noisy crowd. The summer months of 1814 were to go down in history as " the Summer of the Sovereigns ", when the Allied monarchs visited London to celebrate their triumph over Napoleon Bonaparte ; and on that day the members of White's Club had organized a patriotic fête. Henrietta lost her head in a mob of sight-seers, who jostled, ogled and stared at the tall, awkward, anxious-looking foreign girl. Presently she also lost her way ; and it was in a state of tremulous agitation that she eventually reached Byron's door. She rang for admittance and Fletcher appeared—Byron's rustic Leporello, "such a good man", Henrietta thought, and certainly an old hand at dealing with the appeals of inconvenient callers. His lordship, he announced, was not at home. Then the miserable face that confronted him must have prevailed against Fletcher's sense of duty ; for he added that his lordship *was* at home, but entertaining a numerous party of gentlemen. Henrietta herself describes the tragi-comic sequel : " I asked him to let me wait, & then call you out in such a supplicating tone that indeed he could not refuse. I stole into a sort of *Pantry* ... Had I been in a *subterraneous, a ruined Chapel, a cave strewn with skulls and reptiles* ... but a Pantry!! a Pantry flanked with mops and brooms! ... I am joking now that my torture is over, but I never supposed the like in my life ... You see now if I could go away as I came. Why did

you say that word ? And you smiled & you laughed when
I was ready to cry ! " *

This disappointment failed to round off the story—there were
further petitions and expostulations ; and Byron's biographer
does not finally lose sight of Henrietta d'Ussières until she learned
that he was about to marry Miss Anne Isabella Milbanke, and on
a sheet of expensive gilt-edged paper, which she allowed the
tears she was shedding to blister and stain, she summed up all
that she had felt and suffered in a passionate valedictory message :
"Farewell (she concludes) to the hand that shall open this letter,
cherished and beloved, though it broke my rosary, you remember ? That hand I kiss—I bless, imploring again forgiveness
and remembrance without severity ". But she appended a characteristic question : did he suppose that his future wife " would
object to my resuming the same intercourse in 13 years time—
we'll then be very old—upon any condition, restriction she should
think proper to dictate " ? Naturally, she received no encouragement ; and within thirteen years Byron was already dead,
while Henrietta had sunk into her former place, deep in the un-
charted background of history. Meanwhile, beneath the beam
that he cast, she seems momentarily to breathe and move—
darting through the summer streets, wearing a white veil, to
collect his longed-for letter from a Mayfair post office ; struggling against the purposeful embrace that broke the thread and
scattered the beads of her rosary ; trembling in Fletcher's pantry,
amid a grim assemblage of mops and brooms, as she listened to
a distant hubbub of convivial masculine talk and laughter. But
Mademoiselle d'Ussières, between appearing and disappearing,
has done the biographer some real service. Apart from her
interesting mention of the crucifix that hung on Byron's wall,
she illustrates the strength of the influence he exercised over those
who met him face to face, reminds us that his personal influence
was firmly rooted in his literary legend, and shows that the
legend and the underlying character often worked at cross pur-

* Op. cit.

poses. If Byron sometimes bewildered those who loved him, he just as frequently astonishes those who seek to write of him. How can so diverse and fluid a subject be dealt with in the compass of a single study ?

The biographer's best plan, I believe, is to build up two entirely separate portraits, hoping that, while they develop, the contrasted impressions may begin to merge ; and, during my long pursuit of Byron, that was the method I myself followed. Byron the man of the world, the cynic, the sophist, is quite as significant a personage as Byron the romantic visionary ; and neither of them can be fully understood until we have examined both with the same degree of attention. The man of the world is easy to evoke—far more easily evoked, for instance, than his friend and fellow exile Shelley, whose features, when we attempt to fix their outline, seem to melt away into a shifting luminous blur. Of Byron, " in habit as he lived ", there are very few details that we cannot definitely establish, from his height, his weight and his colouring to individual tricks of gesture and speech. Physically, he was not very large—just under five feet eight inches high ; but he was accustomed to walk on his toes, in order to conceal his slight limp ; and, before dissipation had spoiled its grace, he possessed a remarkably compact and muscular body, completed by squarely set shoulders and a round, curly, classically shaped head. His eyes, we are told, were bright " but dissimilar "; his fine nose was slightly bulbous at the tip ; his face, nevertheless, had a statuesque charm, particularly attractive if observed in profile, with his small hand clenched under his chin and the thick dark curls clustering around his brow. Byron was proud of his curls, naturally a deep auburn, but darkened by the use of macassar-oil—during his dandified youth, Scrope Davies claimed, he had found the poet asleep in curl-papers ; and he was equally proud of his white, even, almost perfect teeth and of the transparent " moonlight pallor " of his skin, which he did his best to keep clear and smooth by swallowing enormous purgative doses. Other advantages that caused him satisfaction were the whiteness and smallness of his hands. He regarded them as a sign of aristocratic birth; and that they were indeed strangely diminutive we can see from a yellowing pair of kid gloves, now preserved in the wonderful collection of Byroniana, housed behind Mr. Murray's solemn front door, at Number Fifty Albemarle Street—gloves much too small for the average modern woman's fingers. But the same collection, besides the waistcoat and the frilled shirt that, like the kid gloves, he wore on his unlucky wedding day, includes one of the curious surgical boots with which he supported his defective ankle. Byron's lameness sometimes went unnoticed; contemporaries agree that his limp was slight; but in his own mind that minor deformity had become the rallying-point of many different feelings—his sense of guilt, his sense of isolation, his sense, above all, of the hereditary load he had been carrying since early childhood.

Byron's attempt to control such feelings had an important effect upon his personal character. The man of the world was, in part, a representation of the kind of man he would have liked to be—virile, uncomplicated, unselfconscious, boldly exploiting the pleasures of the moment. Until the end of his brief but crowded life, it was the rôle he very often played; and at Genoa in 1823, while he awaited the fatal summons from the Greek patriots and lazily prepared for an expedition that he was well aware might prove his last, he confronted a new friend, Marguerite Blessington, under his most mundane and unpoetic guise. Lady Blessington, an attractive adventuress, had recently married a tipsy Irish peer; but she cherished literary ambitions, was keeping a travel-diary and had looked forward to lengthy instructive dialogues on moral, intellectual and sentimental topics. Byron, however, although he appreciated her beauty, refused to gratify the eager diarist's whim. He preferred, she noted with dismay, to be regarded as an " *homme de société* rather than as a poet "; and his small talk, which was copious and indiscreet, usually took the form of social gossip : of anecdotes about his early adventures in the ball-rooms and drawing-rooms of a bygone

160

London, where he had paid his court to "poor dear Lady Jersey", enjoyed the cynical wisdom of Lady Melbourne—how thoroughly she might have enslaved him, had she been a few years younger!—listened to Germaine de Staël, the cleverest woman he had ever met, and, despite his Whiggish, even revolutionary, views, admired the surpassing elegance of the Prince Regent.

Far from appearing reserved and melancholy, the poet seldom drew breath : and "were I to point out (Lady Blessington recorded in her diary) the prominent defect of Lord Byron, I should say it was flippancy, and a total want of that natural self-possession and dignity which ought to characterise a man of birth and education ". Like his London gossip, the clothes he wore seemed by this time a trifle out of date. The tartan coat he affected hung loosely round his wasted frame ; for, having been florid and fat during his stay at Venice, he had subsequently grown spare and pale. An important member of the Blessingtons' suite was Marguerite's Parisian lover Count Alfred d'Orsay, and to d'Orsay we owe a memorable pencil-sketch of Byron in his last period. It exhibits an anxious-looking, somewhat haggard face, the hair receding from his lofty forehead ; and Byron's curls, we know, before he left Italy, were already thickly streaked with grey. He looked old, and he said that he felt old— "sixty in mind " at the age of thirty-six ; and, as he talked of his vanished youth and revived the scandals of past London seasons, there was nothing about him to suggest the heroic figure that had once haunted Marguerite Blessington's fancy. Nevertheless, being sensitive and perspicacious, she discovered the heroism that lay beneath the pose. Thus he announced, quietly and casually, that he did not expect he would return from Greece. " There was a helplessness about Byron (she noted), a sort of abandonment of himself to his destiny as he called it, that commonplace people can as little pity as understand ". For Byron, his idea of his destiny had replaced the Christian idea of a divine providence ; and here is the solution of many of the problems that beset his twentieth-century biographer. With tremendous physical and nervous energy, he had a strain of fatalistic self-abandonment ; and the resulting conflict both fostered his genius—a hidden conflict is implicit in the creation of every work of art—and helped to shape his personal character and the varying disguises that his personality assumed. Now he is Childe Harold, the gloomy wanderer who grandiloquently accepts his fate : now Don Juan, the man of the world who spars against it with defensive irony : now, having abandoned verse-writing, he confronts us as the way-worn traveller, still a man of many different moods, flippant and fatalistic, resolute and disillusioned, yet prepared to sacrifice his existence to a cause in which, he admitted himself, he did not always quite believe.

From these images the biographer's task is to produce a comprehensive literary pattern. But first he must consider the sense of powerlessness that underlay Byron's ebullient zest for living—a line of enquiry that soon takes him back to the dismal circumstances of the poet's childhood. That he was deformed, he could never forget ; and his mother's reproaches kept the wound open. Meanwhile, he had been roughly initiated into the secrets of adult physical pleasure. " My passions (he remarked in a notebook jotting) were developed very early—so early that few would believe me, if I were to state the period . . . Perhaps this was one of the reasons which caused the anticipated melancholy of my thoughts—having anticipated life." The initiation that had such far-reaching results occurred, in fact, before he went to Harrow. Of the two Scottish sisters who governed his nursery, Mary was both a harshly devout and a drunken and promiscuous woman ; and Hanson, the family lawyer, afterwards confided to Byron's staunch supporter, John Cam Hobhouse, that she had been dismissed not only for ill-treating her charge but, when he was nine years old, for making him her partner in minor sexual malpractices. Besides arousing his dormant passions, she managed to infect him with her Calvinist sense of sin ; and Mary Grey's example, strengthened by that of his vulgar and tempestuous mother, must have done much to determine his ambivalent attitude towards the opposite sex, in which attraction was mixed with hatred, and physical susceptibility with moral repulsion. Byron's mistresses were obliged to pay the penalty for the vices and short-comings of his early guardians.

This experience also encouraged his cult of " ideally beautiful, unpossessed love, which (says his latest biographer) had numerous embodiments, male and female ", during the remainder of his amatory life.* There was his romantic devotion to a series of very young girls, Margaret Parker, Mary Duff and, later, Lady Charlotte Harley ; and there was his " violent, though *pure*, love and passion " for his Cambridge disciple, Arthur Edleston, the youthful chorister whom, at the " most romantic period " of his existence, he declared that he loved " more than any human being ", and whom he seems eventually to have transposed into his mysterious heroine " Thyrza ". That Byron had a bi-sexual temperament no biographer could now deny. Probably at Harrow and Cambridge, certainly on his Levantine tour—when, among the luxurious Turks, he made love as the Turks did—he would appear to have given fairly free rein to his homosexual impulses, while the last passion from which he suffered was inspired by Loukas Chalandritsanos, his Greek page.† As a rule, his homosexual attachments were far more durable and more romantic—they were remembered, at least, with more romantic and nostalgic feelings—than the heterosexual affairs that he indulged in as a Regency *homme à bonnes fortunes*. But, although Byron was not ashamed of propensities that were condoned or shared by various members of his circle, pæderastic love, in

---

* *Byron* by Leslie A. Marchand. 1958.

† Loukas, evidently, did not respond to his master's strong attachment ; and Byron summed up his feeling in the " agonized poem " that was found among his papers at Missolonghi, but remained unpublished until 1887. The following extract reveals its gist :
> " Thus much and more ; and yet thou lov'st me not,
> And never wilt ! Love dwells not in our will.
> Nor can I blame thee, though it be my lot
> To strongly, wrongly, vainly love thee still."

the contemporary social system, was still a very grave offence ;
and, despite his defiance of the established moral code, Byron
retained a reluctant respect for convention. His early discovery that he possessed a bi-sexual nature, with all the hidden
stresses it provoked, may have added to the hereditary burden
that he felt he was condemned to bear.

This burden he described as his " heritage of storms ", be-
queathed to him at birth by a violent, erratic family. Among a
precious collection of unpublished papers, which not long ago
were still hidden away in the vaults of a bank and the lumber-
rooms of a secluded English country house, but to which a particularly enterprising and energetic student has recently contrived
to gain access, lurks the private correspondence of " Handsome
Jack " Byron, the poet's dissolute, unhappy father. Knowing
his foolish mother much too well, Byron had idolised his father's
memory. How soon (a biographer would like to know) did he
turn these scrawled and angry pages, the miserable outpourings
of a worn-out spendthrift, besieged by his creditors in a dreary
French provincial town, where almost his only companion,
was a sluttish and maltreated servant-girl ? But Captain Byron
had kept in touch with a sympathetic married sister ; and their
communications are said to provide hints that the affection between brother and sister was not entirely passionless. Thus
incest, Byron may have believed, was also part of his disastrous
heritage ; and the belief may perhaps have strengthened his own
impulse towards self-destruction, when, after years of silence
and absence, he once again encountered Augusta Leigh and—
whether in a spirit of perverse daring or from a desire to possess
and subdue a human being who so closely resembled himself,
who had inherited the same blood and was burdened by the same
destiny—he embarked on the " strange summer adventure " that
terrified his worldly confidante Lady Melbourne, an episode, he
told Tom Moore, of which he did not often care to think . . .

The notorious " Byron mystery "—always more apparent than
real—has at length been reduced to its correct proportions. But

during my youth, rather than accept the theory that the poet's half-sister became his mistress, students were still propounding alternative theories, to account for his sense of guilt and the disastrous breakdown of his marriage, which involved them in an infinity of labour but threw very little light on the problem at issue. Thus I heard of an aged scholar who had devoted many years to defending Byron against the charge of incest, and whose tragi-comic story might, I think, have attracted Henry James. Apparently, his hypothesis rested on the assumption that Byron, while still young, had been tricked into a discreditable secret alliance, which would have invalidated any subsequent marriage and bastardized Lady Byron's child ; and one day he thought he had grasped a clue that led directly to the centre of the labyrinth. Alas, he had put it aside, called away by some urgent private business ; and, when again he sat down at his desk, he found that, during the interval, he had utterly lost the thread. Of course, he remembered the relevant passage ; what he had forgotten was where it lay concealed ; and the remainder of his laborious existence passed in a desperate search that had no end. After his death, the scholar's widow felt it her painful duty to carry on the quest ; and she, too, spent many years among mountains of Byronic archives ; but the *genius loci* was evidently determined on baffling and frustrating her. All that remains to-day is a hurried transcription of a few ambiguous, unsigned words, suggestive yet far from conclusive, presumably a scrap of an unknown letter. The letter itself has now completely disappeared.

Yet who can be sure that it will not reappear just as suddenly and unaccountably, and by doing so necessitate a thorough revision of our previous views on Byron's early life ? Most biographical judgements are necessarily somewhat tentative, since fresh sources of information may at any juncture come to hand ; no biographer, it follows, should profess to tell the whole truth ; and we must remember that, while our subject is humanity and the vicissitudes of a human mind and heart, the best that we can hope to provide is an imaginative reconstruction rather than a definitive delineation. Not only does an individual move through the world on several different outward guises; but we must distinguish between the man his contemporaries knew—or, rashly, liked to think they knew—the man he supposed himself to be, and the more heroic personage he may at times have wished to be. As we accompany our hero upon his life-long quest for self-knowledge—and we cannot expect to understand him until we have joined him in his struggles to understand his own mind— we must attempt to pin down the unifying quality that gave his nature its coherence and its force. Byron's chief virtue, I have always imagined, was his unflagging self-awareness. The " common soul ", Pope reminds us, finds it enough to " peep out once an age ", a " dull, sullen " captive of the body, shackled by the chains of prejudice and habit. But a man of genius, even a man of talent, is perpetually awake and indefatigably alive; and Byron's was a passionately inquisitive spirit, whether he was considering himself or analysing the experiences of his fellow men. " Anything (he wrote) delights me that confirms, or extends one's observations on life and character . . ." And from Venice, during a particularly dissipated period : " I never strike out a thought of another's or of my own without trying to trace it back to its hidden source ". He valued dissipation, indeed, and the violent responses and reactions it provoked, because it intensified his consciousness of being alive and strengthened his hold upon his own identity : " the great object of life is sensation —to feel that we exist, even though in pain ". And his follies and misadventures were the price that he paid for driving his sensations to their furthest limit.

Byron's temperament, however, was not immune from doubt and fear ; like Pascal and Baudelaire, he could not forget the gulf that always yawned around his footsteps. " Why (he demands) at the very height of desire and human pleasure . . . does there mingle a certain sense of doubt and sorrow—a fear of what is to come—a doubt of what *is*—a retrospect to the past, leading to a prognostication of the future? . . . I know not, except that on a pinnacle we are most susceptible of giddiness . . ." No human being, I have already suggested, can be fully described or conclusively explained; but in these sentences I seem to detect a hint as important as the hint that Lady Blessington supplies. Clearly, Byron was not an intellectual of the stamp of Coleridge, Shelley and Wordsworth. He had read much, and read with enthusiasm; but his reading had been confined within a rather narrow circle; and he knew more of the English dramatists (from whom he very often quoted) than of the poets and historians of antiquity or of contemporary European writers. Similarly, his critical intelligence was neither acute nor far-reaching. He preferred Rogers to Keats, since Rogers, he believed, was a true disciple of Pope; and he expressed an unbounded detestation for the pretentious " tadpoles of the Lakes ", their pseudo-metaphysical excursions and mawkish efforts at sublime simplicity. Compared with Coleridge, he had a notably ill-furnished, compared with Keats, a somewhat shallow intelligence; but his genius and his gift of projecting it were rooted in the matrix of his personality—in the conflict between the worldly hedonist and the visionary fatalist, between his astonishing natural vigour and his strain of moral lassitude, between his pride, his vanity, his self-love and an inherited tendency towards self-destruction. While the ordinary man attempts to smother his conflicts—which he does all the more quickly and easily because his understanding of his essential self is often very slight and vague—the man of genius brings them to the surface and there translates them into a series of imaginative symbols, as Byron did when he produced Childe Harold and afterwards raised the ghost of Don Juan, who speaks not for the *lacrimæ rerum* but for an element of comic absurdity lying at the heart of human life. Both personages reflect the poet's character; each is partial and incomplete reflection. Yet, if placed side by side, they help to form a portrait in which all his varying traits are united—that of a Romantic against his will, a literary artist *malgré lui*, endowed, however, with a poignant self-awareness that drove his intelligence to creative activity, art being the means he employed to reconcile his deep emotional discords. The unending struggle to explore and understand provided the impetus his talents needed.

Byron's problems, of course, in a greater or lesser degree are shared by all creative spirits; and it would be difficult, or impossible, to construct a biography around the opposite type of human character—the individual whose early self-awareuess has soon begun to dwindle and decline, who has omitted to keep an eagle-eyed watch from the central stronghold of his own identity. Almost all the subjects I have undertaken have been self-questioners and self-doubters; and none was more furiously assailed by doubt than that engaging neurotic James Boswell, who possesses the additional interest of having laid down the rules that every twentieth-century biographer follows. He acquired the gift of literary portrayal through his arduous attempts at self-examination; and, although he was never able to answer the series of searching queries that the face he beheld in his glass constantly threw out at him—' Who am I ? What are my qualities and prospects ? On the example of which of my various reverend friends should I seek to re-shape personal life ? '—the habit of painstaking introspection helped to make him a supremely skilled observer. Meanwhile his restless intelligence kept up a feverish, fluttering activity. " I am continually *conscious* (he told Temple, during the year 1789), continually *looking back* or *looking forward* and wondering how I shall feel in situations which I anticipate in fancy "; and his private journal, he ventured to predict, would undoubtedly " afford materials for a very curious narrative ". When, in May 1791, his biography of Johnson at length appeared —despite the chronic alcoholism into which he was gradually sinking, and the fact that his hand was growing so tremulous that very often he could scarcely correct the proofs—Boswell again addressed Temple with a second, and equally shrewd, prophecy. His masterpiece, he assured him, would prove a " very valuable and peculiar volume "; and then, " I am absolutely certain that my mode of biography, which gives not only a

168

history of Johnson's *visible* progress through the world . . . but a view of his mind, in his letters and conversations, is the most perfect that can be conceived, and will be *more* of a *Life* than any book that has ever yet appeared."

The effect of his book exceeded the author's hopes ; for, besides being all that he claimed, it revolutionized the technique of biographical writing and encouraged in writers a completely novel attitude towards the study of human thought and conduct. Previous biographers, such as Walton and Johnson, were the literary exponents of a pre-Copernican system, with a fixed earth, overlooked by Providence and governed by immutable laws of right and wrong. Across the terrestrial board, God's unswerving arm moved His mortal chessmen to and fro ; but, although the fortunes of the chessmen rose and fell, their distinctive attributes showed remarkably little change ; they were interesting, not so much for themselves as for the moral laws they illustrated, for their achievements while they remained on the board and the dramatic circumstances in which they had been swept away. Boswell's feverish self-obsession induced a very different point of view. No human character, he saw, could be portrayed in bold and simple strokes ; his own varied from hour to hour, and was composed of the most diverse materials—vanity, vulgarity, lust, mingled with courage, generosity and pride. Boswell, moreover, had a genuine passion for truth, uninhibited by modesty or false shame. " I have a kind of strange feeling (he once recorded) as if I wished nothing to be secret that concerns myself "; and his love of candour was equally apparent whether he was designing a portrait or a self-portrait. It was the private man who absorbed his attention rather than the public figure ; and, thanks to Boswell's efforts, the treatment of the individual in art began to assume a wholly new form. A man seemed to deserve attention merely because he had existed, thought and suffered—as a representative of the human species, not as an exemplar of humanity's virtues and failings. Thus, having abandoned the standpoint of a Christian moralist, the biographer became a neo-humanist, interested in the smallest details that might tend to bring an individual character to life and, by enlarging our knowledge of the individual, help us to appreciate our common destiny.

A humanist the biographer remains, and must remain so long as his art flourishes. Hence the satisfaction of writing a biography; for in no other literary field is the writer conscious of being less alone. Vanished men and women surround him, demanding to be rediscovered and portrayed; and, although some, like Homer's plaintive ghosts, appeal, beckon, gesticulate, yet never quite materialise, a gifted few, who while they lived had a peculiarly vivid sense of life, seem more real to us, once they have entered our circle, than many of our closest and dearest friends. Incidentally, they are much more communicative—the dead have lost the reticence of the living; and frequently they appear to have looked forward to a literary Day of Resurrection, when every heart would be laid bare and not a secret would be left untold. Thus Byron, who imagined his correspondence " bursting forth " in the mysterious twentieth century, was amused to reflect that it might puzzle his readers if they sought to elucidate his hidden meanings. And then, the dead have ceased to stand on their dignity : the biographer need not profess an unqualified regard for the mighty figures of the past : all they beg is that, without necessarily admiring them, we should exert ourselves to understand them, and should do our best to restore them to life by re-clothing them in vital substance. What they require is an imaginative recognition of their essential human qualities.

Notwithstanding Boswell's influence, the Victorian biographer was often hampered by the social prejudices of his age ; and terrible stories have come down to us of the crimes that he committed against the truth—facts suppressed, documents destroyed, letters edited or expurgated, sentences mangled and revelatory words removed. These crimes, committed in the name of discretion, usually defeated their own object ; for Truth, being one and indivisible, cannot be cut up into a number of convenient scraps, some of which we decide to publish while the remainder are hidden or thrown away. It was Sir Edmund Gosse, a splendid specimen of the late-Victorian literary pontiff, who achieved the prodigious feat of writing an " authoritative " full-length book on Swinburne that contained no mention of the poet's sexual vagaries and hardly a reference, apart from oblique hints, to his early alcoholism, though both factors had had a considerable share in the formation of his poetic imagery. Sir Edmund's attitude towards the great, however, was not as reverential as one might have at first supposed. I remember visiting him, for instance, at his handsome classical house in Regent's Park, where a huge photograph of Tolstoy, bearing an effusive dedicatory message, occupied a dominant position from which it immediately attracted his visitors' notice. Until I said goodbye, my host had maintained a tone of mild Olympian benevolence, gravely advising and warning me about the difficulties and dangers of a literary life, and solemnly " praying God " (I recollect) that I might be spared some of the personal hardships that—presumably as the Librarian of the House of Lords—he himself had undergone. But, when I rose and, with majestic courtesy, he insisted on accompanying me to the head of the stairs, we were confronted by Tolstoy's impressive photograph, which produced a rapid and remarkable change. His eyesight at the time was weak ; and one of the lenses of his spectacles was made of black, or dark grey, glass—a detail that tended to give him a vaguely rakish and piratical air. Now his expression became almost sinister as he scrutinised the patriarch's bearded face. " That old *humbug* ! " he hissed out fiercely, before extending an aged, dry-skinned hand . . .

There was no doubt, of course, that he had loved and reverenced Swinburne, or that his disingenuous treatment of the poet's failings had been dictated by the very highest motives. But it occurred to me then, and has often occurred to me since, that the reverential attitude towards the dead usually adopted by Victorian men of letters, on some occasions, perhaps, may have concealed a certain basis of repressed resentment. Just as the Victorians' cult of the family sometimes masked their private hatreds, so the deep regard they exhibited for the noble figures they delighted to praise and excuse may overlaid have a fund of primitive antagonism, hidden far beneath the surface of their minds. Twenty or thirty years later, the covert antagonism broke through ; and in the Georgian age a school of biographers arose who treated their victims with ferocious flippancy, denigrating instead of applauding, demolishing instead of building up, depicting Disraeli as a " strange old comedian " and pretending to reveal Gordon as a surreptitious brandy-swigger. Today, denigration, practised for its own sake, seems no less foolish and disingenuous than unqualified biographical applause. Sympathy is now the trait that we value in the work of any biographer we esteem—the intuitive sympathy that a novelist also possesses, and that enables novelist or biographer to grasp the secret pattern of his subjects' thoughts and emotions, first explaining how, as individuals, they differed from their fellow men, subsequently emphasizing the important relationship between their personal experiences and the experiences of mankind at large.

In this respect, the biographer resembles a novelist ; but, unlike the novelist, when he sets out to interpret, he cannot rely upon imagination. He must deal with facts—frequently unpalatable facts ; and, besides the skeleton of facts, slowly and patiently constructed during his researches into documentary evidence, every genuine biographical portrait needs a firmly drawn historical background. Here the biographer must emulate the historian, and examine the various problems of historical cause and effect. How far is the individual moulded by the age he lives in ? How much does a powerfully gifted mind contribute to the development of his social period ? Obviously, a human being, gifted or ungifted, is to some extent a product of his age ; but the man of genius is a little ahead of his epoch, or has anticipated the forward movement of history, and so contrives to catch and condense a mood that was already hovering in the air, as Byron did when he caught the Byronic mood and expressed it through his literary legend. Yet our study of his personal character shows that he undertook the task with some reluctance and that, had he been able to escape from pressure of forces over which he himself had no control, he might, in the drama of his age, have played a comparatively unassuming part. It was his "helplessness", his self-abandonment, that gave him the status of a tragic hero : in Greek tragedy, the hero owes his distinction to his conscious acceptance of an unavoidable fate. But, although Byron had inherited a sense of fate, he had also inherited a passionate thirst for living ; and the two, so long as he breathed, kept him in a state of constant tension. From that tension sprang his poems and his letters—the protests he uttered against an unwelcome destiny. He was still protesting when he reached Genoa and settled down to await the last summons—a recalcitrant hero, meagre and travel-worn, with his grey-streaked curls and his faded tartan jacket.

VII

The First Person Singular

THE ETRUSCANS are one of those ancient races whom we invest with an air of deep mystery. We are wrong to do so, announces the most distinguished of modern Etruscologists, who assures us that they are only mysterious because we have not yet learned to read their language. In the present state of our knowledge, however, all that we know about them helps to increase the impression—their attitude towards death and the after-life, their curious modes of living and thinking, even the strange circumstances said to have attended their lamentable decline and fall. They arose and disappeared according to a rhythm pre-established by their ancestral soothsayers; their destiny had long been written; and when, eighty-eight years before the birth of Christ, a noise like the hoarse blaring of a brazen war-trumpet resounded across Central Italy, they recognised that the eighth, or penultimate, period in the life-span of their race had come to its appointed end; while, forty-four years later, the flashing tail of a comet heralded the conclusion of the last cycle. Luxurious lovers of life, they were intensely preoccupied with thoughts of death. Natural sensualists yet inveterate fatalists, they believed that human destiny was governed by an unknowable, unmentionable group of powers, too dreadful to be named, whom they spoke of merely as " The Hidden Ones ". Beneath the Etruscan's enjoyment of the world lurked an enervating sense of hopelessness and loneliness, " a feeling of the nonentity of man before the divine will " (suggests Professor Massimo Pallotino) that the creative Greeks and the imitative, acquisitive Romans neither experienced nor comprehended. Images of death always haunted their feasts ; and, in the brilliant scenes of drinking and dancing that decorated their homely tombs—pictures that show them revelling among their women and their favourite slaves, under the beneficent influence of the wine-god *Fufluns*—two demonic presences are often depicted, come from the regions of the underworld to cast a shadow over human joy. Here *Charu*, the ancestor of Charon, threatens a carefree and beautiful girl ; there a hideous spirit, known as *Phersu*, casts his fatal sling around an athlete's legs. He is the enemy of pride and strength and grace, an ambassador of that " undiscovered country " which every traveller must at length explore.

Phersu is represented wearing a mask ; and the Romans, being great admirers of the people whom they conquered and eventually destroyed it was from Etruria, *genetrix et mater superstitionum*, that they borrowed both the arts of divination and such details of civic pageantry as the ruler's gilded laurel wreath and purple robe, the lictors' fasces and the ivory curule chair—adapted the ominous demon's name, which in Latin finally became *persona*, the word used to designate the mask worn by actors on the Roman stage. During our own epoch, it has again been utilised to describe a certain aspect of the adult personality. In Jung's system (writes a contemporary psychologist),* the " persona " is " that part of the consciousness which is exposed to the gaze of the outer world. It may correspond closely to what the individual conceives himself to be ", the equivalent of Freud's ego-phantasy ; but " it is not . . . the same as his character, which includes important unconscious elements "; and, " in so far as the individual regards himself as identical with the ' persona ' "', his understanding of himself must be considered " minimal ". Self-expression is sometimes assumed to be one of the creative

* *Psycho-Analysis and its Derivatives*, by H. Crichton-Miller.

writer's chief objects ; but, when he exhibits his personality, he should bear in mind the antique origin of the word and remember its former association with the idea of deliberate deception and disguise. Europe has a magnificent literature of self-revelation and self-portrayal ; and the literary self-portraits it has produced may frequently be described as masks. Yet—so extraordinary is the effect of literary genius—the mask with which a writer hides his face often represents an aspect of his nature that the face beneath it is endeavouring to conceal. Thus Byron confronted the world in the romantic mask of *Childe Harold*, for which he presently substituted the tragi-comic mask of *Don Juan* ; and each mask seems to have reflected some essential characteristics of the inner man, far more accurately than the worldly face that his friends and his boon-companions saw. The " pose " that he dropped in private, but assumed for public literary purposes, was a genuine representation of the poet's secret doubts and struggles. What some of his critics have dismissed as affectation was an effort to translate into symbolic literary shape—true, now and then, the symbols were badly chosen and the artistic result was clumsy and stilted—feelings that the pressure of social opinion otherwise obliged him to keep carefully hidden away.

English literature is particularly rich in its records of individual feeling ; and this perhaps may have something to do with the English form of the first person singular. Through the Book of Exodus, translated into English, rolls Jehovah's thunderous affirmation of his unique and undivided identity : "I am that I am "—how much more significant a sentence than " *Je suis celui qui suis* " or " *Je suis celui qui est* " ! *Je* and *Io* have comparatively little weight, beside *I*, formed with a single stroke of the pen, the emphatic mark that an English writer inscribes when he wishes to distinguish himself, and all the emotions and convictions that have helped to make him the man he is, from the innumerable surrounding selves who demand his notice at every hour of the day, often endeavouring to submerge, but never

176

quite absorbing him. That single stroke proclaims his independence ; from the moment he has executed it, he stands alone ;
but whether the figure he cuts is impressive or absurd must
depend, of course, on his artistic abilities—on whether he has
acquired the gift of tempering egotism with imagination, of
seeing himself as at once unique and an infinitesimal detail of the
gigantic human background. In my youth, T. S. Eliot uttered
some eloquent protests against the " cult of personality "; for
our personalities, he asserted, were " disorderly and mostly
silly ",* and a dedicated writer should disregard the self and turn
to loftier and less impure concerns. At the time, I was shocked
and stimulated, since I came fresh from the poems of Rupert
Brooke ; and his work had done much to colour my adolescent
day dreams, which fed greedily on his constant references to the
vicissitudes of his own emotional career, lavishly sprinkled with
the attractive pronouns that Eliot now insisted that it was my
duty to despise. But I respected the wisdom of the Anglo-
American seer ; and my views of poetry and the poetic life
underwent an immediate transformation.

Not until I was growing up, and had left Oxford, did I begin
finally to escape from the master's influence. After all, were
there not hundreds of noble passages, both in ancient and in
modern literature, to which the abhorred first personal pronoun
gave much of their poetic beauty and their dramatic poignancy ?
What, for example, of the celebrated fragment of Sappho where
she speaks of her lonely and cheerless bed, when the Moon and
the Pleiads have sunk beneath the horizon, midnight approaches
and time goes creeping by, and she lies, solitary and forgotten,
listening for the step of some unfaithful lover ? What of Alcman's
equally moving verses, in which he bids goodbye to his own
vigorous youth and compares his sad plight with that of the
carefree ceryl—as Greek zoologists called the cock-halcyon—
whom the females he has gathered around him support on their

---

* " To reduce one's disorderly and mostly silly personality to the gravity of a
jeu de quilles would be an excellent thing . . ."
A Brief Introduction to the Method of Paul Valéry, 1924.

devoted pinions, and who flies with them " over the flower of the wave ", the " sea-blue bird " of an eternal Spring ? And then, there were the Roman elegaic poets—studied in a convenient edition that published parallel English and Latin texts. Catullus and Propertius can scarcely have shared the prejudices of the author of *The Sacred Wood;* for they did not hesitate to give their poems a strikingly individual and egocentric form, and made no attempt to shake off the Self, their awareness of it being enlarged and exalted by their experience of pleasure and misery alike. Catullus has left behind him an autobiographical record in the series of lyric poems he addressed to Lesbia, the frivolous and promiscuous *femme du monde,* whom he had met and adored while he was still very young. Lesbia—in real life, Clodia, sister to Clodius, the wild patrician demagogue—was encumbered at the time with an elderly respectable husband ; and a friend named Allius smoothed the path of love by offering Catullus and Clodia a refuge in his house. Later the poet remembered how his " white goddess "—*candida diva*—would sometimes hesitate as she crossed the threshold, " with shining foot posed upon the slender sandal-tip ". But although *candida*—which, I am told, has an additional connotation of good fortune—the woman Catullus worshipped was never *casta.* She deceived the young poet no less readily than she had cuckolded her ageing husband—Catullus had fallen into the common mistake of supposing that an unchaste beloved will be unchaste in our arms alone—and rumours soon reached him that she was seeking enjoyment with a host of vulgar unknown rivals. Then the playful lyrics in which he had celebrated their secret meetings under his good-natured friend's roof—*Vivamus, mea Lesbia, atque amemus* of which the untranslatable sixth line, *Nox est perpetua una dormienda,* could only have been achieved in Latin—give way to a long series of magnificently vituperative poems where passionately regretful tenderness goes hand in hand with savage jealousy, and declarations of undying love are thrown into sharp relief by the use of obscene colloquial phrases, as in the celebrated poem that begins *Caeli, Lesbia nostra, Lesbia illa,* but concludes by picturing the idolised Lesbia now utterly oblivious of Catullus and his kind, abandoned to the embraces of vagrant amorists at street-corners and down squalid alleys.

Nearly a thousand years after the fall of Rome, when the huge open metropolis that Catullus knew had become a battlemented mediæval city, an intensely personal voice was once again heard in European literature. Again it was raised to vent a passionate protest—the voice of a poor young scholar who, like Catullus, had always hoped for better things, yet always, driven by his destiny, felt an irresistible compulsion to choose the worse. François Villon vanished from record at the age of thirty-two, having been ordered to leave Paris " in consideration of his evil life "; and it seems probable that he died on the road, was murdered during a tavern row or hung as a petty thief by some provincial court of justice. Meanwhile he has sunk to the depths of the Parisian underworld ; and at one period before his sentence of expulsion, pronounced in January 1463, he was attached to a brawny prostitute whom her customers called " *la grosse Margot* ". Villon's *Ballade de la grosse Margot* is a memorable and terrible account of the life they shared, with its refrain— " *En ce bordeau ou tenons nostre estat* ": in this brothel where we keep our state—its glimpses of violent quarrels if Margot came home empty-handed ; of ignominious reconciliations followed by drunken log-like sleep, and its closing lines in which he looks back to the " honour " he has irremediably lost :

" *Vente, gresle, gelle, j'ay mon pain cuit.*
Je suis paillart, la paillairde me suit.
Lequel vault mieulx ? Chascun bien s'entresuit.
L'ung vault l'autre; cest a mau rat mau chat.
Ordure amons, ordure nous assuit;
Nous deffuyons onneur, il nous deffuit,
En ce bordeau ou tenons nostre estat "

The Sign of the Fish

Literary parallels are often delusive; and vague talk of a poet's "influences" should always be regarded with some suspicion, since what excites a poet in the work of his predecessors is usually not so much their gift of "thought"—an element that, for lecture-room purposes, the average academic critic is never tired of discussing and defining—as some far less easily definable gift, implicit in the texture of their style. Baudelaire, no doubt, had studied Villon; but he does not refer to the *Testament* or the *Ballades* in any of his major critical essays. Yet one can scarcely read the *Ballade de la grosse Margot* without remembering *Les Fleurs du Mal*—first published in 1857, almost four hundred years after François Villon had left Paris—more especially that dark and tragic poem, among the group entitled *Spleen et Idéal*, which was evidently provoked by his impressions of a similar "journey through the underworld":

> "*Une nuit que j'étais près d'une affreuse Juive,*
> *Comme au long d'un cadavre un cadavre étendu,*
> *Je me pris à songer près de ce corps vendu*
> *A la triste beauté dont mon désir se prive . . .*"

Here, as in many of his other poems, we find the same sense of self-abandonment, the same nostalgic tribute to the hopes he has thrown away and the credit he has forfeited, the same admission of a painful dichotomy between contrasted and conflicting selves. While Villon had his beloved Catherine—the well-brought-up Parisian girl who had renounced him at her honest parents' command, and against whom he took a neurotic's revenge, not only making her the victim of his obscene and scurrilous verses, but punishing himself (which was meant to punish her) by his commerce with such sordid associates as *la grosse Margot*—Baudelaire continued to cherish and abuse his romantic visions of an ideal love, embodied first in his adored mother, who betrayed him, when he was still a child, by marrying his hated step-father, and afterwards in a succession of women who tem-

180

porarily usurped his mother's rôle, Marie Sabatier, the voluptuous *Présidente*, and the young actress, a remote and shadowy
figure, known as " Madame Marie X . . ." Baudelaire's Margot
was *l'affreuse Juive* or his dusky mistress, the half-caste Jeanne
Duval.

Both a writer's virtues and his vices contribute to the production of a work of art ; for the creative processes have their own
mysterious economy which absorbs and transmutes into artistic
form the most discordant types of raw material. " *Nostre
bastiment, et public et privé* (Montaigne declared) *est plein d'imper-
fections: mais il n'y a rien d'inutile en nature, non pas l'inutilité mesme
. . . Nostre estre est cimenté de qualites maladifves . . .*"* Thus, the
unhealthy qualities in the composition of a Catullus, a Villon or
a Baudelaire—unhealthy from a social or from a moral point of
view—once they have been subjected to the alchemy of art re-
emerge under a very different guise ; weakness becomes a source
of strength ; masochistic and self-destructive traits help to quicken
the artist's creative impulse. France, however, has developed a
tradition of unsparing self-analysis for which it would be difficult
to find an exact equivalent in the literature of other races. The
Anglo-Saxon character may be as deeply troubled ; but it is
inclined to approach the problem of the Self with a greater degree
of literary caution ; and Coleridge considered that the poet's
apparent selflessness was one of Shakespeare's chief merits—he
shaped his dramatis personæ " out of the nature within ; but we
cannot so safely say, out of his own nature as an individual
person . . . Shakespeare . . . had no *I*, but the *I* representative . . ."†

---

* *Essais:* Livre III.

† *Lectures and Notes on Shakspere.* If, in this context, Coleridge fails to mention
the *Sonnets*, it seems probable that he had some very good reason. For, although
they are scattered with personal references, they include nothing that could be
described as a comprehensive self-portrait ; and generations of scholars have
been unable to establish the outlines of the underlying story. Indeed, I have sometimes been tempted to assume that " Mr. W. H." was the original author, being
the " onlie begetter of these insuing sonnets " in as much as he might be said to
have fathered them on the imagination of " our ever living poet ", who had reshaped
and immensely improved the rough drafts that his friend supplied, and thus ensured
them that " eternitie " of which the publisher, the " well-wishing adventurer ",

Certainly, the Ego makes a somewhat spasmodic appearance in English sixteenth- and seventeenth-century verse and prose. John Donne's tumultuous self-assertion is followed by Milton's majestic self-suppression. Perhaps Milton speaks in *propria persona* through the mouths of Samson and the Fallen Angel ; but his lament for his blindness, which rises from the Fourth Book of *Paradise Lost*, strikes on our ears as strangely and unexpectedly as the voice of the Ghost from beneath the Elizabethan stage.

Yet, despite these obvious reservations, the English pronoun is at once more potent and more pervasive than its Gallic counterpart. The self-examination that writers practise may be less intense and less unsparing; but it is far more generally diffused in English than in French literature, and embraces a wider aspect of the artist's personality. For it is not confined to professional self-analysts, or gifted lyrical poets tormented by a sense of sin. Whereas the *Grand Siècle* produced Racine and Corneille, who expressed their attitude towards life in splendidly impersonal terms—La Fontaine alone sounded the note of personal regret and sorrow—the English Augustan Age bred Alexander Pope, who set a standard of classical dignity but did not refuse to enrich his poems and letters with lively references to his own emotions. Admittedly, the Augustan writer is very seldom off his guard and expresses his private feelings only in the stateliest language. But, once at least, he drops his defences and confronts us in a very different rôle—as a man who had discovered that genius and fame were poor substitutes for the pleasures of satisfied love, and that the beauty of the gardens he had planned beside the Thames served merely to remind him of their emptiness and loneliness :

> " Ah friend, 'tis true—this truth you lovers know—
> In vain my structures rise, my gardens grow ;

---

speaks. So thoroughly did Shakespeare re-shape his material, adding a quantity of material drawn from his own experience of life, that the thread of continuing narrative was for ever broken.

In vain fair Thames reflects the double scenes
Of hanging mountains, and of sloping greens . . .
What are the gay parterre, the chequered shade,
The morning bower, the evening colonnade,
But soft recesses of uneasy minds,
To sigh unheard in to the passing winds ? "

Compared with the human happiness he knows he can never
achieve—the uneasy occupant of a sickly and deformed body—
his own loneliness and frustration seem to bear down upon him
with a double weight. But Pope's view of the importance of
happiness is shared by many English writers, and would appear
to have characterised the Anglo-Saxon temperament since the
early eighteenth century. In the literature of no other people
does the idea of happiness bulk so large, and nowhere are such
an immense variety of meanings condensed into a single noun.
Other races have sought to distinguish between the different
states that the English word covers. The Greeks, for instance,
established a careful distinction between happiness, cheerfulness
and joy or mirth, inventing six words to describe the first, and
five to help us evoke the second ; while even the grave and sententious Romans knew that happiness, joy and delight were
entirely separate modes of being, and that to experience *felicitas*
was not necessarily to enjoy *gaudium* or *lætitia*, which again were
not to be confused with *delectatio* or *voluptas*, the sensuous or
sensual delight that stirs both the emotions and the senses.
Felicitas, of course, suggests good fortune, like *bonheur* in the
French vocabulary ; and such was the original significance of the
all-inclusive English word ; for, when our ancestors spoke of a
" happy event " or a " happy thought ", they wished their
audience to understand that it had turned out to be a stroke of
good luck, not that it had calmed and refreshed the heart and
lifted their spirits towards the heavens. But the word gradually
changed colour as the Romantic movement began to invade
England—which occurred during the lifetime of Pope, a classicist

whose finest verse and prose reveal some strikingly romantic traits—and the ideas associated with it slowly spread across the Western literary world. " Happiness is a new idea in Europe ",* said Robespierre's friend Louis de Saint-Just. The handsome young revolutionary died under the guillotine on July 28th 1794; and eighteen years earlier the American patriots who issued the Declaration of Independence had laid down the " pursuit of happiness ", together with the enjoyment of life and liberty, as an unalienable human right. This imaginative re-definition of humanity's chief aim and purpose—no longer to qualify for supernatural bliss, but to seek the reward we deserve within the limits of our own minds—was echoed and adapted by a host of nineteenth-century English writers, each dominated by Saint-Just's " new idea " and determined to explain how the promised reward had so far failed to come his way.

Latin writers, with their Catholic background, have proved somewhat less susceptible. Certainly, the idea would seem to have haunted Rimbaud. " *Le Bonheur!* " (he exclaims) " *Sa dent, douce à la mort, m'avertissait au chant du coq . . . dans les plus sombres villes:*

> *O saisons, ô châteaux!*
> *Quelle âme est sans défauts!*
>
> *J'ai fait la magique étude*
> *Du bonheur, qu'aucun n'élude . . .*"

But French poets of an earlier period stated their claim in far more modest terms; and La Fontaine, in his celebrated invocation asks for happiness as a grace, rather than demands it as a personal right :

> " *Volupté, Volupté, qui fut jadis maîtresse,*
> *Du plus bel esprit de la Grece,*

* Quoted by Albert Camus : *Combat,* 1944.

The First Person Singular

Ne me dédaigne pas, viens-t-en loger chez moi;
Tu n'y seras pas sans emploi:
J'aime le jeu, l'amour, les livres, la musique;
La ville et la campagne, enfin tout; il n'est rien
Qui ne me soit souverain bien,
Jusqu'au sombre plaisir d'un cœur mélancolique "

And then, *volupté* is not happiness, so much as a pleasurable
awareness of life, a heightened sensitiveness—sometimes tinged
with melancholy—to all the joys that the body and the spirit can
offer. An Englishman, on the other hand, when he speaks of
being happy—or an Englishwoman when she complains that
husband or lover has not " made her happy "—envisages a state
of inward contentment that includes animal euphoria without
excluding a random touch of ecstasy. It is a frame of mind that
need not take into account such abstract conceptions as virtue
and honour ; the happy man is not happy because he feels that
he has been victorious in the battle of life, but because, having the
English gift for compromise, he has finally arrived at a working
agreement both with his circumstances and with his own nature,
thus achieving a state of inward concord that he accounts superior
to all other blessings.

Before he can achieve it, the pursuer of happiness has to
contend against many insidious foes. Doubts emerge that
threaten to disrupt his plan ; for happiness depends on a sense
of individual one-ness ; and we very few of us feel altogether
sure that our personality forms a single self-contained unit, but
are apt to see it, at least in despondent moods, as a chance-met
assemblage of miscellaneous flotsam, the small idiosyncrasies we
have acquired ourselves and the strange quirks we have inherited.
These doubts were recently expressed by a distinguished modern
English critic :

" A stone lies in a river ; (muses the pensive Palinurus) a piece
of wood is jammed against it ; dead leaves, drifting logs, and
branches caked with mud collect ; weeds settle there, and soon

birds have made a nest . . . Then the river rises and the earth is washed away. The birds depart, the flowers wither, the branches are dislodged and drift downward . . . Such is our personality ".*

Far more unexpected is the argument of H. G. Wells, who, in a pamphlet published at the very end of his career, entitled *A Thesis on the Quality of Illusion in the Continuity of the Individual Life,*† followed an equally pessimistic line. Despite the cock-sparrow-like self-assurance so characteristic of his youth and middle age, he dared to suggest that " there is not and never has been such an original mental unity " as is implied in the conception of selfhood, and that all " consolidations " of our personality are therefore largely artificial. Nor do these contemporary doubters stand alone. James Boswell, though inflamed by self-love, was simultaneously racked by self-doubt. Who was he ? How could he claim to exist as an individual human being, when his mental shape constantly changed under the influence of other human characters ? His face in the glass frequently attracted him, but at no period did it unreservedly please. He could not become himself—whatever that self was—except by becoming someone else ; and again and again he attempted to discover himself by identifying his own irresolute being with that of a personage whom he had elected to love and admire—the stern Lord Auchinleck, Samuel Johnson, Pasquale Paoli. In his eyes, they had a sharp and dignified outline that the reflection in the glass had always wanted.

Boswell, however, had the strength of his failings : from the fluidity of his protean temperament sprang his greatest literary virtues. He remained in a state of perpetual oscillation ; but he was destined never to collapse entirely ; and it is among the writers whose reason at length collapsed that we find the saddest records of the Self struggling to defend its separate status.

---

* *The Unquiet Grave,* Part I.   Hamish Hamilton, 1945.
† *A Thesis on the Quality of Illusion in the Continuity of the Individual Life in the Higher Metazoa, with particular reference to the Species Homo Sapiens.*

Deranged poets are more often English than French. Even Gérard de Nerval, who admitted that he had " three times crossed the Acheron "— that is to say, had thrice been committed to a private madhouse—traversed the gloomy stream as a poetic conqueror and returned home, through the Gates of Ivory and Horn, with an array of curious and beautiful trophies. He is still himself in *Aurélia*, though not quite so self-possessed as he had been in *Sylvie*; but English poets who suffered the same misfortune, perhaps because they held a different view of the Self, describe their experiences in a far more pathetic style. They are not conquerors ; they are shipwrecked sailors—Clare writing from the dismal wards of Northampton County Asylum, a derelict visionary, tossed by his fate—

> " Into the nothingness of scorn and noise,
> Into the living sea of waking dream,
> Where there is neither sense of life, nor joys,
> But the huge shipwreck of my own esteem . . ."

and Cowper, who launches his *Castaway* on to the surges of a wild Atlantic storm with a hint that he is just such a " destined wretch " as the miserable author in his country cottage, then proceeds to develop that hint until he reaches a resounding climax :

> " No voice divine the storm allayed,
> No light propitious shone :
> When, snatched from all effectual aid,
> We perished, each alone :
> But I beneath a rougher sea,
> And whelmed in deeper gulfs than he."

The eighteenth century being an age of prose, Cowper does not omit one or two soberly prosaic observations. We are told of the practical measures with which his devoted comrades on board prolong the castaway's last despairing struggle :

The Sign of the Fish

"Some succour yet they could afford;
And, such as storms allow,
The cask, the coop, the floated cord,
Disdained not to bestow "

And we are also reminded of the psychological motive that has inspired the composition of the poem; for—

"Misery still delights to trace
Its semblance in another's case "

Every literary work is an effort to share experience, and to establish a connection between our own plight and the sufferings of the world at large; and the effort becomes particularly marked when a writer makes use of the word *I* and, discarding all symbolic imagery, addresses the reader in his proper person. The more difficult he finds it to establish contact, the more anxiously does he set about his task; and great introspective writers often prove to have been men, cursed with a life-long sense of personal and moral isolation, who attempted to explain, and escape from, their solitude by looking inward and describing what they saw. This is especially true of English nineteenth-century self-portraitists, of Coleridge, for example, and Thomas De Quincey, both artists who sought in literature a consolation that they were denied in life—an assurance that they were not alone, and that around them, wherever their voices carried, they had spiritual companions and fellow-sufferers. To the English preoccupation with the idea of happiness they added a Romantic absorption in the cult of youth. Happiness and youthfulness, according to the Romantic poets, were inextricably bound up together. The discovery that he had outlived his boyhood Byron remembered as "one of the deadliest and heaviest feelings " of his whole existence; while Wordsworth's regrets for his vanished youth overflowed from *The Prelude* into *Intimations of Immortality*. Although, like Baudelaire, Coleridge believed that the exquisite freshness of childish sensations could be recaptured by the man

of genius at will,* he did not pretend that he had himself succeeded in recovering such lost delights or in returning to the
state of imaginative purity that had lent his youthful visions so
exquisitely keen an edge. His eye reflects ; the heart refuses to
respond ; Nature has become a painted show :

> " All this long eve, so balmy and serene,
> Have I been gazing on the western sky,
> And its peculiar tint of yellow green :
> And still I gaze—and with how blank an eye !
> And those thin clouds above, in flakes and bars,
> That give away their motion to the stars . . .
> Yon crescent moon, as fixed as if it grew,
> In its own cloudless, starless lake of blue,
> I see them all so excellently fair,
> I see, not feel, how beautiful they are ! "

Thus the English introspective seems to have developed a
character that distinguishes him at once from other European
artists. His mood perhaps is less heroic ; for instead of begging
that he may be granted the moral strength to contemplate his
mind and his body without revulsion—

> " *Ah! Seigneur! donnez-moi la force et le courage*
> *De contempler mon cœur et mon corps sans dégoût!* " †

—he dwells, angrily or resignedly, on the loss of happiness and

* " To carry on the feelings of childhood into the powers of manhood ; to
combine the child's sense of wonder and novelty with the appearances, which every
day for perhaps forty years had rendered familiar . . . this is the character and
privilege of genius, and one of the marks which distinguish genius from talent."
                            Coleridge : *Biographia Literaria.* Chap. **IV.**

" Rien ne ressemble plus à ce qu'on appelle l'inspiration, que la joie avec laquelle
un enfant absorbe la forme et la couleur . . . Le génie n'est que *l'enfance retrouvée* a
volonté, l'enfance douée maintenant, pour s'exprimer, d'organes virils et de l'esprit
analytique . . ."   Baudelaire : *Un Peintre de la Vie Moderne.*

From these passages, and another closely connected pair, it seems obvious that
Baudelaire must at least have looked into Coleridge's major work of criticism,
though from his biographer, Dr. Enid Starkie, I learn that there is no external
evidence to support this belief.

† Baudelaire : *Voyage à Cythère.*

the inevitable passage of youth. He is less apt to generalize than to comment and particularize ; and this trend is vividly illustrated by the gifted author of *The Unquiet Grave*, one of the most original pieces of introspective writing published during the last few years. " Palinurus " is a type of the unashamedly self-centred Englishman—with an added strain of Celtic nostalgia derived from his Anglo-Irish birth—who makes himself the measure of the world and confers on his own immediate response to life the dignity of an absolute critical standard. This attitude may sometimes be exasperating ; but it is also oddly stimulating. While Europe and Asia smoked or blazed, Palinurus continued to execute his clear nostalgic flute solo. Had he forgotten (I have heard a detractor ask) that, even as he mourned and mused in his sitting-room above the tree-tops of a London square, hundreds of thousands of his fellow human creatures were fighting and dying amid the ruins of embattled Stalingrad ? But Palinurus refuses to be distracted by any specious humanitarian appeal. The destruction of armies, he reminds us, and the violent vicissitudes of revolutionary change, are much less moving to a writer than the experience of the individual spirit ; for, whereas men in the mass may command our pity, only the fate of the individual arouses deep imaginative sympathy ; and that sympathy cannot be dispensed with if we aim at the creation of a work of art.

On ears half-deafened by propaganda, the soloist's message fell like heavenly music. Bullied, advised, over-persuaded by a dozen vociferous " organs of opinion "—*The Unquiet Grave*, written " between the autumn of 1942 and the autumn of 1943 ", appeared in 1944—a reader suddenly remembered that he had still his separate life to enjoy, and that no collective effort could ever take the place of his own private aspirations towards happiness and truth. Hence the far-reaching charm that Palinurus exercised—an egoist not ashamed of his egoism if he felt that it safeguarded his intellectual liberty. His book made some strange converts and helped to perform some unexpected cures. I recollect, for instance, discussing the author with a much advertised photographic model who, although little interested in works of current literature, told me that she had found his text an unceasing source of personal comfort, and that, at one moment, she had had three or four copies, which her friends had subsequently borrowed or stolen. *Angst*, during the mid-nineteen-forties, threatened to become a fashionable modern disease, from which the most unlikely persons claimed proudly that they had long been suffering ; and the book achieved a popular success, that, as popular acclamation often does, tended to obscure its real qualities. Hostile critics, on the other hand, adopted an equally misleading view. They asserted that it was a mere anthology, regardless of the uncommon skill with which Palinurus had bound his well-chosen series of extracts together, so as to provide a vivid, if indirect, illustration of the spokesman's changing tastes and interests. He himself has described it as a " signal of distress "—the author, while he wrote, was suffering from an acute private sorrow—and the effect that it produces is occasionally lugubrious, sometimes even lachrymose. Cyril Connolly is a Man of Feeling in the eighteenth-century sense of the term ; and one thinks not only of Jean-Jacques Rousseau but, now and then, of James Boswell, whom Johnson sternly warned against what he was pleased to call the " hypocrisy of misery ".* Yet, on almost every page, some luminous shaft of intelligence filters through the clouds of remorse and regret. Palinurus may write as gloomily as Coleridge of the physical disadvantages of growing old—" this drooping gait, this altered size " form the subject of many a tragi-comic reference—but such laments are usually followed by a sunny suggestion of the will to live, and painful recollections of the unhappy past by exquisite descriptive passages that reveal both his relish of happiness and his unaltered affection for natural beauty. The Man of Feeling is also a man of

* " Dear Sir, I hoped you had got rid of all this hypocrisy of misery . . . I love every part about you but your affectation of distress. Come to me, my dear Bozzy, and let us be as happy as we can . . ."
                                                    Johnson to Boswell, March 14th 1781.

sense, lucky in the possession of a well-schooled academic brain ; and from the combination of those two different characters springs Palinurus the introspective artist.

It has been my good fortune, over a period of thirty years, to watch him gradually developing. When, about 1924, I first encountered Cyril Connolly at Oxford, I was immediately fascinated by the gift he already displayed of lending colour and poetic significance to the smallest episode. Thus a nocturnal expedition down the Oxford Canal—we despised the comparative banality of green-fledged Thames and Isis—provided at every turn of that dark and stagnant waterway, every glimpse of a street-lamp or of an elder tree athwart a crumbling wall, new vistas into the realms of literature or the paradise of the imagination. From a journey to Western England, I seem to recollect, where he had been attending an aunt or a grandmother at Bath, he brought back a lively account of how he had visited Bristol in pursuit of Thomas Chatterton, and had wandered along the quays beneath gigantic shuttered warehouses, still redolent of the rum and spices and hides imported by eighteenth-century merchant-adventurers. Vitality and imaginative sympathy were always among his most endearing traits ; and that sympathy is extended not only to his fellow human beings—whose relationships he studies and analyses with the perspicacity of a born novelist—but to the animal and vegetable world, of which he writes so feelingly in *The Unquiet Grave*, "slobbering melon, downy quince and dew-dusted nectarine ", and the series of fox-faced, black-gloved lemurs whom, during the 'thirties, he used to keep as pets. He has described them at some length in the latter section of his book ; but he does not refer to the graceful attitude they adopted when they were warming themselves at the bars of an electric stove, and sat poised on their elegant rumps with thick black-barred tails curved up behind them, stretching out small, delicate, marvellously human hands, like children before the nursery-hearth. This, he would explain, was the lemurs' attitude, at dawn amid their native tree-tops, when they gather to enjoy the rising sun after a chilly night below the leaves and utter a " sun-greeting call ", from which is said to have originated the word " Ra "—the name of the Egyptian sun-god and perhaps one of the earliest syllables in any human language.

Evidently, there is a close connection between Cyril Connolly in *The Unquiet Grave* and Coleridge as we know him through his letters and his notebooks. Each of them shows great mental activity combined with a disposition towards extreme sloth ; and, during the course of years, Connolly's indolence has become a well-established popular legend. But it is a legend he has done nothing to discourage ; and, being possessed of unusual strength of character, he has never allowed it to be held against him and, far from appearing to regret that he has published so little, he has often succeeded in convincing his friends that their own haphazard publications have been very much too numerous. ". . . The true function of a writer (he points out) is to produce a masterpiece . . . no other task is of any consequence "; and *The Unquiet Grave*, whether it succeeds or fails, is planned as a deliberate work of art, in which an attempt is made to lift the Self and its sorrows on to the level of imaginative literature. Such an attempt provides the impetus of every form of auto-biographical writing ; but only if the writer is a genuine artist can he finally transcend the limitations of his theme by exploring those aspects of the Self which link the ego with humanity at large—the essential, unchangeable elements of selfhood that Art alone can discover and display. For this purpose, he need not necessarily resort to the use of the magnetic pronoun. Most novels, we are frequently reminded, rest on some kind of autobiographical basis ; and there is no type of literary exercise in which the author completely conceals his identity. However impersonal his aim may be, however conscientiously he seeks to discard the Self, the desire to understand it, and come to terms with it, remains a dominant human preoccupation.

The Sign of the Fish

Among other services, the art of writing acts as a sovereign method of self-discovery and, at the same time, as a means of compensation for the flaws and weaknesses that self-analysis reveals. It is to his sense of personal insufficiency that we can trace many of a writer's virtues—he has resolved that he will cultivate in art the fine qualities that he was denied by Nature; and even his physical blemishes—Byron's twisted foot, Pope's deformed spine, Gibbon's smallness and undignified waddling gait—may exert a decisive effect upon the evolution of his literary style. Astrology is one of those pseudo-sciences which incorporate a number of provocative half-truths; and, born myself under the sign of Pisces, I am conscious of exhibiting several of the characteristics that an astrologer would attribute to me, and of endlessly waging war against them through the medium of the written word. On the credit side, the children of Pisces are said to be imaginative and intuitive; and from their ranks spring poets, actors and dancers—all people who enjoy variety and movement, abhor monotony and dread boredom. Simultaneously, they are described as creatures of habit, patient and persevering in the fishy manner; while unfriendly observers complain that they are also somewhat cold-blooded. Worse, under that wavering, watery spell, they lack consistency and intellectual clarity; and, to counterbalance their rare moments of intuition and illumination, they are hampered by a strain of muddle-headedness that often envelops them in a dense subaqueous fog. They show very little aptitude for any of the exact sciences; and, although their memories are extremely retentive of trifles, names, dates and similar important pieces of information constantly elude their grasp. It is because their mental processes are inclined to be slipshod that they admire stylistic definition; and their interest in style, as the years go on, may eventually affect their handwriting, until the business of shaping letters has become a form of primitive magic—if they write carefully, without blots or erasures, they imagine that the ideas they express may be correspondingly definite and clear. Like their fellow writers, they have a double aim—both to capture the essence of the Self and to escape from the baffling limitations of the individual temperament. Only thus can they hope to develop a heightened awareness of their own identity and create for themselves a literary *persona* that reflects the face beneath the face.

VIII

Crime and Punishment

DURING THE last fifty years, I suppose, I must now and then have set eyes upon an undetected murderer; but only two murderers, convicted of their crimes, have I ever watched across a court. The first wore a pale-plum-coloured suit and an expression of handsome, upright innocence : the second, a neat brown suit and a perhaps faintly dishonest, yet good-humoured and disarming, air. The name of the first I have long ago forgotten— possibly I failed to learn it; the newspapers paid him little attention ; and I had entered the court with a barrister I knew when he was appealing against the death sentence, and went out again, in time for a comfortable luncheon, while the issue was still unresolved. The young man's offence was that of matricide ; he was alleged to have cut his mother's throat with a razor as she lay asleep in bed, then walked quietly to the local police station, told the sergeant what he had done and pulled the razor from his coat pocket. He could not accompany it, however, with any coherent explanation of his act ; and, although in the past he was said to have had epileptic seizures, his crime remained almost as inexplicable as the events of some particularly hideous dream. One received the impression that he had woken from a nightmare, put out his hand and felt blood.

So there, bemused by his dream, he stood patiently behind the barrier of the dock, looking lonely yet stolid and reserved, wearing the " best suit ", with high padded shoulders, that he must have bought in some big provincial store. He was a miner and came of a large family ; and several members of his family had volunteered to give fresh evidence, the chief witness being his youngest sister, who, until I left the court, was standing huddled in the box. An unattractive and underdeveloped girl, twelve or thirteen years old, she had an expressionless, very white face, thrown into relief by her dismal black clothes ; and she was answering the questions of a tall young Scottish barrister, pink and robust beneath his threadbare wig. His method was to repeat her answers in his loud resonant Caledonian voice ; at which the senior Judge, a gentle old man, like one of the kindlier creatures of a Lewis Carroll fantasy, would re-echo the barrister's echo and, with a pencil unusually long and thick, slowly and deliberately write them down :

" Will you tell us what happened then ? "

" 'E got into bed with me."

" He got into bed with you."

" He—got—into—bed—with—you. You may proceed, Mr. Mackintosh."

Counsel for the defence next attempted to establish who had got into the witness's bed. It was her father. But how did she know it was her father ? " 'E was 'eavier ", replied the witness in the same husky, unaccented tones. The barrister's voice was deep and masculine : hers so thin and hoarse and low that we might have been listening to a grub or beetle, raked up from a pile of wet leaves and suddenly endowed with powers of speech. " He—was—heavier ", recorded the Judge ; and every word spun out the atrocious story—the story of a back-to-back house in some disconsolate northern mining town, where endless, aimless ribbons of streets stretch over the Yorkshire or Cumbrian ridges, and at the bottom of a bricky slope runs a dark and sluggish river. It was the House of Atreus or the House of Oedipus. The witness seemed unable to remember a time when either her father or her brother was not likely to invade her bed,

197

although her father, who was a cripple, slept in the scullery beside the sink. On the night of her mother's death, she continued to assert, dully but obstinately, that she had heard him crawling upstairs.

Her married sisters were now following her evidence ; it was they, apparently, who had instigated the appeal—two neat respectable-looking young women who would appear to have emerged from the same household without a blemish or a moral scar. They listened and watched and approved ; while the prisoner in the dock retained his stolid handsome poise, and the Judge's pencil crept over the paper, or momentarily he laid his pencil down and joined his aged hands upon the surface of the desk. Deeply impressive is the mechanism of Justice, measured and grave and unemotional ; but how difficult to avoid the suspicion that it had failed to capture certain elements of the story! The matricide or patricide is a recognised monster, whom the ancient Romans punished by drowning, having previously sewn the criminal into a sack that also contained a live ape. But there was nothing recognisably monstrous about the young man who now occupied the dock, no hint of brutal depravity about his commonplace proletarian features. But then, if the defence had at length succeeded in shifting the burden of guilt from the son to his bed-ridden father, might not the father himself have presented just as difficult a problem ? Hunted out of his scullery-refuge, he might have confronted us under the guise of a benevolent, though incestuous, patriarch, his genial face pitted with coal-dust and surmounted by a thatch of silvery hair.

As it was, the young man occupied the dock and eventually heard his appeal dismissed ; and my recollections were already becoming dim when, some twenty years later, I again entered a British court of justice and saw Crime and Punishment personified in an almost equally improbable set of figures. John George Haigh was one of the strangest personages ever associated with the profession of killing. At first sight, he suggested a motor-car salesman or perhaps a pedlar of domestic appliances, who had spent his life bustling to and fro along privet-hedged suburban roads or pattering up the concrete paths across innumerable tidy front-gardens. True, after his trial, a rumour went about that he had once been the boon companion of Neville Heath, a murderer of a very different and possibly far more dreadful breed, and that both had been attached to a minor drinking-school that met at a public house off Knightsbridge. There in an atmosphere of Air Force slang, pink gins and cigarette-smoke, Heath would casually expound his idiosyncratic views on love and women, recommending the pleasures of flagellation, which, he said, promoted masculine energy, while the ordinary approach to sexual enjoyment involved a kind of intimate defeat. But Haigh himself, despite his alleged regard for his crony, was a modest, unassuming character ; and the crime reporters, who wrote up the story of his life, found it impossible—though some strenuous efforts were made—to provide the copy they produced with the right degree of " love interest ". His last habitat was a quiet residential hotel, the type of hotel at which guests in the restaurant seldom speak above a half-whisper and pass their evening hours amid the palm trees of the lounge completing the *Times* crossword puzzle. In these surroundings he exerted his charm upon an elderly widow named Mrs. Durand-Deacon, who, I am told, had been accustomed to inform her nieces that a gentlewoman was known by her ability to keep her photograph out of the newspapers, but who had succumbed to the ingratiating small-talk of her gentlemanly acquaintance at the next table. She agreed to visit his laboratory-shed in Sussex, where he had arranged for her a hideous and ridiculous end.

Haigh's arrangements show the keen attention to detail that distinguishes a good domestic manager—he had previously drawn up a pencilled shopping-list : suitable drum, handy stirrup-pump, apron, pair of rubber gloves, as well as a fresh carboy containing ten gallons of sulphuric acid ; yet with his executive gifts went a remarkable strain of recklessness or carelessness. No sooner had Mrs. Durand-Deacon crossed the threshold of his squalid backyard laboratory, in which—a macabre invention—he had told her that he proposed to manufacture artificial finger-nails, than he shot her through the base of the skull, stripped her of her jewellery and fur coat, consigned her body to the empty drum and left it there while he ordered a light meal, which included a pot of tea and a poached egg on toast, at a local eating-place oddly entitled "Ye Olde Ancient Priors' Restaurant". Having eaten, he returned to work and carefully filled the drum with acid ; then, once the corpse had begun to disintegrate into the form of animal residue known as " sludge ", ordered and ate a second meal and placidly drove home to London. Yet, although among his previous exploits were five profitable murders accomplished by much the same method, he had forgotten that even sulphuric acid might fail to destroy the evidence completely—it spared, in fact, a set of false teeth, three gallstones, numerous corroded fragments of bone, a metal lipstick-case and the plastic handle of a bag; and he was also singularly rash or incautious when Mrs. Durand-Deacon's friends, noticing that she had suddenly disappeared, raised a public hue-and-cry. So eager and talkative were his offers to assist the police that he eventually aroused their slow suspicions. Simultaneously, they happened to learn that he had served various brief terms of imprisonment as a petty swindler. Haigh was arrested, interrogated and, after some bland enquiries about the chances of being released from a criminal lunatic asylum, volunteered to make a full statement.

There followed his trial at Lewes Assizes in July 1949 ; and for the occasion, with a friendly editor's help, I became a front-page crime-reporter. Naturally enough, I received very little encouragement from my fellow journalists. The court was small; tickets of admission were extremely hard to come by ; and until the close of the first day it proved almost impossible to pass the obstinate country policemen at the door, and I spent a good deal of my time sitting in a tap-room opposite, watching the comings and goings of barristers and reporters as they darted importantly up and down the steps. Much earlier, the personification of Justice had appeared and deliberately climbed those steps, very old, swaddled in ermine and scarlet, accompanied by a ritual fanfare ; and, before I could claim my ticket and persuade the policemen on guard to let me enter the gallery, the prosecution's case against John George Haigh had already reached its final stages. From my post, I could not see the prisoner—only the Judge, counsel, jury and the witness then occupying the box were completely visible; and at that moment a witness was being asked to identify some mysterious objects in a cardboard container, which I afterwards discovered to have been Mrs. Durand-Deacon's false teeth. A neat middle-aged person, she was bending over them with apprehensive interest, as if she felt that these deathly relics might still possess a malevolent life of their own. Elsewhere no flicker of emotion disturbed the heavy atmosphere of the court. A broad bar of sunshine, full of luminous specks, slanted athwart it from the central glass roof.

Then the Judge rose ; and the group of grey-pated, rook-winged barristers rose in unison and spread their rusty plumage. As I had not yet been able to see Haigh, I hurried at once to the front of the gallery, and found that I stood immediately above him, and that he had turned and was now gazing upwards. A smile, gentle, positively beatific, illuminated his neatly modelled, undistinguished face—a smile that came direct from the eyes, with nothing behind its candid effulgence that might possibly have suggested shame or fear. It was a look of affectionate recognition, intended, I saw, for a rather pretty young woman standing close beside me. Haigh had been married at the age of twenty-four ; but the marriage had soon broken down ; and during his later years he had become devoted—with a devotion that remained wholly innocent—to the young daughter of a businessman who employed him in his engineering firm. Their friendship, Haigh wrote from prison, had provided the mainstay of " five happy years "; she would always be in his thoughts; "you know I have been proud of our association : it has always been an honourable one." * The young woman's privacy, however, was not respected by the British press ; an enterprising group of journalists had popularised her as "Haigh's girl friend "; and in that rôle she had been brought to Lewes and occupied a seat above the dock. Haigh was evidently glad to see her ; gladness and gratitude warmed his smile. Their encounter afforded a curious contrast to the impersonal atmosphere that had prevailed in court, where any display of human feeling would have seemed irrelevant and slightly suspect. They exchanged glances ; then he turned away and walked off quietly towards the cells below.

The second day of the trial at Lewes was even stranger than the first. Again tickets were difficult to come by, and some hours had again to be passed in the hotel just across the street, which was crowded with lawyers' clerks and miscellaneous feature-writers, among whom were two popular novelists, Peter Cheyney and Louis Golding—Cheyney distinguished by an eye-glass and a boldly coloured check waistcoat : his colleague, small and hirsute, exhibiting an air of dusky eastern wisdom. From time to time, some piece of news arrived—for example, that the Prosecution had dealt severely with an expert witness, the only witness that the Defence had decided to call, since their efforts were entirely concentrated on obtaining a verdict of " Guilty but Insane ". Before I could enter the court, the expert witness had vanished ; and now I found a different seat. It was exactly behind, and a little above, the dock, with the well of the court and the judicial bench beyond. Facing me sat the judge, the octogenarian Mr. Justice Humphreys, his pale, narrow, deeply lined face all the paler for his scarlet robes ; on my left, the patient jury—eleven men and a motherly woman, whose name I discovered to be Mary English, and who wore an exceedingly

* *The Trial of John George Haigh.* Edited by Lord Dunboyne. Notable British Trials Series.

202

English-looking straw hat; below me, between the prisoner and
the judge, a group of grey-and-black counsel. Blanketed in
heat and stillness, the court-room resembled a huge aquarium;
the dusty sunbeams that fell from the roof glistened on its
varnished woodwork; and the low panelled partitions that enclosed the dock shone a sticky chestnut-brown. Haigh was
leaning negligently back; it seemed clear that he was feeling
drowsy.

He alone appeared to take very little interest in the business
that absorbed the court—the closing speech for the Prosecution
delivered by the Socialist Attorney-General, Sir Hartley Shaw-
cross, its counterpart, the speech for the Defence, by Sir David
Maxwell Fyfe, and the Judge's carefully detailed summing-up,
which handed the case over for the jury's decision. Each of these
weighty protagonists had his own mannerisms and his own style;
and together they formed a variegated pattern of personal characters and legal points of view. Thus the tall, fine-featured
Attorney-General was elegant, incisive, caustic, an exemplar of
the practised legal intelligence, concerned with facts, contemptuous of speculations—" the speculations and the opinions and
the theories of the psychiatrists and the psychologists and the
alienists and the medical specialists ", professors of an alleged
branch of science that " bears upon its face the motto that ' a little
knowledge is a dangerous thing ' ". Our law, in its wisdom and
experience, had laid down " certain specific tests which juries
were invited and indeed directed to apply when they are considering . . . whether a defendant who seeks so to do has made
out and discharged the onus of proving that he is insane and
therefore entitled to be excused from criminal responsibility . . ."
The tests that he referred to were incorporated in the famous
McNaghten Rules, " laid down a very long time ago and considered time and again in decisions since they were originally
promulgated ". According to those rules, " it is for the Defence
to show . . . that by reason of some disease of the mind . . . the
prisoner either did not know what he was doing, did not know

the nature and quality of his acts, or . . . did not know that that which he was doing was wrong." *

Sir David Maxwell Fyfe, addressing the jury, had had a far more difficult and unwelcome task ; and, as he spoke, he often reminded me of a fully armed mediæval warrior, courageously attempting to hack his way through the cobwebs and shadows of some enchanted forest, where the foliage dripped with blood and boughs bristled with obscene symbols. But, broadly built, bull-necked, resolute, he continued indefatigably to thrust ahead, pausing now and then to make some brief remark on the sheer unpleasantness of such a mental journey, so remote from the habitat of ordinary decent men and women. It was distasteful to anyone, he observed in an apologetic aside "—believe me, it is distasteful to me—when the examination of a byway of the mind leads into the approach to matters which are profound in their effect on our lives ; but I have to consider it, just as an infinite line of lawyers . . . have had to consider it, because it is our duty to investigate the case in front of us and try to present its different facets to you . . ." The prisoner had claimed that he committed homicide, impelled by a desire to drink his victim's blood ; he also claimed that, since his youth, he had been accustomed to drink his own urine ; and he had spoken of terrible and sanguinary dreams that preceded every attack of homicidal mania. The expert witness, whom the Defence had called, had described Haigh as suffering from a paranoiac constitution, and explained that the paranoiac " becomes a living anachronism " who reverts to the reprehensible customs of his savage ancestors, maintaining that they increase and improve " the vital force in him which answers to the spirit which controls him." Here Sir David introduced a passing, almost a deprecatory, reference to Frazer's work *The Golden Bough*—a " repository of savage practices ", he said, that he did not pretend to have studied himself and doubted if any of the jury had studied. Haigh had adopted those practices, obeying the dictates of a radically

* Op. cit.

diseased mind; he had developed "the delusion and precon-
ception that he was specially controlled by the divine mystic
force behind the world . . . and from that came the delusion that
this force compelled and demanded that he should commit the
murders and drink this blood. By reason of that . . . I submit
to you there is only one conclusion, that he did not know that
he was doing what was wrong ".*

Another three or four measured sentences, and Sir David
closed his case. Meanwhile the "living anachronism" in the
dock was quietly fidgeting through the long, hot day. As he
leant back, his sleek round head rested against the panelled
half door—the door that divided the dock from the staircase to
the cells below. Occasionally, it threatened to swing open and,
with a lazy, slightly irritable movement, he turned his shoulders
to refasten it. Otherwise he did not change his position; never
did he lift his head and bend forward—even when the Judge was
delivering his charge to the jury, and the case built up for the
Defence was being slowly, methodically broken down. The
Attorney-General had kept his speech quiet, clear and low-toned;
Sir David had permitted himself some touches of oratorical
gusto; the Judge's method of speaking was notably quiet and
restrained, but here and there he seemed to remove an irrelevance
as if he were flicking aside a scrap of paper. Gravely paternal in
his attitude towards the jury, he appeared, like Dr. Johnson, to
be inviting them to rid their minds of cant; and, indeed, there
was something that recalled the eighteenth century about this
twentieth-century minister of Justice—the large forehead above
heavily pouched eyes, the dark furrows of that octogenarian mask,
the deep lines that curved from the nostrils past the corners of
the wide mouth with its reflective drooping underlip.

He, too, carefully recapitulated the provisions of the dread
McNaghten Rules, and suggested that the jury should remember
that the expert witness called by the Defence—" a highly qualified
gentleman; there are many, one is happy to know, in this

* Op. cit.

country who have given their lives to mental diseases rather than to rheumatism or any other bodily disease, and no doubt they know a good deal about it "—had himself at length been obliged to admit that the prisoner had understood the nature of what he was doing and understood that it was wrong. " Members of the jury, if I were to say to you that you ought to follow the opinion of Dr. Yellowlees, that would be in terms telling you to find a verdict of guilty . . ." From that moment his listeners perceived how the decision must inevitably fall, and that any attempt to portray Haigh in the guise of a crazy paranoiac theorist could be discounted as mere delusive verbiage. The expert witness had told them that Haigh revealed a " cheerful, bland indifference to the crime "; but he had agreed that it was " not at all uncommon that a man who has committed murder is quite indifferent for some reason or other, quite callous about the matter, and this man is." Haigh was also said to have displayed the demented æsthete's cloven hoof, when he asserted, discussing his previous convictions, that now and then he had derived an " artistic joy " from scoring off the people he swindled. " If that is artistic, well and good ", commented the Judge with telling emphasis. Nor was he impressed by the assertion that Haigh's lack of sexual ardour revealed a lack of mental balance. True, it had helped to make an unpleasant case perhaps a little less intolerable ; it was " really rather a comfort in a way ; one gets rather tired in these courts of sex complexes . . ." *

At twenty-three minutes past three, the jury retired to consider its verdict ; and the journalists, except myself—I had been warned that, if I gave up my place, I might be unable to enter the court again—trampled out into the street beyond. A sudden alarm brought them hurrying back ; the jury, we heard, was returning after only seventeen minutes ; and in filed that respectable assemblage of ordinary level-headed citizens charged with the most extraordinary duty that they had ever been called upon to undertake. As they settled down and formed

* Op. cit.

a silent row, the atmosphere of the court-room became doubly dense and still. Their foreman stood ; the prisoner stood; the Clerk of Assizes put the expected questions. Were they agreed upon their verdict ? The foreman answered that they were. Next : " Do you find the prisoner, John George Haigh, guilty or not guilty of murdering Mrs. Durand-Deacon, or do you find him guilty but insane ? " " Guilty of murdering Mrs. Durand-Deacon ", replied the foreman in a somewhat hesitant and breathless tone. " Is that the verdict of you all ? " " That is the unanimous verdict ". Whereupon the machinery of justice seemed to recoil for a prodigious final move, and its attention swept towards Haigh, standing planted at the front of the wooden dock. He might have himself been sculptured in wood, a small statue of painted and varnished deal—hair so glossy and un-ruffled that it resembled neatly painted hair : roundish shoulders, straightened to meet his audience, beneath a trim uncrumpled coat : his hands linked at the base of his spine like the hands of an infantryman ordered to " stand easy ". So long as he stood there, he neither shifted nor flinched ; and, if he was feeling any strong emotion, it did not appear until he spoke. Asked whether he had " anything to say why sentence of death should not be passed upon him according to law ", he responded quickly : " None at all ", when " Nothing at all " * were the words that he had evidently meant to use. His voice was high and fluting ; he had a noticeably refined accent.

Now, of course, there was nothing to do but perform the last terrific rites. I had imagined that the " Black Cap " was some kind of decorative antique head-covering, and was astonished to watch a rectangle of cloth—no more impressive than a black duster—being arranged by his attendant across the summit of the Judge's wig, where it stuck or hung somewhat precariously as if it had been dropped from heaven by a passing bird. The ancient formula of the death sentence for murder, as it was still

---

* These words are attributed to him in the printed account of his trial. At the time, however, I was impressed by his slip. Apart from his plea of " Not Guilty ", it was the only phrase that he pronounced in court.

employed ten years ago, is an admirable specimen of pre-Romantic English prose, a long-drawn continuous array of syllables running heavily towards its climax, with a single semi-colon to mark the brief pause between the pronouncement of doom and the final expression of hope :

> " John George Haigh, the sentence of the Court upon you is that you be taken from this place to a lawful prison, and thence to a place of execution, and that you there suffer death by hanging, and that your body be afterwards buried within the precincts of the prison in which you shall have been confined before your execution ; and may the Lord have mercy on your soul."

Although the Judge did not dramatise his phrases—his voice remained cool and quiet and steady—they were as deeply chilling, in the effect they produced, as the crucial phrases of the Burial Service, which commit dust to dust, and ashes to the realm of ashes. But Haigh accepted them calmly, if one could judge from the motionless slope of his shoulders ; and, when he turned for the last time to descend the stairs, his face displayed a faint unchanging smile—the smile of a man, charged with a minor motoring offence, who had expected a fine of ten or fifteen guineas, but found, to his half-amused dismay, that conviction would set him back a good deal more. A smile " on the wrong side of his face "; yet unmistakably a smile it was.

In May 1817, during his only visit to Rome, Byron decided to attend an execution. It was an occasion of considerable pomp and ceremony—" the *masqued* priests ; the half-naked executioners ; the bandaged criminals ; the black Christ and his banner ; the scaffold ; the soldiery ; the slow procession, and the quick rattle and heavy fall of the axe ; the splash of the blood, and the ghastliness of the exposed heads . . ." But, although two of the felons "behaved calmly enough", the first to approach the guillotine " died with great terror and reluctance, which (he notes) was very horrible "; his hand shook so violently that he could scarcely hold his opera-glasses ; and he felt "quite hot and thirsty" when justice had at length been done. I experienced much the same sensations as I stumbled forth into the sunshine of Lewes High Street—an odd dryness of the throat and palate, accompanied by a tremulous tightening of the nerves. Yet there could be no doubt that the prisoner at the bar had received a fair and careful trial ; no doubt that, according to definition laid down in the McNaghten Rules, the jury, however merciful their mood, could scarcely have been expected to find him guilty but insane. Each of the crimes he was known to have committed had brought him in a substantial reward ; except for his own evidence, there was not the slightest proof that he had experienced sadistic dreams and delusions ; and at the police station he had made some artful enquiries about the possibility of being released from Broadmoor. What other conclusion could the patient jury have reached ? And yet Haigh himself still presented a problem completely insoluble in the terms of criminal law.

The law, after all, must pronounce on facts, with a secondary regard for motives ; it does not—it cannot—attempt to investigate the secrets of a human character ; and Haigh's secret lay hidden beneath a bland, disarming smile—the warm smile that I had intercepted when he looked up towards his friend in the gallery : the faintly rueful, yet unaffected, smile that he had displayed as he prepared to leave the dock. Years later, among Turgenev's reminiscences, I read his memorable account of how, during the January of 1870, he attended the execution of the French mass-murderer Tropmann, visited him in his cell on the morning of his death, and watched the condemned man being made ready. Turgenev's first impression was of a "young, black-haired, black-eyed face, which, moving slowly from left to right", surveyed his visitors with "huge round eyes". But that air of intensity soon diminished ; he observed the small crowd that occupied the room "calmly, almost somnolently"; and Turgenev was now impressed by the strangely commonplace look of the young man whom the warders were stripping and binding. Tropmann's face "could have been described as handsome but for the unpleasantly full lips, which made his mouth protrude a little too much and turn upwards funnel-like, just as with animals, and behind his lips were two rows of bad, sparse, fan-like teeth. He had thick, slightly wavy, dark hair, long eyebrows, expressive protruding eyes, a wide clear forehead, a regular, slightly aquiline nose, little curls of black down on his chin . . ." If one had happened to meet such a man outside prison, the impression he produced might not have been un-favourable ; there were hundreds of such young faces to be seen in factories, schools and institutions. Tropmann resembled an "overgrown boy, and, indeed, he was not yet twenty. He had a natural, healthy, slightly rosy complexion . . . He did not raise his eyes and his breathing was regular and deep, like a man walking up a steep hill. Once or twice he shook his hair as though wishing to dismiss a troublesome thought, tossed back his head, threw a quick glance at the ceiling and heaved a hardly perceptible sigh." *

Of the commonplace quality of Haigh's appearance I have written in an earlier passage. It was uncommonly smooth and neat—those were the adjectives that at once occurred to me : a round skull, covered with smooth hair ; a smooth, decently proportioned forehead : neat ears set close to the head : sharp eyes placed respectably far apart : a small neatly trimmed mous-tache above an unaggressive mouth-line. By some stretch of the imagination, one might perhaps have claimed that he looked a trifle shifty ; but it was not a shiftiness that would necessarily have struck the observer who was unacquainted with his criminal record ; and that ready smile would probably have disarmed even the most cantankerous and suspicious housewife, who answered a ring at her suburban door and found him waiting bag in hand, prepared to sell her an insurance policy or distribute free samples. "A person very well dressed, very well spoken, with

---

* *Turgenev's Literary Reminiscences and Autobiographical Fragments,* translated by David Margarshack.

a moustache " was the description given by a witness at his trial, on whom Haigh had called to collect an acid-resistant steel drum —the drum that he had bought to employ for the liquidation of Mrs. Durand-Deacon. He was a gentlemanly representative of a section of society in which " gentlemanly ", like " well-dressed ", is a powerful and important word. Had he been un-gentlemanly, bohemian or " common ", he could scarcely have captured his last victim, a gentlewoman proud of her ability to avoid any form of public notice. His accent, as I heard myself, had a dulcet Kensingtonian ring.

Yet Haigh, as we subsequently learned, was not a product of the London middle class. He had been born in the industrial Midlands, where his father was employed first at an electricity works, afterwards at a colliery. His parents, poor and upright, were pious members of a nonconformist sect, the Peculiar People, whose stern religious beliefs coloured every action of their daily lives. " They lived by precepts (he remembered), and they talked in parables. It is true to say that I was nurtured on Bible stories, mostly concerned with sacrifice ". Later, having developed a taste for music, he became a chorister at Wakefield Cathedral. There the services in which he joined were " highly ritualistic "; and the Defence put forward a suggestion, when he stood his trial at Lewes, that the sudden change in his surroundings, between the ages of ten and sixteen—from his parents' " harsh and circumscribed " household to the splendiferous background of a High Church cathedral, with its chants and its pageantry and the effigy of a bleeding Christ on which he said that he had often gazed—had somehow radically distorted the growth of his adolescent mind, encouraging the development of those paranoiac delusions, dreams of blood and forests of blood-stained crosses, that would presently impel him to commit murder. That was the theory of the expert witness, which Counsel for the Defence had courageously expounded ; and in conversation with his legal advisers Haigh seems to have given them all the help he could ; though whether he was " playing up " and following the psychiatrist's lead, exaggerating the vague fantasies that had haunted his youth because he had discovered that they had a legal value, or telling the true story of his paranoiac torments, since he has paid the penalty it is now impossible to determine. But, as seen from a layman's point of view, Haigh did not appear " mad ". He asserted—the assertion was never substantiated—that, among the murders he had committed, two at least had had no mercenary motive ; but the others—six in all—increased his bank balance by several thousand pounds. They were carefully planned and precisely executed. Nor, considering his aims and methods, did they involve any unnecessary loss of life. Having murdered both the Hendersons, he took good care of the dog they had left behind. At times, however, he was unduly reckless ; and this, according to his own account, was the result of relying on super-natural guidance : " I felt convinced there was an overseeing hand which would protect me ". But then, such a conviction has also been held by many great and famous personages—by Cromwell, for example, who saw the Will of God plainly manifest through everything he did. In Haigh, it may have been merely the sublimation of a profound and ineradicable conceit.

Plainly Haigh's was a calculating spirit, adroit and acquisitive rather than self-destructive ; and, despite all his fiendish actions, he impressed me as a curiously trivial character, distinguished from the rest of humanity not by his temperament but by his deeds, by what he happened to have done under the influence of a way of thought that contemporary psychologists have not yet explored. A Christian moralist presumably would equate that influence with the power of Evil. But to depict Haigh as devil-possessed is not only to allow him a dignity he did not deserve : it implies that his brain was the vehicle of some positive rebellious energy. His nature, I think, can best be explained in terms of the characteristics that his make-up lacked, of the blank spaces—patches of mental darkness—where his kindlier instinct could not function. Nothing will persuade me that he was unrelievedly

Crime and Punishment

cruel, or that his crimes had a genuinely sadistic origin : there seems no doubt that he was capable of affection, and that with his gift for disinterested affection went an aptitude for human sympathy : his courage at his trial would have been noted and admired had he faced the court as a political prisoner. If his virtues were few, there was no disputing them. They were un-co-ordinated, however, in any emotional and intellectual scheme.

To vary the image, the criminal's mind should perhaps be represented as the keyboard of a piano, in which some keys respond to the touch, while others remain permanently dead. Thus, although Haigh was capable of feeling, on certain subjects he registered no emotion ; for the men and women he murdered he seems to have felt neither hatred nor pity ; at the most, the feelings they aroused may have amounted to a mild contempt. The phenomenon is not so rare that a writer, interested in more far-reaching problems of human conduct, can afford to dis-regard it. Since 1914 we have lived through a period of tremen-dous international crimes ; and a good many of these crimes have been planned and committed by politicians and busy civil servants. The twentieth-century Genghis Khan very often sits behind a desk, and hands on his projects of destruction to the bureaucrats outside his office, who accept the liquidation of an entire race or social group as merely part of their official duties, and in their turn produce a typewritten directive, which, at a lower level, sets their subordinates to work marshalling " death trains ", arming execution squads and building concrete gas-chambers. For every sadistic executioner, there are several dozen bureaucrats ; and even the executioners are sometimes activated by an impersonal devotion to duty rather than an inbred love of cruelty. How illuminating is the account, pub-lished in a recent book on the Hitlerian régime,* of Tremblinka extermination camp ! Here the director and his staff were partic-ularly proud of their efficient methods, and disdained the rough-and-ready procedure employed in less enlightened institutions.

* *Gestapo : Instrument of Tyranny*, by Edward Crankshaw.

The " self-contained Diesels " that kept the gas-chambers humming were all of the latest and trimmest pattern. Better still, the entry to the camp was a " very smart 'Potemkin' railway station ", a perfect model of an ordinary station built at the end of the fatal siding, with bogus posters and railway time-tables plastered cheerfully across its walls. Passengers who alighted on the brightly lit platform had the impression that they were simply changing trains ; they did not discover, until they had been shepherded into the camp, that they had reached a deathly terminus. Hence all unnecessary trouble was avoided ; there were no confusing and distressing scenes. The staff of Tremblinka Camp piqued themselves on their superior humanity. One thinks of Haigh feeding and exercising his victims' favourite red setter.

Just as significant, however, as the nature of these international tragedies is the reaction they have often provoked among modern Men of Good Will. Before the outbreak of the Second World War, Hitler's treatment of the Jewish race found not a few apologists, who either denied the existence of concentration and extermination camps, or declared that the evils of the Nazi régime had been monstrously over-emphasized. And then, on the other side, we have all of us listened to some pained and angry Fellow Traveller, earnestly explaining away Russian policy towards the kulaks or defending, as " rough horse medicine ", the disciplinary methods adopted by the existing Chinese government. They, too, our Men of Good Will, like the liquidators and the executioners, would appear to have lost, or deliberately tampered with, some of the keys in their emotional keyboard, curtailing its range of responsiveness and gradually diminishing their gift of sympathy. At such a moment, the artist has a doubly important part to play ; for, although he has sometimes been described as a dangerous natural anarchist—and anarchists and criminals have frequently been lumped together—the chief object of his creative efforts is to extend our limited emotional range, to explore old feelings, elicit new emotions and generally heighten our awareness of the horror and the beauty of the world in which we live. Despite the antagonism he often provokes and the aggressive form that his vision of life may assume, he sympathizes, constantly and intensely, with the experience of his fellow human beings, with their defeats and their victories, their degradation and their pride alike. Two anecdotes that I read not long ago seem to illustrate the character of the artist's mind, and underline the eternal division between the imaginative artist and the mundane opportunist. The first of them concerns a famous painter who, during the troubled period that followed the liberation of Paris, when he heard reports of mysterious shootings in the streets, declared that his own allegiance, regardless of party, lay with " the people being fired on ". The second story is related of Talleyrand, that arch-politician, who possibly engineered, and certainly condoned, the execution of the Duc d'Enghien, one of the darkest crimes committed by Napoleon and his ministers. During the Revolution of July 1830, while a chaotic street-battle was being fought beneath his windows, " I see that we are winning " he remarked to his attendants. " Who are *we*, Monseigneur ? " they asked. " Hush ", said the shrewd old man, " I'll tell you tomorrow ".

IX

Maladies and Professional Hazards

EVERY WRITER must sometimes envy the chaotic profusion of a painter's studio and, despite grit and rubble underfoot and dusky cavernous spaces overhead, the austere cathedral-like surroundings in which a sculptor battles against clay or stone. By comparison, how airless and characterless is the setting of the average writer's work—a single smallish room that has as its focal point a bleak oblong of unwritten paper, islanded on the surface of his desk amid the meagre apparatus of his trade ! Humanity learned to think and feel when our first ancestors began to use their hands ; and a strange satisfaction is still to be discovered in any form of expert manual labour. But very little of this satisfaction rewards the movement of the hand that holds a pen ; for, whereas the painter and the sculptor can translate their inward struggle into bodily terms—their chosen medium becomes a friendly adversary : the battle that they wage is at once physical and intellectual : they depend not only upon " inspiration " but upon varying degrees of technical accomplishment—a literary artist is obliged to wage his wars inside the narrow circumference of his own head, while he does so transmitting a series of reports through a range of cramped and unco-operative fingers, which perform their task with none of the zest that accompanies the handling of a brush or the direction of a chisel. His sheet of paper is merely a patient victim : there is nothing physically pleasurable in the act of covering and disfiguring it.

Hence, I have often suspected, much of the irritability and nervous instability that are apt to overcloud a literary life. Literature is not a health-giving business ; and there are moments, indeed, when the annals of literature suggest a view of some gigantic hospital, where all the diseases are represented as a visitor passes down the wards. In successive periods, different agents of death have helped to fill those gloomy chambers—in the early nineteenth century, the tubercule bacillus, which took so large a toll of the Romantic artists : at a later stage, the insidious spirochæte, which riddled and destroyed so many gifted brains. And then, besides diseases that cannot be directly linked with the hazards of the literary calling, there are a host of mysterious illnesses that appear to be reserved for writers, or to be far more prevalent among writers than among any other group of men. According to a French physician, men of genius are particularly vulnerable in the region of the liver; and equally undefended are the stomach and the intestinal tract. One remembers the Goncourts, who left an exhaustive record of their painful and unnerving symptoms : Coleridge, whose disorders included severe attacks of nervous dyspepsia, which were the effect, presumably, as well as the cause, of his habitual state of irresolution : and De Quincey, whose agonizing stomachic cramps first drove him to abuse drugs. Even the scientists and philosophers have frequently succumbed to psychosomatic maladies ; Darwin was regularly confined to his sofa by an internal affliction that defied cure ; while Herbert Spencer, most prosaic and pragmatic of the great Victorian prophets, although his stomach and liver seem to have escaped harm, experienced during early middle age what he called a " cerebral congestion ", which, as he grew older, made it quite impossible to work uninterruptedly for more than three hours. Should he do so, he suffered from a sensation in his skull—" not pain, nor fulness, nor tension, but simply a sensation "; and he was therefore obliged to take his amanuensis out on to the waters of the lake in Regent's Park, " row vigorously for five minutes and dictate for a quarter of an hour ", after

217

which another burst of activity would be followed by a further explosion of ideas.*

No less significant, however, are the maladies that affect the mind alone, the spells of melancholy, lassitude and despair that have always troubled the creative artist, especially the artist who deals with words and with the impalpable images that words evoke. For, above everything else, he values definition ; and the clarity of outline at which he aims repeatedly eludes his grasp ; words turn traitor and revolt against his command ; a hopeful project sinks back into the matrix of chaos from which he has been struggling to disengage it. After such struggles, the baffled creator may feel a catastrophic loss of faith and hope—of faith not only in the art he serves but in the meaning of his own existence. Temporarily, at least, he ceases to believe that he has any individual talents, and is overwhelmed by that sense of general hopelessness and powerlessness, of despondency combined with sloth, known as *acedia* or *accidie*. Once again Coleridge, our foremost literary invalid, describes the condition in a moving passage :

> " A sense of weakness (he wrote to Robert Southey, on August 1st, 1803), a haunting sense that I was an herbaceous plant, as large as a large tree, with a trunk of the same girth, and branches as large and shadowing, but with pith within the trunk, not heart of wood—that I had power not strength, an involuntary impostor, that I had no real Genius, no real depth. This on my honour is as fair a statement of my habitual haunting, as I could give before the tribunal of Heaven. How it arose in me, I have but lately discovered . . . The whole History of this feeling would form a curious page in a *nosologia spiritualis* . . ."

Though his correspondence includes many revealing hints,

* Thomas Huxley considered that Spencer's symptoms might be due, not to overwork but to excessive chastity, and advised him to try the effect of " gynopathy ", or marriage. See *Herbert Spencer: The Philosopher of Evolution* by J. W. Burrow. *History To-day*, October, 1958.

Maladies and Professional Hazards

Coleridge's spiritual case-history remained unwritten ; and it is difficult to decide whether he failed in the work he meant to do because he was burdened throughout his life by a weak digestion and ill-functioning nerves, which the remedies he adopted usually tended to exasperate : or whether his health was defective because some psychological obstacle always interposed between the artist and his plans. But it is clear that his brain and his body conspired to one another's disadvantage, and just as clear that, had he been sound and healthy, his occasional flashes of genius might have lacked their peculiarly vivid colouring. His strokes of creative energy show all the pent-up force of an intensely frustrated and disappointed man.

From habits of sloth and the sense of guilt they bred sprang the inspiration of *The Ancient Mariner*, already several years old when Coleridge composed his letter to Southey, in which the way-worn pilgrim, the poet himself, fastens with neurotic obstinacy upon the apprehensive wedding-guest—as Coleridge was accustomed to fasten upon the helpless recipients of his table-talk—and the albatross symbolises the load of remorse that he had been carrying since his early manhood. Evidently, the hypochondriac and the man of genius were too closely connected ever to be disentangled ; and an old problem, often debated in the past, confronts the sympathetic, but healthy-minded, reader. Are sickness and literary talent part of an identical human pattern? Do certain morbid conditions encourage the genesis of works of art ? Some support for this theory may be found in the critical writings of various gifted poets. Besides comparing the artist to a child, equipped with adult intelligence and adult critical perceptions, Baudelaire also likens him to a man who has lately recovered from a grave illness—a convalescent who is rediscovering the world, which reappears in all its pristine splendour; whereas the child, on the threshold of life, examines it for the first time through fresh unclouded eyes. Similarly, T. S. Eliot, who composed *The Waste Land* during the period of convalescence following a serious physical shock, has expressed the belief that

" some forms of ill-health, debility or anæmia, may (if other circumstances are propitious) produce an efflux of poetry . . .   To
me it seems that at these moments . . . what happens is something
negative: that is to say, not ' inspiration ' as we commonly think
of it, but the breaking down of strong habitual barriers . . ." *
Illness has simplified the business of living and, while he was
still concentrated on the task of keeping alive, has freed the
poet's mind from supernumerary cares.   Thus he recaptures
the innocent vision of youth, which he proceeds to translate
into words with adult discrimination and an adult grasp of
language.

Other experiences may produce the same result by breaking
down our mental barriers ; and here troubles that afflict the mind
prove as efficacious as disorders that attack the body.   I have
already mentioned the moods of melancholy and lassitude that
are apt to descend upon every imaginative artist ; but some of
these moods, although the symptoms they engender are apparently weakening and disabling, may tend, before the mood has
passed, to give his imagination a new and sharper edge.   Melancholy, of course, has many different faces ; and, under the
heading " The Sick Soul " and " The Divided Self ", in his
Varieties of Religious Experience, William James has portrayed
them at length, ranging from *anhedonia,* which designates a condition of universal joylessness, to the " worst kind of melancholy
. . . that which takes the form of panic fear." He quotes Tolstoy's
Confession as an admirable account of how *anhedonia* affects the
spirit.   The novelist was then fifty years old and at the height of
his immense creative powers ; but " I felt (he writes) that something had broken within me on which my life had always rested,
that I had nothing to hold on to, and that morally my life had
stopped . . .   It cannot be said exactly that I wished to kill
myself, for the force which drew me away from life was fuller,
more powerful, more general than any mere desire . . .   All this
took place at a time when so far as all my outer circumstances

* *The Use of Poetry,* quoted by John Press in *The Fire and the Fountain.*

went, I ought to have been completely happy . . . And yet I could give no reasonable meaning to any actions of my life." Every support appeared to have fallen away ; that life was meaningless and absurd, he decided, " is the only incontestable knowledge accessible to man."

With Tolstoy, the desperate seeker for truth, James contrasts John Bunyan, the devoted fugitive from Hell. During my own childhood, I was often deeply alarmed by Doré's illustrations in a copy of *Pilgrim's Progress*—Christian weeping and trembling, having deserted all whom he knew and loved, standing bowed beneath the ominous load he carried against a night-sky dimly streaked by flames. A sense of terror pervaded the engraver's work ; and just as acute is the feeling of apprehension that radiates from Bunyan's autobiography :

" I was both a burthen and a terror to myself ; not did I ever so know, as now, what it was to be weary of my life, and yet afraid to die. How gladly would I have been anything but myself ! Anything but a man ! and in any condition but my own."

James also quotes from the evidence provided by an anonymous French writer, who for some time, he explains, had been labouring under a mood of " general depression " and " philosophic pessimism : "

" Whilst in this state . . . I went one evening into a dressing-room in the twilight . . . when suddenly there fell on me without any warning . . . a horrible fear of my own existence. Simultaneously there arose in my mind the image of an epileptic patient whom I had seen in the asylum, a black-haired youth with greenish skin, entirely idiotic, who used to sit all day on one of the benches, or rather shelves, against the wall, with his knees drawn up against his skin, and the coarse grey under-shirt, which was his only garment, drawn over them enclosing his entire figure. He sat there like a sort of sculptured Egyptian cat or Peruvian mummy, moving nothing but his black eyes. This image and my fear entered into a species of combination. *That shape am I*, I felt, potentially."

Fear as acute and devastating as this may have been experienced by comparatively few writers ; but there is a striking parallel between the sudden rush of panic that engulfed James' unknown correspondent and the spiritual sufferings that have been put on record in one of the strangest of nineteenth-century novels. George Borrow, a temperate and athletic man, was often distracted by a state that he entitled " the Horrors " or " the Fear ", which first overwhelmed him at the age of fifteen and recurred at regular intervals throughout his adult life. While an attack lasted, he was incapable of coherent speech or thought, and his handwriting (as a specimen shows) degenerated into a feeble shapeless scrawl. Vainly he appealed to his friends for the help he knew they could not give ; and thoughts of suicide, to which he had always been prone since he had imbibed the pessimistic doctrines of a metaphysical acquaintance named William Taylor, returned with redoubled strength and constantly pursued him in his wanderings. But what did he fear ? Of that he was never certain. This " dark feeling of mysterious dread " was not (he insisted in *Lavengro*) " the concomitant of disease—the result of shattered nerves ". Rather his sufferings proceeded from the " principle of woe itself, the fountain-head of all sorrow coexistent with man, whose influence he feels when yet unborn, and whose workings he testifies with his earliest cries . . . for, as the sparks fly upward, so is man born to trouble, and woe doth he bring with him into the world, even thyself, dark one, terrible one . . . In the brightest days of prosperity . . . how sentient is the poor human creature of thy neighbourhood ! how instinctively aware that the flood-gates of horror may be cast open! . . ." And Borrow—he is still writing of his youth—concludes with a passage of dramatic dialogue in which the speakers are a boy and his mother, and the woman endeavours to rationalise the strange

terrors that her son feels, suggesting that he may be alarmed by
an hallucination, the phantom of a physically disturbed brain ;
whereas the boy protests that his mind is clear, that he knows that
she is beside him and can see an Italian volume on the table, but
that he is weighted down and reduced to despair by an unanalys-
able sense of apprehension. " Mine is a dread of I know not
what "; and there the ultimate horror lay.

A modern psychiatrist, who examined this passage, would no
doubt decide that Borrow's sufferings were due to a series of
acute " anxiety states "; but at the present moment there is no
consensus of opinion as to the source from which anxiety springs.
Its symptoms, nevertheless, colour the background of many
works of modern literature. Imaginative artists are particularly
subject to the fear that has neither shape nor name ; and I remember discussing its origins with a well-known contemporary
critic who had himself experienced its full force. Seated, he said,
in the stalls of a theatre during an unexpectedly lurid production
of a Sophoclean tragedy, he was overcome by a surge of alarm,
accompanied by mounting waves of claustrophobia, that nearly
swept him into immediate flight. At another time, interviewing
a foreign scholar for the newspaper he represented, his sudden
sense of anxiety was so acute and pervasive that he was obliged
to turn where he stood and examine a map on the wall, until his
panic fears had subsided and he could again pick up the threads
of the conversation. To my friend's testimony I can add some
personal notes. The anxiety state, or whatever else one may call
it, frequently approaches by very gradual stages, like an earth-
quake travelling towards us through the upper layers of the
ground. It is apt to start with an infinitesimal tremor, a vague
suspicion of something mysteriously wrong. But the tremor
grows ; the sense of alarm increases ; and little by little the
entire organism begins to register a profound upheaval, as the
whole universe appears to change and assumes a lugubrious or
darkly threatening air. A thin glassy veil seems to descend
between the spectator and all the objects that surround him.

Two or three minutes ago, they were familiar and friendly. Now they confront him in an alien and hostile shape.

I recollect, for instance, walking across a garden and brushing the rampart of a massive yew hedge. Instantly, from the dusty interior thicket, sprang a pestilential swarm of flies, large, bulbous, fast-moving insects, clad in glittering green armour, which, as they burst into the light, emitted a deep-toned menacing hum—

Le bourdon farouche de très sales mouches

—a noise that recalled the courts of Beelzebub rather than an English garden in the height of August. On a subsequent occasion, an Elizabethan gate, standing opposite my bedroom window, a somewhat fantastic piece of local brickwork, topped with a pair of decorative apertures that resembled huge spectacles, acquired so portentous and ominous a look that I found it necessary to draw the curtain. Luckily, such attacks of unreasonable dread have not often come my way ; but for fairly long periods, while otherwise sane and sound, I have experienced the unpleasant condition known to psychiatrists as one of " floating anxiety ", in which the sufferer awakes with a sense of anxiety he can neither explain nor shake off, a day-long obsession that follows him into his dreams and continues to harry him throughout the hours of sleep. Now these visitations, I believe, have a literary, as well as a clinical, interest ; for they produce a mood of aggravated sensibility, or unnaturally acute impressionability, not unlike the frame of mind that we recognise in most imaginative writers. Among the symptoms of this disturbing state is a tendency to see the world by flashes ; each flash of vision discloses a new alarming or repulsive detail ; and every detail on which the eyes rest has the sharpness and the vividness of something never seen before. The ground that we tread is not a prosaic stretch of urban footpath, but an assemblage of curiously jointed quadrangular stones, littered with odd scraps of multicoloured rubbish, smeared with gouts of yellowish-grey slime.

Ugly buildings suggest the architecture of Hell ; their blackened sculptures become as strikingly unattractive as the devilish decorations of some satanic prison-house. Our familiar universe, safe and dull and limited, suddenly disintegrates into a heap of fragments.

Very similar is the effect of dissociation achieved by the greatest imaginative writers, who break through the commonplace shell of existence to reveal the beauty and the terror that lurk beneath. Ordinary mortals inhabit a world of concepts—the *street* they are at present hurrying down : the *office* that awaits them at a certain number : the *job* that will absorb their energy until the lamps have gone on and dusk has descended. None of the abstract ideas they carry around with them is treated to a close scrutiny—their gifts of observation and analysis have been overlaid by years of habit—unless an imaginative artist should happen to intervene and destroy or dislocate the whole conceptual pattern. Then, indeed, for a moment, the *homme moyen sensuel* may see men as " trees walking "; he is faced no longer with the world that he has grown accustomed to and supposes that he understands, but with a new world that the artist has re-created, far more beautiful or far more terrible, in which every object, separated from its familiar context, acquires a novel and surprising value. A great artist revolutionises our vision of life because he has never lost his own capacity for astonishment, and has never ceased to feel the emotions that accompany it—awe and doubt and primitive alarm. Is there not some valid connection, in fact, between the artistic and the neurotic personality ? Both find the planet they live on a mysterious, and often a dangerous, place ; neither can reconcile what he sees with what he has been informed he *ought* to see if he is to play his part as a healthy and right-minded citizen. Finally, the artist is anxious—about his work, about his personal existence, about the position he occupies in the general scheme of things ; and it is that anxiety, I think, which impels him to creative effort.

If the artist is a " self-cured neurotic "—Cyril Connolly's

illuminating phrase—the state of mind that produces works of art might perhaps be described as a condition of controlled anxiety. Although psychiatrists cannot agree on the causes that underlie the clinical " anxiety state ", they appear to be at one in assuming that it arises from a hidden conflict. I have already expressed my belief that the writer is a man who loves and loathes life with an equal strength of feeling, and whose contradictory emotions are not only unusually violent but extraordinarily well-matched. From these ambivalent impulses may originate the conflict that provokes anxiety, which in its turn sharpens his perceptions and helps to foster his gift of seeing the world anew. " He is over-sensitive ", sighs almost every parent whose child has developed literary ambitions. " He seems to lack a skin : he is apt to be dreadfully morbid : I do wish sometimes that he would take more interest in sport." Such parental forebodings are often fully justified when the young scribbler becomes an adult artist ; and yet the hypersensitiveness that annoys his family and his friends is an important adjunct of his literary gifts. Poets, said Horace, were an " irritable race "; and it is by refining on their nervous irritability that they may succeed at length in developing an individual sensibility. Their most harmonious and untroubled poems reveal signs of constant nervous tension ; and that tension, which assumes a variety of forms according to the poet's character, is reflected both by his view of life and by all the distinctive qualities of his poetic style—the rhythms that he prefers to employ and his peculiar choice of words and images. However zealously impersonal a poet may be, the work that he leaves behind him contains some of the elements of a self-portrait.

Consider, for example, Alexander Pope, to whom nineteenth-century Romantic writers attributed many of the worst faults of eighteenth-century neo-Classicism—its aloofness, its artificial elegance, its lack of sympathy with ordinary human emotions. Examined from a twentieth-century standpoint, Pope displays a far more troubled face. " Pope's most sensuous descriptive poetry (remarks a modern English literary critic) is seldom independent of physical irritation. It is the *suffering* eye which stings Pope into his most elaborate luxuriance of vision." * He has himself described the exquisite anguish of seeing too acutely and sympathising too intensely, for an observer " tremblingly alive " in every fibre of his nervous system.† Here the Augustan master anticipates Keats, whose reference to the " snail-horn perception of beauty " recalls certain of Pope's favourite images—the spider at the heart of its web, " feeling along the line " as the poet feels along his nerves : the fragile nautilus, again a symbol of the poet, bowing its translucent sail beneath the blast. Keats' own poems, though much less finely organised, show a somewhat similar poetic temperament and the same hypersensitive snail-horn response to even the lightest touch of pleasure or pain. But then, Keats' consumptive disposition played a part in developing the imagery of his verse. Pope was externally deformed, Keats radically diseased ; and over the landscape of his imagination the disease spread an atmosphere of feverish languor ; so that a billow, toppling above the sand, breaks and dissolves to a lazy voluptuous rhythm—

> " As when heav'd anew
> Old Ocean rolls a lengthened wave to the shore,
> Down whose green back the short-liv'd foam, all hoar,
> Bursts gradual, with a wayward indolence "

—and, in the *Ode to Melancholy,* the goddess' worshipper " gluts his sorrow " on the sight of rainbows and roses, and derives a sleepily sensuous satisfaction from provoking and contemplating his beloved's rage, since she reminds him that beauty and death are as closely linked as pain and pleasure, and that " Joy's grape " must be brutally crushed before it can be fully tasted.

Besides the tactile imagery employed by Pope and Keats, one remembers the spatial imagery and the images of movement that

* *On the Poetry of Pope* by Geoffrey Tillotson.   † *An Essay on Man.*

characterise the work of Coleridge and Baudelaire. Each of these two unhappy poets bears the stigmata of some profound neurosis; but each translated his secret obsessions into terms that have a grave impersonal dignity. Throughout his later life, Baudelaire was expecting the crisis that finally destroyed his reason at the age of forty-four ; and to the attacks of physical vertigo that heralded the approaching catastrophe can no doubt be traced his desperate preoccupation with the idea of a dark unlimited gulf— the abyss that he had carried around with him, like the gulf that had always accompanied Pascal.* It is mentioned in his private notebooks and haunts the splendid symbolism of his verse :

> *Pascal avait son gouffre, avec lui se mouvant.*
> *Hélas! tout est abîme,—action, désir, rêve,*
> *Parole! et sur mon poil qui tout droit se relève*
> *Mainte fois de la Peur je sens passer le vent . . .*

> *J'ai peur du sommeil comme on a peur d'un grand trou,*
> *Tout plein de vague horreur, menant on ne sait où;*
> *Je ne vois qu'infini par toutes les fenêtres . . .†*

Coleridge was another poet who dreaded the experiences of sleep, and traversed the threshold of waking consciousness as if he were plunging into some horrific cavern. " While I am awake (he told Tom Wedgwood on September 16th 1803), by patience, employment, effort of mind, and walking I can keep the fiend at arm's length ; but the Night is my Hell . . . Three nights out of four I fall asleep, struggling to lie awake—and my frequent Night-screams have almost made me a nuisance in my own House. Dreams with me are no Shadows, but the very Substances and foot-thick Calamities of my Life . . ." Because he dreaded

---

* After a serious carriage-accident, Pascal was haunted by the belief that, wherever he went, a prodigious gulf perpetually yawned upon his left-hand side.

† The fourth line of this poem, *Le Gouffre*, contains a tragic prophecy ; for, when the last warning of his breakdown reached the poet, he recorded that he had felt "the wind of the wing of imbecility " sweeping by across his head.

his nightmares and his waking dreams were almost equally oppressive, the images he employed reflect his longing to escape from a physical and mental prison. Everything flickering, flame-like, evanescent, swiftly moving and as swiftly vanishing, had for Coleridge an especial charm. On a journey across the Mediterranean, he had watched with wondering delight the play of phosphorescent surges :

" A beautiful white cloud of Foam at momentary intervals coursed by the side of the Vessel with a Roar, and little stars of flame danced and sparkled and went out with it ; and every now and then light detachments of this white cloud-like foam dashed off . . . each with its own small constellation over the Sea, and scoured out of sight like a Tartar Troop over a wilderness." *

In *The Ancient Mariner*, the shining water-snakes, as they wreathe and undulate through the phosphorescent calm, represent the spirit of poetic happiness and freedom ; and, when the Mariner, rooted to his death-ship, calls down a blessing on their innocent animal beauty, the Albatross, symbol of guilt and fear, drops from his rugged salt-scurfed neck. Beauty, in Coleridge's mind, was usually associated with the idea of movement—the movement of the wind, of clouds and shadows, above all with the flight of birds ; and, whatever subject he happens to be discussing, he often falls into an ornithological comparison, whether he is likening himself to an ostrich that abandons its eggs in the desert sands of existence, or describing his interminable vacillations between the demands of philosophy and the claims of poetry :

" I wished to force myself out of metaphysical trains of thought . . . and when I wished to write a poem, beat up Game of a far other kind—instead of a covey of poetic Partridges with whirring wings of music, or wild Ducks shaping

* *The Friend,* November, 1809.

their rapid flight in forms always regular (a still better image of Verse) up came a metaphysical Bustard, urging its slow, heavy, laborious, earth-skimming Flight, over dreary and level Wastes."

Yet it was the predicament against which he rebelled that provided Coleridge with the impetus he needed ; and there seem to be few writers who do not subconsciously cherish the burden of anxiety they are doomed to bear. His tremor, announced Goethe, was the finest and most interesting part of a man. "*Une chose surtout donne de l'attrait à la pensée des hommes*", wrote Anatole France in *Le Jardin d'Epicure:* "*C'est l'inquiétude. Un esprit qui n'est point anxieux m'irrite et m'ennuie.*" "*J'ai cultivé mon hysterie avec jouissance et terreur*", recorded Baudelaire in his *Journaux Intimes;* "I am not sure ", Byron observed, " that Fear is not a pleasurable sensation "; while a modern writer, Henry de Montherlant, has told us that he " loves his fear ". From one point of view, the imaginative artist is a permanently displaced person ; yet his knack of sympathising with and understanding the world in which he finds himself gives him a remarkably firm attachment to every portion of the earth on which he sets his feet. He surveys the landscapes across which he moves both as an outcast and as a conqueror ; and those who knew Tolstoy, for example, during his storm-tossed and distracted old age, were struck not only by the veteran creator's look of restlessness and solitude—already he was preparing to drag up his roots and leave his home to die in exile—but by his air of belonging to the world, of having measured it and mastered it. He was as much the master of an alien landscape as of his own familiar fields and woods. ". . . In the flaunting scenery of the Crimea (we read) . . . he was at once both in his place and out of place. He seemed a very ancient man, master of all his surroundings—a master builder who, after centuries of absence, has arrived in the mansion built by him . . . He walked the paths and roads with the business-like, quick step of a skilled explorer of the earth ", from whose magisterial inspection " neither a single pebble nor a single thought could hide . . . He looked, measured, tested, compared." * The world might be a spiritual wilderness. At the same time, it was his private patrimony, in which as a man of genius he walked at ease.

Almost to the end, he retained his powers of enjoyment ; and, in any portrait we draw of the ailing and neurotic artist, we must take into account the capacity for pleasure that underlies his gift of suffering. Every poet enjoys the splendour of the world ; many prove to have been strongly sensual—Byron and Victor Hugo, their biographers tell us, had the omnivorous appetites of sexual giants ; and even writers as miserably handicapped as the crippled and consumptive Leopardi, listening to Silvia's " incessant song " in the courtyard far beneath his window, appear to have regretted the sensuous satisfactions from which they felt they had been cut off by life. The artist, Gautier declared, was a man for whom the visible world existed ; but he is also particularly sensitive to the rich texture of its material substance. Besides being much more acutely developed, his senses are more harmoniously arrayed, and co-operate more smoothly and readily, than those of the ordinary ungifted man. One sense, having been pleasurably excited, soon invokes another's aid, until he believes that he can taste a scent—say, the honeyed scent of lime-flowers—distinguish the colour of a sound or hear the arabesque of sounds that colours produce. However chaste the conduct of his personal career, the imaginative artist remains a hedonist ; although works of art are brought forth with anguish, they are invariably conceived in pleasure ; at least, some spark of remembered delight has fertilised their composition. Thus the artist's apparent weakness often conceals an unexpected

* *Reminiscences of L. N. Tolstoi* by Maxim Gorky, translated by S. S. Kotellansky and Leonard Woolf. Compare with this passage Adler's description of Paul Klee, quoted by Cyril Connolly in *The Unquiet Grave:* " I have never seen a man who had such creative quiet. It radiated from him as from the sun. His face was that of a man who knows about day and night, sky and sea and air. He did not speak of these things. He had no tongue to tell of them."

strength—the strength that enables him, if not to dispel anxiety, to control and canalize it for his own purposes. The human condition may be generally painful; but the artist possesses a supreme advantage. Unlike the vast majority of his fellows, he has begun to understand, and can sometimes use, his pain.

Epilogue

A SMALL hollow object in rugged dark bronze stands opposite me on the corner of my desk. Not much bigger than a large Victorian thimble, it is certainly over two thousand years old and may possibly have been created during an even more remote period ; nothing about it reveals its exact age ; it is the casual everyday product of an extraordinarily long and vigorous tradition. Besides worshipping at Bubastis the cat- or lion-faced goddess Bast, the ancient Egyptians kept a multitude of cats which ran freely around their palaces and houses, and placed cat-heads as decorative finials on many pieces of domestic furniture. Such a head I happen to have acquired ; and innumerable similar relics are now distributed through the world's museums. No expert Egyptologist would allow my head a second glance : in its context it is almost as unimportant as a late-Victorian door-knob. Yet, for its owner at least, it possesses a mysterious gift of stirring the senses and quickening the imagination. That the household cat remains a wild animal, the Egyptian craftsman makes completely clear. Deep, dusky triangular eye-sockets—once filled with coloured faience eyeballs or perhaps with fragments of semi-precious stone—give the narrow, thin-cheeked mask a look of fierce, unblinking expectancy. The muzzle is lengthy but blunted, as in the modern Abyssinian breed ; and the tall flattened, thick-furred ears—each pierced towards the base to receive a miniature jewelled ring—project sentinel-wise from the rounded cranium, as the cat raises its lean neck to confront some unfamiliar challenge. The Egyptians, unlike the Japanese, very seldom portrayed a cat asleep. What they admired in the half-tamed animal was its attitude of vigilant, aggressive pride—the pride of life peculiar to a race cherished and protected by the mighty mother-goddess Bast, who numbered " The Lady of Life " among her various solemn titles. On that aspect of the splendid creature before him, the craftsman dwelt with especially loving care. Between himself and its alien existence he seems to have established a strong imaginative bond ; and from the contact sprang a sudden minute explosion of the life-enriching quality we call " art ".

Microscopic the spark is ; yet there it still gleams after twenty centuries—imperishable and unmistakable as a scrap of pure gold in a barren, dried-up stream-bed ; and to have caught and fixed even that single spark few efforts would not be worth enduring. The theme of the present book is the background of art, studied chiefly through the art of literature ; and although, while I pursued my subject, I have often wandered very far afield, the time has now come to cut short my journey and prelude its close with an unashamed confession. For nearly as long as I can remember, I have wished to be some kind of artist, and have believed that no other activity brought the same rewards or had quite the same value. In my early youth, I suppose, I should have agreed with Cyril Connolly, whose stern dictum I have already quoted—that the " true function of a writer " is simply " to produce a masterpiece " and that no less ambitious aim is of the slightest consequence. To be memorable, I thought, a work must also be " great ", an achievement of heroic magnitude, large and grandiose and breath-taking as *Paradise Lost*, Michelangelo's *Night* and *Day* or Piero della Francesca's painted visions at Arezzo. Today, however, the scale of a work seems relatively unimportant, partly no doubt because I no longer expect to succeed in creating a masterpiece myself, partly because my ideas of the artist's function have since undergone a gradual change. Thus I have begun to think of art as a quality that may illumine the most trivial objects, and to value an artist both for his ability to raise us high above the world and for his gift, simultaneously exercised, of intensifying and enlarging our sense of life. This he may help to do, if he is an imaginative writer, by encouraging us, in our own experience, to distinguish the essential from the inessential. Art is the essential residue of life : literature, a record of experience from which the inessentials have been carefully removed, the essential elements being further purified during their translation into imaginative imagery. An artist cannot unriddle the universe ; but he alone formulates an insoluble problem in terms that the human mind can grasp. Shakespeare's tragedies provide no answers ; but they put forward a series of age-old questions with such commanding grace and skill that they reconcile us to the unaltered human condition and deprive uncertainty of half its terrors.

" As the influence of religion declines ", once suggested Aldous Huxley, " the social importance of art increases ". And, were the artist to drop out of the social system, who nowadays could take his place ? Not only does he illuminate the landscape of the present ; but he throws an airy bridge between the present and the future. In a thousand years, if our descendants can reach us, it will be through the works of art that we have left behind, just as we ourselves, handling a scrap of bronze cast a thousand or two thousand years ago, enjoy a sensation of electric sympathy with the artificer who kneaded the wax model. Nothing else remains of him—neither his religious beliefs nor the political system under which he lived and died. Faiths expire ; political systems collapse ; the elaborate structures planned by science and philosophy are reduced to picturesque ruins. Then, among the ruins, appears some broken artifact that reveals the imprint of human desires and feelings—an Egyptian statuette : a strip of tarnished metal that shows a procession of stout Sumerian dignitaries advancing to the sound of music : a fragment of an early Greek vase, with charioteers, wrestlers and a frieze of helmeted warriors bearing huge heraldic shields : an Athenian koré whose smile still warms the heart : a grim-visaged Maya seer or the scowling features of an Aztec priest.

From an ethical point of view, the Maya and Aztec worlds now seem particularly remote and strange ; for the Maya priesthood were obsessed by Time—an obsession with which I can vaguely sympathise, since in my childhood I was troubled by hideous dreams about unending Time and illimitable Space— and devoted their genius to the composition of extraordinarily detailed and extensive calendars, afterwards engraved upon monumental blocks of stone ; while the Aztecs imagined that their ferocious gods were constantly meditating the destruction of mankind, and that at any season the rains might cease to gather and the maize crop wither in the dusty fields, unless the divine tyrants who ruled their fate received a gigantic daily tribute of blood and suffering. Fear dominated the Aztec world ; and fear and its concomitant, cruelty, are reflected in all the manifestations of their art. Now and then, the creative spirit is obscured by a coarse and ugly realism ; and we are confronted by the statue of a dancing priest who carries around with him the flayed-off skin of the human victim he has sacrificed, peeps through the eye-holes of the scooped-out mask and wears the flaccid hide of the dead man's torso tightly strapped about his body. There is not a smile in the Aztec pantheon, though sometimes a broad sadistic grin ; and equally cold and unsmiling were the human types that the Mexican sculptor chose. The Aztecs, in their curious view of life, although they cultivated pleasure and recognised beauty, found little room for hope or joy ; but again and again we encounter a statue, hewn out of dusky porous rock, to which the frowning brows and the close-shut mouth lend an air of tragic human dignity. The illusory terrors that haunted the Mexican craftsman have now been superseded by very different fears—we dread, not the vengeance of heaven, so much as a mushroom-shaped cloud arising from the earth. Yet Fear, in one of its many disguises, still overshadows the twentieth-century mind ; and it was the Aztec's staunch acceptance of an almost intolerable fate that gave his masterpieces their darkly impressive character.

If art is a universal language, as Ruskin—at war with his contemporaries' view that works of art were a mere decorative addition to life—never tired of pointing out, the artist himself is none the less deeply involved in the transitory problems of his own existence. The writer who fulfils his mission—which is to justify the ways of Man to men, and to produce an æsthetic harmony from the savage disorder of the world we know— would appear as a rule to have originally shouldered it for reasons that concern his own life, his own fears, his own anxieties, his own aspirations towards security and peace. His work may benefit mankind ; but he is a supremely undeliberate benefactor, like the alchemist who adds to the wealth of nations during his laborious attempts at self-enrichment. In his life-time, he frequently forfeits the respect of saner and solider human beings, when they observe how small his rewards are, how disastrous his private losses, and how surely every increase of knowledge seems to be counterbalanced by some increase of doubt. Oddly enough, though, doubt is a condition that generally stimulates the creative intelligence. Thus Keats discouraged his fellow poets from seeking to arrive at definite conclusions : " the only means (he wrote) of strengthening one's intellect is to make up one's mind about nothing—to let the mind be a thoroughfare for all thoughts, not a select party "; for it is to his doubts, his self-confessed ignorance, that the creative artist owes his independence. " I doubt ; therefore I am " is his emended version of Descartes' famous phrase.

In a society where to be able to make up one's mind is commonly accounted an important virtue, the artist, with his lack of fixed opinions, often cuts a somewhat unheroic figure. Keats himself, a fiercely proud young man, who had a particularly exalted view of the grandeur of the poet's task, was obliged to admit that the poet was " the most unpoetical of anything in existence . . . he has no Identity—he is continually . . . filling some other body. The Sun, the Moon, the Sea, and men and women, who are creatures of impulse, are poetical and have about them an unchangeable attribute ; the poet has none . . ." For his awareness of himself, being especially vivid, is apt to reveal him his own character in all its native incoherence ; while the gift of sympathy, that becomes his greatest asset—his power of feeling with and re-living the lives of others—entails a constant loss of identity and little by little may blur the Self's outline, just as an actor's real face is slowly obliterated by the impress of the multiple parts he has played. Oscar Wilde summed up the writer's predicament in an unexpected flash of insight . . . " He who lives more lives than one (declares the prisoner of Reading Gaol) more deaths than one must die "; and, although it was Wilde's hybristic conceit, not his modest share of creative talent, that presently accomplished his personal downfall, he is speaking here for every imaginative artist who has allowed his imagination to range too widely, whose nervous system is linked at too many points to the sufferings of a world that he both loves and loathes.

*   *   *

I am concerned in this book with the art of writing, as seen by a middle-aged professional writer ; but among the various penalties of planning and producing books is the fact that a book, once it has definitely taken shape, seldom bears a very close resemblance to the more ambitious features of the original design. Thus a series of chapter-headings, successively discarded, strew the pathway of the present volume. I had hoped, for example, to say something about the difficult relationship between the artist and the moralist, suggesting that, although the artist is neither a teacher nor a preacher, and himself rarely leads what the moralist would consider a markedly dignified or virtuous life, his appreciation of moral values is often reflected in the distinctive qualities of his style. " *Il y a une sorte de netteté et franchise de style* (observed Joseph Joubert in his miscellaneous thoughts on writing) *qui tient à l'humeur et au temperament, comme la franchise au caractère.*" But the virtues that a writer puts into his work are frequently those he has failed to display in his conduct ; and one thinks of Pope, whose venomous personal character was belied by his great and generous gifts, and whose style achieved a splendid breadth and unity of which we can find scarcely a trace in any description of the private man. It seems clear, nevertheless, that moral and artistic virtues spring from much the same source, just as the religious and the creative emotions are inspired ultimately by the same instinctive needs—the need to justify and understand, coupled with a deep-rooted desire to express our sense of fear and wonder. "*Il y a de l'oraison en toute grande œuvre* (writes Alain), *et même dans les romans de Voltaire*". Every genuine work of art enlarges the dimensions of its subject ; and Tolstoy, in his criticism of *The Darling*, points out that Tchehov, when he began his story, would appear to have intended to draw the portrait of a thoroughly commonplace and stupid woman ; but that, as his theme developed and his knowledge of his heroine grew, he gradually lost sight of his destructive purpose, until a gathering wave of imaginative sympathy had lifted his petty subject on to the plane of art.

Something should also have been said about the writer's sexual interests, about the affinity between the human erotic impulse and the mood that urges him to the act of literary creation ; each is inspired by a yearning for personal release, by a vision of the decisive moment of truth, when a multitude of conflicting energies suddenly fuse into a single burst of feeling. Yet " it is a significant fact (a modern anthologist notes) that so few poets should even have tried to render the exaltations and agonies of physical love ".* Apart from Marlowe's *Hero and Leander*, no long erotic poem that deserves re-reading has yet been written in the English language ; the poet's description of amatory experience usually transcends the act itself ; and what he pursues in love is not only the realisation of present pleasure—though the pleasure-principle

---

* Aldous Huxley : *Texts and Pretexts.*

is closely bound up with every aspect of creative activity—but a means of escape and fulfilment that will carry him far beyond the customary limits, and transport him to a mysterious realm of emotion, where sensation and imagination blend. Because the writer's amatory adventures have a symbolic as well as a sensual significance, they are often considerably more calamitous than the exploits of an ordinarily sensual man. A million other men have wasted hope and energy upon a Marie Sabatier or a Jeanne Duval. None but an artist of Baudelaire's temperament would have made these two prosaic females the starting-point of an endless imaginative journey, during which, as he contemplated the animal splendour of her body, observed the cold metallic flash of her eyes, or absorbed the heady aroma of her hair and skin, the woman he adored became a whole landscape, peopled by the poet's reveries, regrets and desires, and the transient creature of flesh and blood was soon lost in the expanding beauty of the image. It is not to be wondered at that both Marie and Jeanne should have found the poet an unimpressive lover ; nor could they have been expected to understand his insatiable need for self-punishment ; to sympathise with the cynicism that caused him to announce that loving intelligent women was a pederastic joy—an artist should spend his time in the company of " *les filles ou les femmes bêtes* "—or with the romanticism, fed on memories of childhood, that had implanted a lasting suspicion of the flesh. For Baudelaire's life provides an extreme example of a tendency that many writers have displayed. Whatever the circumstances, they feel obliged to rebuild a similar self-punishing situation. It is the situation, their genius or daemon warns them, in which they are somehow most themselves.

Yet another chapter, planned but unwritten, was to have dealt with the writer and the natural world. Of one well-known novelist I have heard it said that he is entirely unresponsive to the life of nature ; and, indeed, I have watched him, a cigar in his mouth and a large straw hat crammed on his angry head, wearing a striped suit that increased his resemblance to a rich plantation-

owner of the last century, stumping ponderously along a Caribbean beach without a glance for the spectacle of sea and sky,
despite the humming-birds that played through the hedge or the
liquid aquamarine of glassy wavelets that slid up against the
blanched sand. But the average writer is peculiarly wide awake
to the magnificence of the world in which he lives; and the
quality he admires is not its familiarity so much as its unending
strangeness. " How do you know but ev'ry Bird that cuts the
airy way, (runs the " Memorable Fancy ", published by Blake in
The Marriage of Heaven and Hell) is an immense world of delight,
clos'd by your senses five ? " And it is as an immense world of
delight—world within world, a tremendous constellation of
separate points of feeling—that one would prefer to regard this
alien universe which surrounds us at every moment of our days.
Even a mallard drake washing its plumage on the edge of a pool in a
crowded urban park, beating its wings and rearing its burnished
neck amid a circumference of spreading concentric ripples, is an
apparition that seems to fling wide some long-unopened mental
window. Henry de Montherlant is not a story-teller who often
pauses to evoke a natural detail ; but in *Les Célibataires*, when the
younger of his two wretched protagonists lies dying in the
gardener's room, he describes, with admirable effect, the tumultuous passage overhead of a great flock of migratory wild
geese, which represent, as they approach and recede, the strength
and gaiety and freedom of Nature, while the unhappy Count,
alone on his truckle bed, typifies the fears and the frustration
of Man.

Reading this passage, I remembered an experience of my own,
during a holiday below the foothills of the Maritime Alps, which,
if the day were particularly hot and calm, flung down their marbly
shadows across the sea. Up the Gulf of Beaulieu, arriving from
Italy, came a column of slowly travelling birds—not in extended
order, as wild geese fly, when they travel at night above the
Scottish lowlands, but linked one by one in a gently undulating
chain like the floating tail of a vast celestial kite, the drifting

streamer that might follow an archangel or a loose ribbon
attached to the chariot of Venus. They were flamingoes making
for the marshes of the Camargues, where, amid the lagoons and
the reed-beds and the salt pastures of wandering black cattle,
they are still permitted, even in the twentieth century, to lead
their harmless unnecessary lives, and brighten the mud-banks on
which they descend with a scattering of delicate rosy feathers. A
soft ashy rose was the colour of the procession that now drifted
between sea and sky, far above the sea and at a cautious distance
from the land, but shaping its course by the ridge of mountains
that march heavily south to join the Ligurian coastline. They
were flying in unison; and every rhythmic pulse of their wings
momentarily revealed the rosy under-surface; so that the celestial
streamer not only changed its shape—an exquisite arabesque
forming and re-forming through a variety of beautifully broken
curves—but, at the same time, was constantly changing its hue
as it traversed the brilliant background of the heavens, now
greyish, faintly flushed with rose, now the vivid rose of an unclouded summer dawn.

A concluding section of the book I meant to write was to have
been devoted to the curious subject of dreams—both our day-
dreams and the apparitions of sleep, amid which willy-nilly we
spend so large a part of our lives, when we are stripped of most
of our mental privileges and, as it were, brutally reduced to the
ranks. Have a writer's dreams any significant relationship with
the imagery in which he expresses his waking emotions? Personally, I know that my dreams are full of bewildering and disconcerting contrasts; that at one moment I re-live the anxieties
of youth and quarrel bitterly with half-forgotten foes, or wander
off into hideous regions where all my adult sins are remembered
and recounted; while at others I become the romantic tourist
exploring a succession of lovely and unreal scenes—prospects
that must no doubt be derived from journeys in France or Italy
or Greece, radiant bays closed by rugged highlands and odd
fragments of noble antique architecture, often cropping up on

Epilogue

the outskirt of some grim and ominous industrial city. I study
these ancient edifices with the utmost minuteness and sometimes
comment on their historical origin : such-and-such a ruined
country house was evidently built by the architect of a house
I know in waking life : I admire a casement, a group of statues,
a chimney, the proportions of a spacious roofless hall. But around
the corner of the Mediterranean bay lies a second, and lovelier,
bay I cannot hope to reach. There is a doom on the mouldering
house I visit : a voice informs me that it is soon to be pulled
down. . . .

Having disposed of the volume I originally planned, I must
find room for a last important question. Since I have frequently
referred—perhaps at tedious length—to the penalties and pains
of writing, a critic may reasonably ask if I do not sometimes
regret the early choice I made. Certainly I regret my repeated
failures to produce the books I wished to write, just as I regret
the hours, totalling entire decades, that it has been my ill-luck to
spend engaged in various types of modern hackwork ; although
from hackwork there is often much to be learned about the uses
and the abuses of language. But I do not regret having adopted
the literary profession, for the very good reason that, besides
keeping me alive, it has also enriched and enlightened the experience of living. I continue to assume that the life of the writer is
greatly preferable to any other form of life, and that the smallest
scintilla of art, if the artist can apprehend it and, having appre-
hended it, can impose it on his raw material, will always shine
out from the disorder of the present and the accumulated rubbish
of the past. In that respect, creative art is timeless ; and the
writer himself enjoys some of the vicarious advantages of
inhabiting a world where Time has lost its power. Not that he
cherishes hopes of immortality—he has watched the decay and
collapse of too many literary reputations ; but he is acutely conscious of the vital link that connects the works of the past with
the works of the present day, and has discovered how little
humanity changes through all the changes of our temporal

setting. Meanwhile, in his private existence, he becomes aware of some undiminished passions. Should he love clarity, elegance and order, he knows that he has loved them from his youth ; if he is sufficiently moved by a face or a landscape to attempt to fix it with the help of words, he may discover it has already a counterpart, awaiting resurrection in the deepest levels of his memory. But gradually, as he begins to grow older, he relinquishes the hope that he may still achieve wisdom. " I have learned nothing from life (acknowledges Omar Khayyam, in a quatrain that Fitzgerald left untranslated) except my own amazement at it." But the Persian poet did not despair ; nor should a modern writer despair, when obliged to make the same confession. Amazement, after all, is a state of mind that betokens a healthily active intelligence, and suggests that our sense of delight and wonder has not yet been overlaid by habit. So long as amazement can induce us to open our eyes, we need not fear that we shall lose the gift of seeing.

INDEX

Index

Index

Index

Quennell.

Sign of the fish.